Provided by
The Library of Congress
Special Foreign Currency Program.

Dr. Amrut Wasudeo. Nakhre was born in Sagar, Madhya Pradesh. He received his M.A. in Political Science from the University of Sagar. He taught briefly at Vikram University and later, at Christian College, Indore, for about six years, before leaving for the U.S.A.

Later, having obtained his Ph.D. from the University of North Carolina, Chapel Hill, he joined the Political Science Department of Atlantic Christian College, Wilson, North Carolina, where he is continuing now as a Professor.

Dr Nakhre has devoted several years to the study of nonviolent action, and has conducted extensive research on the subject.

He has published his research papers in such international journals as *Bulletin of Peace Proposals*, *Journal of Peace Research*, *Gandhi Marg* and others. His other works include *Selected Political Thinkers*, co-authored with Dr. Nagpal.

SOCIAL PSYCHOLOGY OF NONVIOLENT ACTION
A Study of Three Satyagrahas

By the same author
SELECTED POLITICAL THINKERS
(Co-authored with Dr. O.P. Nagpal)

Social Psychology of Nonviolent Action
A Study of Three Satyagrahas

AMRUT W. NAKHRE

Chanakya Publications
Delhi

SOCIAL PSYCHOLOGY
OF
NONVIOLENT ACTION
A Study of Three Satyagrahas

Copyright © 1982 Amrut W. Nakhre

First Published 1982
by
CHANAKYA PUBLICATIONS
F 10/14 Model Town, Delhi 110009

All Rights Reserved

Rupees Seventy

Printed in India by
Kay Kay Printers
150 D Kamla Nagar Delhi 110007

To the Memory of
the Loknayak
SHRI JAYAPRAKASH NARAIN

ACKNOWLEDGEMENTS

Intellectual stimulation for this study was provided by Professor Lewis Lipsitz whose own admiration of Gandhi was only matched by his passion for understanding the socio-psychological underpinnings of 'satyagraha'. It was in his upper level graduate seminars on Gandhi, at the University of North Carolina at Chapel Hill, that the idea for this study took shape in my mind. Much of the data and information used in this work were originally collected for my Ph. D. dissertation which I wrote under his guidance. Chapters 5, 7, and 8 are modified versions of my articles, "Meanings of Nonviolence: A Study of Satyagrahi Attitudes", *Journal of Peace Research*, Vol. 13, no. 3, 1976, "Religion and Charisma in Nonviolent Action", *Gandhi Marg*, Vol. 1, no. 9, 1979, and "Peace Action as Peace Education", in *Bulletin of Peace Proposals*, Vol. 2, no. 2, 1981, respectively.

Johan Galtung provided valuable insights and assistance in the methodological aspects in the preparatory phase of research and planning. I also benefited from the comments of Arne Naess and research scholars at the International Peace Research Institute at Oslo where I spent two very pleasant and fruitful months as guest researcher in the summer of 1975. Professors Gordon B. Cleveland, S. Shepard Jones, Andrew M. Scott, and Jeffrey Obler of the University of North Carolina at Chapel Hill gave assistance at various stages of research and study. Meticulous reading and criticism of the first draft of the manuscript by, late, Dr. Mildred E. Hartsock, Professor Emeritus of English at Atlantic Christian College, enabled me to improve the manuscript considerably.

Professors Hakumat Bhai Desai and Babu Bhai Desai of K.P. Commerce College, Surat and Professor P.S. Jethwa of Saurashtra University, Rajkot, provided indispensable assistance in the preparation of interview schedules and in actual interviewing. Major part of the rank and file interviewing was done with the help of postgraduate students, Messrs M.S. Hanslod J.B. Gandhi, Jayantilal Naik, Harshad Kumar Sidhiwala and Shirish R. Desai of K.P. Commerce College and Misses Jayshree Sheth and Asha Anjharia of Saurashtra University. Together, they developed excellent working relationships with satyagrana participants which proved of inestimable value to the understanding of the satyagrahas. The satyagraha participants themselves deserve special mention. Without their gracious acceptance of the interviewers and responses to their inquiries the project would have been impossible.

To these and numerous others who made this work possible I take this opportunity to record my sense of deep gratitude. For shortcomings and errors I alone am to blame.

Wilson, North Carolina AMRUT W. NAKHRE
March, 1982

PREFACE

The original inspiration for this work came from that indefatigable Gandhian, late, Jayaprakash Narain. A decade back he stated that there had been sufficient elaboration of the philosophical aspects of satyagraha,[1] what was needed was an empirical understanding of the phenomena.

Indeed, nonviolent action for the resolution of conflicts in both social and political arenas has a long history. Yet it has not been subjected to the same dispassionate and scholarly analysis as violent action. The stereotype that nonviolence may be desirable in itself but difficult to attain is almost an obsession with the intellectual and the common man alike. In spite of Gandhi's development of satyagraha, the most systematic and developed mode of nonviolent action, and its dramatic use in India, astonishingly little attention has been paid by social scientists to the processes involved in the workings of a satyagraha.

This lack of attention has given rise to some popular misconceptions about the workings of a satyagraha. The fact that Gandhi developed and interpreted his theory of nonviolent action purely in terms of religion and applied it with dramatic effectiveness has given rise to the idea, particularly in the West, that nonviolent action is typical of Indian culture, and that it has played an important part in Indian development. These misconceptions are held in spite of the fact that for almost one thousand years preceding the advent of Gandhi on the Indian scene, the Indians were involved in continuous and bloody warfare among themselves and against the Muslims and subsequently against the British. Following the independence of India from the British in 1947, Gandhi himself lived to see the worst kind of violence in which thousands of Hindus and Muslims slaughtered one another in communal riots.

In modern India, while the people still continue to pay lip service to the memory of Gandhi, the fact is that acts of political and social violence have assumed frightening proportions. According to census reports, there were twenty thousand cases of riots in India in 1953 compared with close to thirty thousand in 1963. Since then, the growth of violence has taken a turn for the worse.[2] Thus, we see that the popular belief that nonviolence is indigenous to Indian culture is not warranted by facts.

At a time when various countries all over the world are seized with the problem of conflict within their societies Gandhian methods of nonviolent action might provide a civilized method of approach. The purpose of this study is to understand nonviolence—its philosophy, strategy and implications—as perceived not only by the leaders but also by the rank and file participants in a satyagraha. The study is based on a survey of the attitudes on nonviolence of participants in three satyagrahas namely, Bardoli, Rajkot and Pardi which were waged by Gandhi and his followers in the last 50 years. The choice of the three satyagrahas for this study is based upon the fact that they closely approximate the model of satyagraha that has been developed and discussed in Chapter 2.

Insofar as the Gandhian technique has been applied in extremely varied settings, and with varying degrees of success in the developed as well as underdeveloped countries,[3] the result of such a study might be of considerable importance. Of course, one must understand that the conditions surrounding any social phenomena, let alone a satyagraha, are always complex and never amenable to simple generalizations. Even the most rigorous scientific approach might not reveal the truth that would be applicable to the real world in all situations. Nonetheless, this study has been undertaken in the belief that it could at least help to increase our sophistication of thinking and theorising about satyagraha.

Unlike other studies which have analysed satyagraha purely in terms of its main leader, this one looks at it from the point of view of the rank and file participants and the subleaders. As far as known to this researcher this is the first and only study of Gandhian satyagraha tnat has focused on the rank and file participants rather than on the main leaders. Some of the respondents interviewed for this research participated in satya-

Preface xi

grahas as far back as 1928—a few even earlier—and do not strictly satisfy the requirement of a scientific sample. Yet, they were included in the study not only because they were the only ones available or alive but also because of my belief that they could provide a unique perspective in our understanding of the success of the Gandhian phenomena. Also, the fact that some of them were already in their 60s and 70s at the time of interviewing meant that this could very well be the last and only chance to benefit from their insights. How precious was their participation to this study would be clear as the reader wades through the pages of this book. Beyond that the discovery of the moral and spiritual transformation brought about in the lives of these respondents through participation in satyagrahas was, to this researcher, an humbling experience.

NOTES

[1] The term 'satyagraha' has been all along used in a specialized sense to denote nonviolent action in accordance with the principles laid down by Gandhi and as elaborated in Chapter 2.

[2] See in this connection, S.P. Aiyer, ed., *The Politics of Mass Violence in India* (Bombay: Manaktalas and Sons, Private Ltd., 1967): also David H. Bayley, "Public Protest and the Political Process in India" in Joseph R. Gusfield, ed., *Protest, Reform, and Revolt: A Reader in Social Movements* (New York: John Wiley and Sons, Inc., 1970).

[3] Gene Sharp, *The Politics of Nonviolent Action*, (Boston: Porter Sargent Publication, 1973) has described scores of examples of nonviolent action which occured in recent times. See especially Chapter 2.

TABLES

1.	The sample	34
2.	Amount of participation in the satyagrahas	59
3.	Number of hours per week devoted to satyagraha	60
4.	Vegetarian or nonvegetarian	62
5.	Caste status of the rank and file	63
6.	Level of education of the rank and file	63
7.	Occupations of the satyagrahis	64
8.	Respondent's perception of benefits accruing from satyagraha	68
9.	Projective responses on whether nonviolence was a tactic or a creed	73
10.	Projective responses on education BY whether nonviolence was a tactic or a creed	73
11.	Projective responses showing the source of familiarity with nonviolence	75
12.	Projective responses on how nonviolence works	79
13.	Projective responses on perception of nonviolence as a tactic or creed By possibility of violence in case of failure for the Gandhi sample	83
13a	Projective responses on perception of nonviolence as a tactic or a creed BY possibility of violence in case of failure for the Pardi sample	83
14.	Attitude to nonviolence at participation BY effect on opponent for the Gandhi sample	85
14a	Attitude to nonviolence at participation BY effect on opponent for the Pardi sample	86
15.	Caste status of leaders	92
16.	Occupation of leaders	92
17.	Projective responses of leaders whether satyagraha was a tactic or a creed	96
18.	Projective responses showing satyagrahis' attitudes to nonviolence By satyagrahis' perception of leader's commitment to nonviolence for Gandhi	107
18a	Projective responses showing satyagrahis attitudes to nonviolence BY satyagrahis' perception of leaders' commitment to nonviolence for the Pardi	108
19.	Projective responses on the question whether the parents, teachers, friends and relatives participated	151
20.	If father liked son's participation	151
21.	If mother liked son's participation	152

CONTENTS

Acknowledgements	vii
Preface	ix
List of Tables	xii

1. CONFLICT, VIOLENCE AND SATYAGRAHA   1
Conflict Theory and Satyagraha	2
Why Nonviolence?	5
Theory of Mass Society and Satyagraha	7

2. THEORY OF SATYAGRAHA   13
Developing the Satyagraha Model	13
Satya	14
Ahimsa	15
Tapasya	16
Satyagraha as a Way of Life	18
Satyagraha, a Doctrine or a Policy?	18
Coercion and Nonviolence	19
The Practice of Satyagraha	20
Preparation for Satyagraha	22
Stages in the Development of a Satyagraha	23

3. METHODOLOGY   28
Interviews	30
The Interviewers	30
The Interview Schedule	31
The Sample	32
Drawbacks of the Study	35
Bardoli (1928)	37
Rajkot (1938-39)	41
Pardi (1953-64)	46
Conclusions Regarding the Three Movements	53

4. PARTICIPATION, SOCIAL BACKGROUND AND GOAL ORIENTATION OF THE RANK AND FILE   58
Participation	58
Social Background	60
Goal Orientation	65
Summary	69

5. MEANINGS OF NONVIOLENCE FOR THE
   RANK AND FILE   71
   Satyagraha a 'Creed' or a 'Tactic'?   72
   Intellectual Grasp of Nonviolence   73
   Nonviolence as a Faith   78
   Satyagraha and Violence   82
   Impact on Opponents   84

6. PARTICIPATION, SOCIAL BACKGROUND
   AND ATTITUDES OF THE LEADERS   90
   Social Background   90
   Meaning of Nonviolence for the Leaders   94
   Nonviolence a 'Creed' or 'Tactic'?   96
   Satyagraha and Religion   103
   Nonviolence as Communication   104

7. RELIGION, CHARISMA AND NONVIOLENCE   111
   Weber and the Concept of Charisma   112
   Gandhi as a Charismatic Leader   115
   Institutionalization of Charisma   117
   Transference of Charisma   119
   Religion and Nonviolence   123

8. IMPACT OF SATYAGRAHA ON THE RANK
   AND FILE   130
   Psychosocial Background   131
   Pardi Tribals as Low Caste   134
   Tribals and Sanskritization   134
   Impact of Satyagraha   138
   Inpact on Pardi Satyagrahis   139
   Satyagraha and 'Self-Suffering'   143
   'Self-Suffering' as Masochism   148
   Satyagraha and Reference Groups   149
   Satyagraha and Constructive Activity   153
   Satyagraha and Frustration   156

9. CONCLUSION   165
   BIBLIOGRAPHY
   APPENDICES   171
   A. Interview Schedule: Rank and File   191
   B. Leader Interview   201

   INDEX   205

As I delved deeper into the philosophy of Gandhi I came to see for the first time its potency in the area of social reform. Prior to reading Gandhi I had about concluded that the ethics of Jesus were effective only in individual relationships. The 'turn the other cheek' philosophy and the 'love your enemies' philosophy were only valid, I felt, when individuals were in conflict with other individuals; when racial groups and nations were in conflict a more realistic approach seemed necessary. But after reading Gandhi, I saw how utterly mistaken I was. Gandhi was probably the first person in history to lift the love ethic of Jesus above mere interaction between individuals to a powerful and effective social force on a large scale.

—MARTIN LUTHER KING
Stride Toward Freedom
(New York: Harper and Brothers, 1958), pp 96-97

1
Conflict, Violence and Satyagraha

This book is primarily concerned with analysis of conflict resolution through nonviolent means, particularly the means used in Gandhian satyagrahas. In this chapter we will first briefly discuss the nature of conflict and follow it with an examination of its relationships with violence and nonviolence. But, before we proceed with the discussion we would like to clarify certain terms which we intend to use as we go along. The term 'nonviolence' has been used by Gandhi in a much wider sense than it is used here. For the purpose of this study we intend to use it in its narrow sense, to mean 'refraining from physical injury to another person or group.' For 'conflict', we intend to use Galtung's definition wherein it is defined as "a property of an action system, viz., when two or more incompatible or mutually exclusive values are pursued."[1] By values we mean in the generalized sense 'preferred outcomes' of the contending groups.[2]

Values have important implications in the theory of action in that they play an important role in organizing the system of action itself. The values influence "the selection from available modes, means and ends of action."[3] In a broader sense values are conceptions explicit or implicit distinctive of a group of that which is desirable or desired. Kluckhohn contrasts the 'desirable' with the 'desired.'[4] We intend to include both the aspects into our definition of value because we believe that anything which is strongly 'desired' is a result of evaluation by an individual or a group that it is desirable and hence, has strong implications for social action. From this point of view, let us say when a group of landless agricultural workers, having evaluated their demands for wage increase against the landowners; or when a minority group, say the low caste, carry on a struggle against the high castes for equality, while the dominant group continues to strive to maintain the status quo; these are examples of pursuing incompatible values. Conflict occurs only when the two incompatible values confront each other within the action system through the behavior of the subordinate and the dominant group.

Having defined conflict thus, the resolution of conflict may be defined as 'absence of conflict.'[5] This happens when only one compatible value comes to be followed. From this point of view, a conflict may be 'intrapersonal' as when a person is on the horns of a dilemma; or 'interpersonal', or 'intergroup' or 'international'. Gandhian technique is claimed to have been used in the context of international conflicts;[6] intergroup conflicts;[7] or social conflicts.[8] The focus of this study is on the attitudes of participants in medium-sized social conflicts. For individuals or groups using nonviolent means for conflict resolution we will use words such as, 'nonviolent group', 'nonviolent actors', 'nonviolent resisters', 'volunteers', 'subordinate group', and 'satyagrahi'. For the individual or groups against whom the nonviolent resistance is being carried out, we will use words such as 'the opponent', 'the target', 'dominant person or group', etc. The terms 'Gandhian technique' and 'satyagraha' have been used interchangeably to describe the carrying on of a struggle or a movement for conflict resolution by nonviolent means and in accordance with the principles laid down by Gandhi.

CONFLICT THEORY AND SATYAGRAHA

Conflicts are endemic to human societies and are as old as mankind itself. Since Karl Marx's analysis of the social conflict in industrializing England, social scientists have devoted increasing attention to developing a conflict theory. Recently there has been a tremendous spurt in conflict literature. Lewis Coser, Dahrendorf and many others have tried to examine the various aspects of conflict.[9]

The factors more or less common in all conflict theories are an emphasis on and analysis of the fragmentation of social systems caused by confrontation of incompatible values and the study of processes by which various interest groups organize themselves around the conflicting values and try to gain advantage over the opposite group. Also, conflict provides an important framework for the study of change; because change usually involves the necessity of promoting or obstructing a value in preference to another, and this necessarily creates a conflict.

Although the above framework has been applied for the analysis of conflict within the whole social system, it can be used to explain the lower level conflicts such as the medium-sized social conflicts we have in mind.

Conflicts occur within a system which has a structure. Hence, to study conflict the first step should be to study the configuration of divergent values among groups which make claims on the power holders within the system.

Next is the problem of interest articulation i.e., the conflicting values have to be translated into decisive influences so as to obtain favourable decision from the opponent. There exist many forms of interest articulation. For example, interest articulation might occur within institutional means, e.g., making use of the legislature, the judiciary, etc. Or interest articulation might occur outside the institutional means as in the case of violent or nonviolent direct action.

If the interest articulation work by subordinate groups is effective enough, it will be followed by deliberative processes in which the conflicting values are resolved into feasible policy. It is in the deliberative process that the conflicting claims confront one against the other. Negotiations might occur, compromises be forged, and rewards distributed. It is in the deliberative stage that a meaningful dialogue is established for resolving the conflicting values. Negotiations are held, compromises are struck, committees are formed, commissions make report; there is bargaining in which the leaders as the power holders of conflicting groups haggle and then only, if at all, emerges an agreed formula. This agreed formula is translated into concrete policy where the last stage culminates in the execution of policy.

Summarizing, therefore, to understand the complex processes involved in the resolution of conflict either by violent means or nonviolent means, one has to study, within the system, all the conflicting groups and values; the ways by which these groups organize themselves around these values, and the means they adopt to put pressure on the dominant groups to accede to the demands of the subordinate groups. The processes of negotiation, bargaining, etc. are ways through which the final resolution of conflict emerges. It would be obvious that the actual tactics used whether violent or nonviolent, will play an important part in activating the above processes.

It seems, however, reasonable to focus only on one aspect of the conflict rather than all. Here, we are concerned with processes involved in conflict resolution by nonviolent means only. Satyagraha particularly in its more militant phase depends, as in the case of violent means, upon activating political processes and putting pressure on the opponent by inflicting economic losses or other inconveniences; but it differs from violent means in the possibility that there might be occasions where the conflict resolution is brought about by a genuine conversion of the opponent rather than through the application of pressure. For a nonviolent direct action to work either through coercion or conversion, the prerequisite is that the participants be nonviolent under all circumstances. The focus of our study here, therefore, is to find out who these participants are and identify the factors which cause them to remain nonviolent at all times.

Gandhi recognized that evils exist in society which result in conflict, and that they must be changed even if they are legitimized by political, social or religious instituations. According to Arne Naess,

> Gandhi always gravitated towards the centre of a conflict— A Karmyogi does not isolate himself from a struggle; he remains at the very heart of it, immersed in the conflicts of his fellowmen as one among men. From the centre of the struggle he tries to bring about a general reduction of violence instead of avoiding it himself.[10]

Moreover, Gandhi viewed conflict in terms of total change in the social system. It involves, through the use of satyagraha, all inclusive change containing the individual, institutions and collective aspects of life. Translated into social science language, what all this means is that each social system contains elements of strain and hence of potential conflict. The potential of conflict increases to the degree that the perception of the contending groups of the incompatibility of values increases. When individuals or groups start pursuing these values, a conflict ensues. These conflicts, unless properly managed and resolved, can become aggravated into dangerous conflicts resulting in an overall disintegration of the total system, although none of the contending groups meant it to be that way. Satyagraha is not only a way of resolving conflicts, but by the very methods it employs, it prevents necessary aggravation of the conflicts, and brings about fundamental change in individuals and institutions comprising the social system.

While the actual tactics employed within a satyagraha will depend upon the circumstances of a situation, the feature common to all the tactics is that they are nonviolent. The focus of this study is on nonviolent attitudes rather than tactics, because we believe that nonviolent behavior of subordinate groups is significantly related to their attitudes on nonviolence. Particularly in the case of Gandhi, the tactics to be used against the opponent are closely related to his views on nonviolence.

WHY NONVIOLENCE?

It should be clear that we do not take the position that conflicts cannot or are not resolved by resort to violent means.[11] But here we are only interested in nonviolent means, because we, with Gandhi, take the normative position that nonviolence is more in conformity with the dignity of the individual. Gandhi goes as far as to consider 'ahimsa' (i.e., nonviolence) as a "supreme duty."[12] Nor are we interested in doing a comparative analysis of costs involved in conflict resolution by nonviolent means as opposed to violent means, for we assume the difference to be qualitative. Gandhi asserts that it cannot be said that violence has ever brought peace to mankind.[13]

Indeed, mankind has watched helplessly as the capacity for planetary destruction has outpaced man's ability to comprehend human violence. Sociologists have produced numerous studies on violence.[14] Their findings report correlations between degrees of violence and certain socio-economic conditions. There would be nothing objectionable about these findings if they were taken to mean that oppressive conditions exist and violence has been one of the most common expressions of dissatisfactions with those conditions. Unfortunately, however, these findings are taken as an indication that violence is the natural and the only reaction to such conditions. Developing a hypothesis that "violence in all its forms, up to and including assassinations is a natural form of . . . behaviour",[15] is only a short step from here.

For the purposes of this study, it seems clear to us that if human beings are capable of violence, they are also capable of conducting themselves nonviolently. It may be that the reason why human beings give expression to their frustrations by indulging in violence has something to do with their perceptions of the values of violence rather than with violence being ingrained in their nature. If the social scientists continue to impress upon us "that nonviolence is a luxury to be afforded only when conflict is not intense, then violence will never be dropped from the repertoire of human responses."[16] Under certain circumstances violence does pay, depending upon the perceptions of the participants, it might even be pleasurable.

In spite of the successful use of nonviolent techniques in a great variety of circumstances,[17] it is unfortunate that their exhaustive study has escaped the attention of scientists. As pointed out earlier, they perhaps still think that nonviolence is only an "interesting ethical notion, but in real life mortals rarely live by such an unworkable dictum."[18] Lewis Coser in his article, "Some Social Functions of Violence"[19] discusses three social functions of violence, namely, "Violence as a form of achievement, violence as a danger signal and violence as a catalyst."[20] It is ironical that the same social functions which Coser attributes to violence have been achieved by nonviolence, through Gandhian techniques. One result of this kind of a dehumanized study of violence is that it tends to suggest not only that violence elicits particular type of responses from the targets against whom it is directed, but also that it is right and proper to use it in order to elicit those responses. Coser in the same article attributes to violence "achievement of personal identity."[21] Yet the same virtues have been claimed for nonviolence. Erikson tells us that violence can achieve only 'negative identity', an identity which is based on distrust, hate and exclusion (or at the cost) of the person or group that is target of violence. On the other hand, Gandhian techniques of nonviolence foster identity, an 'all inclusive identity' which is based on trust, love and harmonious relationships among the nonviolent actors and their targets.[22] Many other writers have suggested this kind of positive effect on the participants in the actions involving Gandhian techniques.[23] We will see how far these observations agree with our study.

THEORY OF MASS SOCIETY AND SATYAGRAHA

In contemporary social science, the theory of mass society has become a very popular theoretical perspective for the analysis of social and political movements. For many, this theory provides the most promising and comprehensive statement of the genesis of modern mass movements. In view of the fact that hundreds of thousands of people participated in the satyagrahas led by Gandhi, one would expect that the theory of mass society would provide a fruitful framework for understanding the dynamics of a satyagraha. But, as we will show below, it is of no great help.

Mass society analysts attribute the proliferation of mass behavior and mass movements in a society to the weakness of the society's integrative functions. The weakening of primary and local associations and groups leave "the nonelites poorly related to society and directly available for mobilization by mass oriented elites."[24] Daniel Bell in his *Critique of Mass Society*, sums it up as one in which "individuals have grown estranged from one another. The old primary group ties of family and local community have been shattered: ancient faiths are questioned; few unifying values have taken their place."[25] In most of the theories of mass behavior there is always an underlying assumption that mass behavior is undemocratic, extremist, pathological and indicative of disruption of primary and intermediate group ties within the society.[26]

The theory has already been subjected to serious criticisms.[27] Suffice it to say that it is irrelevant to the understanding of Gandhian satyagrahas. Far from being the consequence of the weakening of ties at the primary or the intermediate level, the Gandhian satyagrahas occurred in a setting of firm ties of family, caste and clan and were rooted in their ancient faith. Nor were the satyagrahas antidemocratic. The theory of satyagraha is based on respect for legally constituted authority. The participant in a satyagraha, who violates a particular law or laws because he considers the system to be unjust does not do so secretly, nor does he try to escape punishment. He openly declares his intention to break a law and after breaking the law he readily bears the consequences of his act.

Unlike the mass behavior theories, which portray mass behavior as spontaneous, fickle or antidemocratic, some theories on collective behavior e.g., by Neil J. Smelser[28] and Herbert Blumer[29] may provide useful insights for understanding certain aspects of a satyagraha. Thus, Blumer's distinction between collective behavior as in the case of a riot or panic and the collective behavior that is organized and goal oriented can provide a useful distinction between a satyagraha and a riotous mob. Similarly, Smelser provides a useful insight into questions such as what determines whether an episode of collective behavior will occur at all; or if it has occurred, what determines whether one type (e.g., panic or riot) or the other (e.g., purposeful and organized) will occur. The problem is that while the theories of collective behavior may throw some light on why an episode of collective behavior occurs, they do not tell us anything about why it may be nonviolent.

Thus, we see that, where the focus of study is nonviolent behavior, as in this case, the theories of mass behavior are not too much help. Criticizing the theory, Daniel Bell writes,

> When one seeks to apply the theory of mass society, analytically, it becomes very slippery. Ideal types like the shadows in Plato's cave generally never give us more than a silhouette. So too with the theory of 'mass society'. Each of the statements making up the theory... might be true, but

they do not follow necessarily from one another. Nor can we say that all the conditions described are present at any one time or place. More than that, there is no organizing principle—other than the general concepts of a 'breakdown of values'—that puts the individual elements of theory together in a logical, meaningful—let alone historical— manner.[30]

It should be clear from the above analysis that so far there are no theories which can satisfactorily explain all the aspects of nonviolent action.

It is, indeed, regrettable that in spite of the dramatic success of nonviolent action in India and elsewhere, no theories exist which can explain it. As we mentioned earlier, one of the reasons for this sad state of affairs is that the social scientists have not yet chosen to subject nonviolent action to the same dispassionate and scholarly analysis as violent action. This study seeks to take a short step in that direction by investigating some important aspects of nonviolent action through the study of the workings of a satyagraha, the most systematic and developed mode of nonviolent action.

While a satyagraha is an episode of collective behavior and hence it may be relevant to know why a satyagraha (as an episode of collective action) occurs at all, we need not necessarily undertake a comprehensive study of all the aspects of a satyagraha. We can concentrate only on selected aspects. Thus, the focus of our study in a satyagraha is the dynamics of nonviolent behavior. Through a survey of the attitudes of participants in three satyagraha, namely, Bardoli, Rajkot and Pardi, we wish to identify the factors which cause the participants to remain nonviolent at all times. The underlying assumption is that the participants have internalized an ideology of nonviolence which helps them remain nonviolent under even the most extenuating circumstances. We want to investigate how far these assumptions are warranted by facts. We also want to know who these people are and if their social background is in any way significant in their belief in nonviolence.

Similarly, our analysis of the dynamics of nonviolent action shows that all major nonviolent movements, including the Gandhian satyagrahas are characterized by the presence of one or more charismatic leaders. What is the role of a charismatic leader in relation to the nonviolent behavior of the participant? What are the roles of the numerous sub-leaders who actually help in conducting a nonviolent movement? To what extent have they internalized the ideology of nonviolence? How do they affect or are affected by the rank and file participants? Lastly, what is the effect of participation on the participants in a satyagraha? We seek answers to these and other questions through a survey of the attitudes in the three satyagrahas mentioned above. The approach and method of investigation have been elaborated in Chapter 3.

NOTES and REFERENCES

[1] Johan Galtung, "Pacificism from a Sociological Point of View" in the Journal of Conflict Resolution, 3 (1959), 67.

[2] Harold Lasswell, "Conflict and Leadership: the Process of Decision and Nature of Authority" in Anthony de Reuck, ed., *Conflict in Society* (Boston: Little Brown and Company, 1966), 211 fn.

[3] Clyde Kluckhohn, et al, "Values and Value-Orientations in the Theory of Action, an exploration in Definition and Classification" in Talcott Parsons and Edward Shils, *Toward a General Theory of Action* (Harvard: Harvard University Press, 1951), p. 395.

[4] Ibid., p. 395.

[5] Galtung, p. 67.

[6] E.g., Czech resistance against the Russians in 1968; for a description read Ronald J. Tercheck, "Theory Applications of Gandhian Tactics in Three Disparate Environments: India, the U.S. and Czechoslovakia", paper presented at the APSA in New York City, 1969, also India vs. Great Britain in terms of fight for Independence from the British rule.

[7] E.g., industrial conflicts such as 1918 Ahmedabad Mill Strike which Gandhi himself led.

[8] E.g., struggle for the emancipation of the untouchables in India or racial conflicts in the U.S.

[9] Lewis Coser, *The Functions of Social Conflict* (Glencoe: Free Press, 1956); William Gameson, *Power and Discontent* (Homewood, Illinois: the Dorsey Press, 1968); also, "Rancorous Conflict-Community Politics" in *American Social Review*, 31, (February, 1966), 71-81; Lewis Coser, "Social Conflict and the Theory of Social Change", *British Journal of Sociol.*, 8, (September, 1957), 197-220; Ralf Dahrendarf, *Class and Class Conflict in Industrial Society* (Stanford University Press, 1959); Anthony de Reuck, ed., *Conflict in Society*, contains essays on conflict by H. Lasswell, Anatol Rapoport, George de Vos, J. A. Van Doorn,

etc.; J. Bernard "Some Current Conceptualizations in the field of Conflict; in *American Journal of Sociol.*, 70 (1965), 442-54.

[10] *Gandhi and the Nuclear Age* (New Jersey, 1965), p. 39·

[11] Such a position is taken by staunch adherents of nonviolence, e.g., pacifists; see M.Q. Sibley; *Quiet Battle* (Quandrangle Books, 1963); Richard Gregg, *Power of Nonviolence* (Schocken Books, 1966); Arnold Foster, "Violence on the Fanatical Left and right" in the *Annals of the American Academy*, 364, (October, 1966), 141-147.

[12] M.K. Gandhi, *Nonviolent Resistance* (New York: Schocken Books, 1970), p. 42.

[13] The *Harijan*, May 19, 1946.

[14] William A. Weseley, "Escalation of Violence Through Legitimation" in the *Annals*, 364, 120-126; Arnold S. Feldman, "Violence and Volatility: the Likelihood of Revolution" in H. Eckstein, *Internal War*, ed., (New York: Free Fress, 1964); Franz Fanon, *The Wretched of the Earth* (New York: Grove Press, 1968).

[15] A L. Niehburg, *Political Violence* (New York: St Martin's Press, 1968), cited in the *Current*, No. 112, (November 1969).

[16] Elton B. McNeil, "Violence and Human Development" in the *Annals*, 364, 49.

[17] For a description of some of the nonviolent movements carried out in the different parts of the world see M.Q. Sibley, op. cit., and Richard Gregg, op cit.; also Fenner Brockway; *Non Cooperation in Other Lands* (Madras: Tagore and Company, n.d.).

[18] McNeil, p. 153.

[19] *Annals*, 364, 8-18.

[20] Ibid., p. 8.

[21] Op. cit., p. 11. See also Fanon, op. cit., pp. 35-106.

[22] Erik Erikson, "Problem of Identity, Hatred and Non-violence" in the *American Journal of Psychiatry*, 122, No. 3, (1965), 241-250. For the same view see also Edward D. Hoedemaker, "Distrust and Aggression" in the *Journal of Conflict Resolution*, 12 (1966), 72-73.

[23] Christian Bay, *The Structure of Freedom* (Atheneum, (1965); Sally Belfrage; *Freedom Summer* (New York: Viking, 1965); Martin Luther King, *Stride Toward Freedom* (New York: Harper and Row, 1958); J.L. Nehru, *Discovery of India* (New York: John Day, 1959).

[24] William Kornhauser, *The Politics of Mass Society* (Glencoe: Free Press, 1963), p. 115.

[25] Daniel Bell, "America as a Mass Society: A Critique" in his *The End of Ideology*, revised edition (New York: The Free Press, 1966), p. 21. Leading advocates of the theory of mass politics in whole or part, apart from Kornhauser, are Hannah Arendt, *The Origins of Totalitarianism* (New York: Harcourt, Brace and Co.. 1954); Eric Fromm, *Escape From Freedom* (New York: Rinehart, 1941); Robert Nisbet, *The Quest for Community* (London: Oxford University Press, 1953), etc.

[26] Thus, according to Hannah Arendt, "The chief characteristic of mass man is not brutality and backwardness, but his isolation and lack of normal social relations." op. cit., p. 310.

[27] See in particular Daniel Bell, "America as a Mass Society: A Critique", pp. 21-38; Joseph R. Gusfield, "Mass Society and Extremist Politics" in *American Sociological Review*, XXVII (1962), 19-30.
[28] *Theory of Collective Behavior* (New York: The Free Press, 1971).
[29] "Collective Behavior," in J,B. Gittler, ed., *Review of Sociology: Analysis of a Decade* (New York: John Wiley and Sons, 1957).
[30] *Theory of Collective Behaviour*, p. 22.

2
Theory of Satyagraha

In spite of a growing awareness of the use of satyagraha for conflict resolution, there is a widespread confusion about what it means. The following factors are largely responsible for this confusion: (1) Participant leaders in any agitation for change in the status quo within society have used Gandhi's name indiscriminately to justify their tactics. (2) Clarity of thought on Gandhian techniques has often been handicapped by the highly emotional attitudes of the proponents and opponents of these approaches. (3) Gandhi developed his techniques over a very long period of time (almost forty years) and they involve a large variety of conflict situations, and hence, it is hard to square his theory with practice in all conflict situations. (4) Gandhi did not claim any "patent" rights for his techniques and considered them to be absolutely flexible and "evolutionary".[1] This, while helping to develop new techniques in different countries also resulted in contradictory interpretations of the uniting concepts in his theory of nonviolent action. To overcome these difficulties, we first developed a model of satyagraha from the writings by and about Gandhi, and then used it as a criterion for selecting the three satyagrahas for intensive investigation out of the several that we looked at.

DEVELOPING THE SATYAGRAHA MODEL

The word satyagraha, derived from the words 'satya' meaning truth and 'agraha' meaning grip-taking, literally means "holding on to the truth".[2] But in order to hold on to the truth, it is essential to first discover the truth. Thus, satyagraha is an active technique of action in a conflict situation, which consists of a search for the truth and a struggle for its vindication. According to Gandhi, truth is the most important value of the satyagraha system of action. It is the value which is, first, most actively sought and then established. Satyagraha is not just a passive holding on to truth. On the contrary, it is an active technique of action in pursuance of 'right' and 'justice' through nonviolent means. This protracted pursuance after truth occurs in a conflict situation in which the satyagrahis seek to bring about conflict resolution by nonviolent means. They would bring self suffering upon themselves rather than inflict suffering, through violence, against the opponent. Thus the three most important principles of satyagraha are 'satya', 'ahimsa' and 'tapasya', to which we shall now turn our attention in greater detail.

SATYA

'Satya' or 'truth' is the most salient value of the satyagraha action system, whose purpose is the discovery of truth. This would seem to assume not only that Gandhi believed in the existence of truth but also that it is identifiable. He does believe in the existence of an absolute truth which he identifies with God. However, it is not the establishment of the absolute truth to which a satyagraha is geared. Absolute truth can be attained only through self realization, a self realization which cannot occur so long as we are imprisoned in this mortal frame. Gandhi himself never claimed to know the absolute truth. Under these circumstances the best that human beings can do is to keep their minds open on the question of truth. In the absence of the absolute truth we can only have relative truth, which manifests itself in and is a product and an expression of a complex web of interrelations that exist within a social system. These truths are based upon our beliefs in the nature of human needs and the form of the social system that would best satisfy it. Since the different individuals within the social system have achieved different levels of self realization, it is obvious that there will be various versions regarding the truth since it represents human needs. The truth, or rather the relative truth, is to be culled from within the social system, in so far as it serves to draw together, from the beliefs (values) held by various individuals, all that is most useful for the persistence of the social system. The discovery of the relative truth, however, is not a simple process, for it is bogged down in a medley of incompatible and contradictory values. Satyagraha vindicates the right value or the truth by bringing about a confrontation between the lesser values. Thus a satyagrahi, who is convinced that truth is on his side, as he wages a struggle, is indeed only half certain of the truth. As a matter of fact, he is only an ally of truth, regardless of who possesses it. This is to say that a satyagrahi during the course of his satyagraha is prepared to modify his own conception about the truth in a particular matter, in as much as it gives the opponent an opportunity and courage to accept the change.

AHIMSA

If the discovery of truth, i.e., the establishment of right value or values within a conflict situation is the goal of a satyagraha, 'ahimsa' is the means for its discovery and vindication. The word, derived from the combination of negative prefix "a" meaning 'non' and "himsa" meaning 'injury', means "noninjury" and is usually translated as "nonviolence". In this sense nonviolence means refusal to do harm or 'hurt' under any circumstances.[3] However, 'ahimsa' with its negative prefix is not just a "negative state of harmlessness but it is a positive state of love of doing good even to the evil doer".[4] Thus nonviolence has a positive as well as a negative aspect. In the negative aspect it means "complete absence of ill will",[5] 'non injury' against all. In its positive [connotation it includes "affection, sympathy, mercy, generosity, service and self sacrifice."[6] Here, we see that Gandhi identifies nonviolence with love. Thus in its positive aspect 'ahimsa', as Bondurant observes, consists of the concern and active support that belongs to the 'agapeistic' rather than 'erotic' concept of love,[7] a concept which sees an underlying unity in every living thing.

Truth and love are, thus an integral part of Gandhian Satyagraha. "Truth is the end. Love a means thereto."[8] The inculcation of the true spirit of nonviolence is possible only when one has become well versed in the 'law of love'.[9]

According to Gandhi it is easy to know what love or nonviolence is, although it is difficult to follow it. But as far as the truth is concerned 'we know only a fraction of it'.[10] Satyagraha "excludes the use of violence because man is not capable to knowing the absolute truth and therefore not competent to punish."[11] It is for this reason that the search for the absolute truth in a conflict situation has to proceed through a strict adherence to nonviolence. It is only in an atmosphere of nonviolence that the relative truths, as they appear to the contending parties in a conflict, can be tested, thus leading to the higher truth. If, as we observed earlier, truth originates and finds expression in human needs, it cannot be separated from nonviolence. Any use of violence or injury to others in search for truth defeats its purpose. Satyagrahi must convert the opponent to his version of truth with persuasion and gentleness. On the other hand, the satyagrahi should constantly reexamine his own version of the truth in the light of any new facts that might emerge during the course of the satyagraha; and be prepared to accept his opponents' values should they prove to be closer to truth than his own.

TAPASYA

Last but not the least in Gandhi's satyagraha system of action is the principle of 'tapasya' meaning 'self-suffering'. It is an essential expression of nonviolence and truth. It is an essential expression of truth because unless one is prepared to suffer, one can hardly be committed to anything, let alone the truth, as exacting as Gandhi's interpretation will make it to be. In any serious conflict, suffering is always involved for the contending parties. But for a satyagrahi who conducts struggle according to the principles of a satyagraha, there is a greater suffering involved because he does not take a partisan view of truth. Even as he is trying to convince the opponent that satyagrahi's version of values is nearer to truth, he is aware that it is possible that the opponent's values might be nearer to truth than his own. The recognition by satyagrahi of such a possibility in itself puts the use of violent means out of the question. 'Tapasya' is a vital expression of truth and love, both because it embodies a resolution to shoulder as far as

Theory of Satyagraha

possible the burden of suffering oneself rather than shift it to the opponent. Another reason that Gandhi advocates suffering injury in one's own person, rather than inflicting it upon the opponent is his belief in the fundamental unity of the universe. As he puts it, "we are all tarred with the same brush, and are children of one and the same Creator, and as such divine powers within us are infinite."[12] Self-suffering is not just a 'meek submission to the will of the evil doer but it means the pitting of one's whole soul against the will of the tyrant;'[13] it is directed towards moral persuasion of the opponent by awakening his conscience. Implicit in this is the "belief that the sight of suffering on the part of multitudes of people will melt the heart of the opponent and induce him to desist from his course of violence."[14] Apart from the ethical argument that the use of voluntary self-suffering "ennobles those who lose their lives, and morally enriches the world for their sacrifice,"[15] Gandhi gives a utilitarian argument also in its support that "it results in the long run in the least loss of lives."[16]

From the above discussion it should be clear, therefore, that 'truth' which is the goal of satyagraha is in reality a relative truth which grows out of societal needs. During the course of the conflict waged through satyagraha, the contending parties have only a limited view of truth which they cherish as their values. Under these circumstances, to use violent means would be to presume that one has a hold on truth with certainty. But where truth itself is defined as the end product of a nonviolent process, the use of violence will defeat that purpose. From this it should also be clear that the principle of truth in the Gandhian concept of satyagraha is that of relative truth, and is applicable to a social system in terms of its need only at a particular time and place. The proper means for discovering that truth, or the resolution of conflict arising out of the differences of values as to what is truth, can only be pursued through nonviolent action. Love is an important corollary of nonviolence. It is love which sustains a satyagrahi in his resolve to refuse to do harm to the opponent in spite of violence from him. The satyagrahi invites suffering on himself rather inflict suffering on the opponent, as far as possible.

SATYAGRAHA AS A WAY OF LIFE

We have so far tried to elaborate on the meaning of satyagraha only in the context of a conflict. For Gandhi, however, satyagraha being 'soul force' is "the way, the truth, and the Life."[17] It is applicable not only to conflicts but all activities of life. "It is a force that may be used by individuals as well as communities. It may be used as well in political as in domestic affairs."[18] He believes that to make nonviolent action effective in a group conflict, satyagraha has to be practiced "in all aspects of our daily life."[19] Nonviolence, in order to be true, must be a part of our normal life, must be in our thought, word and deed; and must color our behavior. "Nonviolence to be a creed has to be all pervasive." One "cannot be nonviolent about one activity... and violent about others."[20]

Viewed in this context, then, we see that satyagraha is not 'just a means for conflict resolution; it is a way of life; it is the end.' According to Gandhi, to effect an end as lofty as that of satyagraha "nonviolence... cannot be a mere policy. It must be a creed or a passion."[21]

It is a system of social action which has implications for the life of the individual as well as the community. At the individual level, satyagraha is a way of life which gives its practitioner a distinctive orientation. On the societal level, it refers to a system where truth, as defined earlier, prevails and where satyagraha is used as an instrument to manage and resolve conflicts within the social system.

SATYAGRAHA, A DOCTRINE OR A POLICY?

The writers[22] on nonviolent action have sometimes raised the question whether nonviolence in the satyagraha system of action is the ultimate principle of life; or if it is only a policy to be pursued in order to achieve some desirable goals. According to Judith Steim, nonviolent action subsumes two types.[23] Namely, (1) conscientious nonviolence and (2) pragmatic nonviolence. The first is characterized by an ethical or a religious belief which categorically prohibits injury to another. In contrast, the second one is purely goal oriented in which an individual would avoid being wronged rather than avoid wrong.

doing. From what we have so far said about Gandhi, there is no doubt that he belongs to the 'conscientious' category according to the above classification. In the various nonviolent campaigns that Gandhi led or supported Gandhi never tired of reminding the satyagrahis that nonviolence ought to pervade their total lives. This message was constantly brought home to them through various activities, such as constructive work, prayers, speech making, etc., during the satyagraha, till nonviolence as a 'way of life' and 'creed' became a common idiom for the satyagrahis. To be familiar with an idiom is, however, not the same thing as living that idiom in one's life. And it is clear that almost all the nonviolent movements, including Gandhian satyagrahas subsume both 'conscientious' and 'pragmatic' categories. This means that every nonviolent movement comprises participants in which only a few, particularly the leaders, believe in nonviolence as a way of life and the rest believe it is only a tactic, an important tool for promotion of their interests.

On the other hand, it might be argued that there is not and need not be any dichotomy between the two categories because the belief in conscientious nonviolence does not necessarily exclude a pragmatic component insofar as nonviolence is and can be used as a tool for conflict resolution. It is in this sense that for Gandhi nonviolence was a 'means as well as an end.' They were interconvertible terms. As we noted earlier, both of the elements of nonviolent action exist side by side. Even a conscientious believer in nonviolence will have to come up with and adopt pragmatic nonviolent techniques to exert the best possible effect on the opponent.

COERCION AND NONVIOLENCE

Before we conclude our discussion of the theory of satyagraha, it is pertinent at this point to make a few observations on the relation between coercion and nonviolence. Gandhian scholars[24] strongly deny that any element of coercion is involved in satyagraha. But as we said earlier, we believe that satyagraha does carry a positive element of coercion in it. Where it differs from violent tactics is in the fact that, 'its sting is drawn by its nonviolent qualification.'[25] In violence, the force is wilfully used by the subordinate group, in order to injure the opponent and extract submission from him against his will. In contrast, in nonviolent action the subordinate group exercises power to bring about change in the opponent always through persuasion and conversion.[26] This does not mean that nonviolent action always works the way it is intended to work. Measures such as boycott, civil disobedience, strike, etc., can and do, as we shall see later, cause discomfort and injury to the opponent, in the form of loss of business, mental worry, etc. Nor is this state of affairs unjustified; "love, the active state of ahimsa, requires... (one) to resist the wrong doer by dissociating...from him even though it may offend him or injure him physically."[27] There is, however, a basic difference between the coercion engendered by nonviolent as opposed to violent action. In satyagraha, several stages of nonviolent action are specifically directed toward winning over the opponent. It is only in the later stages of the satyagraha that coercive nonviolent methods, such as boycott, civil disobedience, etc...are adopted. The escalation of satyagraha to its coercive stages is gradual, thus giving the opponent at every stage a chance to understand the grievances of the subordinate group. Unlike violent action, the satyagrahi in nonviolent action displays his willingness to take suffering upon himself even as the dominant group is being subjected to it. Even when the conflict resolution is the result of nonviolent coercion, attempts are made after the conflict is over to mitigate the effects of suffering on the dominant group, caused by satyagraha.

THE PRACTICE OF SATYAGRAHA

Corresponding to its philosophy, satyagraha, as a means of conflict resolution, has a technique of action. The techniques vary according to the circumstances and the stage of the conflict. In India, the most general forms of satyagraha action were noncooperation, civil disobedience and constructive program.

In principle noncooperation means refusal to cooperate with evil. Noncooperation might include activities such as strikes, walkouts, emptying statuses, e.g., giving up titles; resignation of jobs, etc. Civil disobedience involves positive violation of the law and might include such activities as nonpayment of taxes, picketing, etc. In this, the satyagrahi invites suffering upon himself by going to jail. The satyagrahi does not try to escape jail-going; as a matter of fact, he considers it deserved in view of his violation of a particular law. Civil disobedience may be of various types—defensive, aggressive, individual, collective and mass. Indeed there are no hard and fast rules as to which specific form a nonviolent action will take to be effective under a particular situation. It depends upon the experience, training, insight and judgment of the leaders of the satyagraha. Over the last fifty years many of the techniques employed by Gandhi have been used successfully in conflict situations in the various parts of the world. Some new ones have been developed. Thus the techniques of 'sit in', 'the wade in', 'going limp' employed in the U.S.A. or the 'reverse strike' employed by Danielo Dolci in Italy are all variations of the techniques which might be employed in a satyagraha.

Since nonviolent action under satyagraha depends for its effectiveness primarily on the moral qualities of those who use it, it is of utmost importance that sufficient attention be paid to how these qualities might be developed. A true satyagraha would be impossible without a strong sense of discipline among its practitioners; a sense that can be developed by proper training. Every conflict brings some suffering to the participants but it should be obvious that the kind of sacrifice and self-suffering which a satyagraha demands would need a tremendous amount of self-control on the part of the satyagrahis.

In Gandhian satyagrahas, this need for training was fulfilled through programs of constructive activities which always preceded and accompanied the satyagraha. The programs of constructive activities were planned and carried out in 'Ashramas'.[28] Gandhi established many such Ashramas all over India. They were used for many purposes connected with satyagrahas such as use as campaign headquarters during active phases of satyagraha, for training of leaders and planning of constructive activities. Gandhi's program of constructive activity ranged from adult education and social reforms to village industries and sanitation. Apart from developing satyagrahi's skills and qualities essential for effective nonviolent action, constructive activities helped to inculcate a 'spirit of service'. For Gandhi, "unaccompanied by the spirit of service, courting imprisonment, and inviting beating and lathi charges becomes a species of violence."[29]

Thus the importance of Ashramas in Gandhian satyagrahas was immense; and as Dhawan expressed, "Ashramas...became the nerve centres of the nonviolent movement...Through them the message of nonviolence filtered down to the masses."[30] Gandhi had so much faith in these constructive activities that he claimed, "Constructive work...is for a nonviolent army what drilling, etc., is for an army designed for bloody warfare."[31] Although Gandhi did not adopt more intensive methods such as the use of psychosocial dramas and other methods[32] (as in the U.S. Civil Rights Campaigns) for training in nonviolence, he considered such methods to be of greatest value for inculcating a strong discipline. Thus he gave approval to a Congress Party Organization called 'Quami Seva Dal' which had its periodical rallies and training camps, its drill, uniforms and national songs.[33] Other methods used for training were propaganda, limited satyagraha campaigns, and the administering of oaths and pledges. According to Gandhi, pledges and taking of oaths are particularly helpful where a population has a strong religious background. They induce a strong sense of discipline among the oath takers. Apart from providing education in nonviolence to simple people, the pledges acquire a still greater value when they detail a comprehensive set of rules of behavior in all possible situations which are likely to develop in a satyagraha. During the 1930-31 Satyagraha, for example, Gandhi published in the Young India a set of rules which was to be observed strictly by all the volunteers in the ensuing campaign. The code was divided into four categories with rules respectively for the individual satyagrahi, for him as a prisoner, as a member of direct action unit, and for his conduct in case of communal riots.[34]

PREPARATION FOR SATYAGRAHA

In addition to the activities noted above, Gandhi insisted on the observance of certain fundamental rules, which he thought were essential to prosecuting a successful satyagraha. The rules are summed up below:[35]

(1) Every stage of the organization of a satyagraha campaign

needs careful preparation. The first and the foremost condition for initiating a campaign is that there must be a grievance. Even when a grievance is clear, the objectives to be achieved by satyagraha have to be chosen with great care. It is essential that the objectives should be clear and tangible. This is necessary because a satyagrahi is committed to open dealing; which in turn is based on the conviction that openness tends to reassure the opponent and reduce his hostility. Also, the demands of the satyagrahis should be based to a minimum consistent with truth; and even these should be open for constant review and readjustment as the occasion demands.

(2) A satyagrahi must shun all compromises which are in violation of the fundamental principles for which a satyagraha was initiated. Before any settlement is reached insistence on fundamentals must be reached.

(3) During the prosecution of a satyagraha, a satyagrahi should utilize all avenues of cooperation with the opponent by helping him. This is essential to convince the opponent of the satyagrahis' sincerity for the cause and goodwill for the opponent.

(4) Propaganda should be an integral part of satyagraha and must continue throughout the campaign. It should be designed not only to arouse and keep the morale of the satyagrahi but also to educate them, the opponent and the public on the merits of the issues in conflict.

(5) Throughout the satyagraha, the initiative should be maintained by the subordinate group. As in the case of a war, the morale of the satyagrahis may be affected if there is a loss of initiative. This may be particularly true where the threshold of opponent's resistance is strong and where the satyagraha, subsequently, does not seem to make much headway. Under such circumstances it requires high ingenuity and skill to retain the initiative.

STAGES IN THE DEVELOPMENT OF A SATYAGRAHA

Since the aim of a satyagrahi is always to convert and never to coerce, it is essential that the escalation of a satyagraha to its more vigorous forms, e.g., civil disobedience, etc., should be gradual and only after milder forms of satyagraha have failed to yield results. The stages through which an ideal satyagraha should pass are briefly summarized below:[36]

(1) Having convinced himself that a genuine grievance exists, the first step in a satyagraha is negotiations. They are initiated for two reasons. First they may bring about conflict resolution by clearing misunderstandings; if not they will at least demonstrate the willingness of the satyagrahis to be polite and their reluctance to use direct action.

(2) If the negotiations fail, agitation for the redress of grievance is the next step. It lifts the morale of the oppressed group; it shakes the opponent from complacency and makes him more responsive to at least looking at the issues which he refused earlier.

(3) After the public attention has been sufficiently drawn to the issues in conflict, the satyagrahis resort to demonstrations. If this fails to get the desired results, an ultimatum is issued which is usually followed by a call for 'hartal'. 'Hartal' is a kind of general strike in which all activities stop.

(4) There is much public prayer and fasting. These are self-purificatory steps. They are also intended to convince the opponent and the public of the movement's morality. As part of this self-purification, satyagrahis might give up honorary titles since they have been conferred by an evil system. They may also resign from their jobs. While resigning from lucrative jobs might hurt the opponent by disrupting his organizational set up, thus causing him financial loss, or even psychological injury, it also shows the satyagrahi's moral purpose of unwillingness to hurt the opponent since he shares some of that suffering 'by inviting suffering' upon himself.

Fasting was a "potent weapon"[37] in Gandhi's armory of satyagraha. He, however, frequently warned about the dangers of fasting indiscriminately. Most of the so-called 'fasts' Gandhi termed only as 'hunger strikes'. No one has a right to fast till he has laid claim to the love of one against whom it is undertaken. Thus Gandhi said he would not fast against a tyrant, a "General Dyer".[38] Minimally a fast may be undertaken by him who is associated with the person against whom he fasts.[39] While Gandhi admitted that an element of coercion was involved in fasting, it was more 'moral' and 'spiritual', since it acts by raising the conscience of the opponent. Gandhi used his fasts for different purposes on different occasions. He either used them to instill satyagraha discipline among the volunteers or wrest concessions from the opponent, or both.

The fastings most commonly resorted to by a large number of satyagrahis, are usually limited to missing a meal or not eating for one whole day and are completely self-purificatory.[40] Fasts of longer duration, i.e., for a week or more, or fasts unto death undertaken by leaders of the satyagraha are considered much more serious. Such fasts are usually undertaken at a much higher stage in the escalation of the satyagraha movement. Often times it is used as a last resort after all the possible steps in satyagraha are utilized and exhausted. According to Gandhi, "Sacrifice of self even unto death is the final weapon in the hands of a nonviolent person. It is not given to man to do more."[41]

(5) Having exhausted its milder forms without getting the desired results, satyagraha now enters into more vigorous form with actions such as economic boycotts, picketing or 'dhurna',[42] a form of sit-down strike. These three forms are particularly useful in labor conflicts. Economic boycott consists of refusal to buy the products manufactured by the opponent. A good example of this came in 1930 when Gandhi boycotted imported cotton goods. By reducing his apparel to a homespun loin cloth, he threatened the whole export business of the British Cloth Industry.

Picketing is usually resorted to with the purpose of demonstrating, advertising and gaining public sympathy.

(6) The next stage is noncooperation which may involve nonpayment of taxes, withdrawal from schools and colleges, even 'hizrat'. 'Hizrat' means mass exodus in which a whole community packs up and leaves. Under these circumstances the opponent, left with no one to exercise power over, may try to bargain and induce the exodees to return.

(7) If this does not work, the satyagrahis can resort to civil disobedience, which consists of violating the law. Great care has to be taken in deciding the law which is selected for contravention.

Beyond these, the other methods suggested by Gandhi are more extreme and apply where the opponent to the conflict is the whole system of government. After the whole machinery of the government has been brought to a halt as a result of nonpayment of taxes, withdrawals from schools, colleges and courts; civil disobedience; the next step is usurping the functions of the government and even formation of a 'parallel' and ultimately an altogether new government. Gandhi did not have occasion to use the last named stages because historic events including granting of independence to India intervened. However, taken as a whole Gandhian Satyagraha provides an elaborate plan for the resolution of conflict at various levels including interpersonal, intergroup, community, national and international. Of course, the exact techniques to be adopted during a conflict by the satyagrahis will depend upon the circumstances, time, purpose and the nature of the opponents. But all the techniques, if it is a satyagraha, have to be practiced within a broad framework outlined above.

NOTES and REFERENCES

[1] M.K. Gandhi, *Nonviolent Resistance* (New York: Schocken Books, 1970), pp. 71 and 6.

[2] M.K. Gandhi, *Political and National Life* and *Affairs* (Ahmedabad: Navjivan, 1968), III, p. 73.

[3] *Nonviolent Resistance*, p. 161.

[4] *Young India*, January 19, 1921.

[5] Gandhi, *Political and National Life and Affairs*, III, p. 113.

[6] S. Abid Hussain, *The Way of Gandhi and Nehru* (London: Asia Publishing House, 1959), p. 13.

[7] Joan Bondurant, *Conquest of Violence* (Berkeley: University of California Press, 1965), p, 24.

[8] *Nonviolent Resistance*, p. 384.

[9] M.K. Gandhi, *Form Yervada Mandir: Ashram Observances*, trans., V.G. Desai (Ahmedabad: Navjivan, 1932), p. 8.

[10] Gandhi, *ibid.*, p. 8.

[11] M.K, Gandhi, *Speeches and Writings of Mahatma Gandhi*, 4th edition, (Madras: Natesan, n.d.), p. 406.

[12] M.K. Gandhi, *The Story of my Experiments With Truth* (Ahmedabad: 1927), II, p. 53.

[13] Gandhi, *Satyagraha in South Africa* (Madras: S. Ganesan, 1928), p. 175.

[14] Gandhi, *National Life and Affairs*, III, p. 171.

[15] Gandhi, *Nonviolence in Peace and War*, 2nd edition, (Ahmedabad: Navjivan, n.d.), p. 49.

[16] Ibid., p. 49.

Theory of Satyagraha

[17] *Young India Selections* (Madras Publishing, 1927-29), III, p. 444.
[18] Ibid., 444.
[19] *Harijan*, June 29, 1949.
[20] *Harijan*, October 12, 1935.
[21] M.K, Gandhi, cited in Thomas Merton, *Gandhi on Nonviolence* (New Directions Paperback, 1965), p. 38.
[22] Theodore Ebert, "Nonviolence: Doctrine or Technique" 11. No. 3, (July 1967), 251-260: Judith Steim, "Nonviolence is Two" in Paul Hare and Herbert Blumberg, ed·, *Nonviolent Direct Action, American Cases: Social Psychological Analyses* (Cleveland: Corpus Books, 1968), p. 447-459.
[23] Op. cit., p. 448.
[24] R.R. Diwakar, *Satyagraha* (Bombay: Hind Kitabs, 1946); K.S. Shridharani, *War Without Violence* (New York: Harcourt, Brace and Company, 1939), etc.
[25] Bondurant, p. 11.
[26] Shridharani, p. 292.
[27] Gandhi, *Nonviolent Resistance*, p. 161.
[28] Ashrama is a place of religious retreat.
[29] *Harijan*, May 18, 1940.
[30] G.N. Dhawan, *Political Philosophy of Mahatma Gandhi* (Ahmedabad: Navjivan, 1957), p. 167.
[31] *Young India Selections*, III, p. 69.
[32] Martin Oppenheimer and George Lakey, *A Manual for Direct Action* (Chicago: Quandrangle Paperback, 1965), Also William Miller, *Nonviolence: A Christian Interpretation* (New York: Association Press, 1964).
[33] Dhawan, p. 178.
[34] M.K. Gandhi, *Nonviolent Resistance*, pp. 78-81.
[35] This description is partly based on Bondurant, op. cit., pp. 38-39.
[36] K.S. Shridharani has abstracted the total plan of satyagraha into about a dozen steps on which the following description is based, op. cit., pp. 5-42. Bondurant's description of the steps is also somewhat similar to Shridharani's, Bondurant, op. cit., pp. 38-41.
[37] Gandhi, *Nonviolent Resistance*, p. 320.
[38] Ibid., p. 183.
[39] Ibid., p. 321.
[40] Fasting has been traditionally recognized as self-purificatory and used as such in Hinduism.
[41] *Young India*, April 23, 1931.
[42] 'Dhurna' has been called the 'Father of sit down strike' where the satyagrahis will refuse to move until their demands are met.

3
Methodology

"What is Satyagraha?" K.S. Shridharani narrates how he addressed this question to scores of illiterate Indian villagers—men and women, and always received the same answer, "Satyagraha is Gandhi's way of fighting the British Raj."[1]

We decided to ask the same question, but this time in greater depth so as to find out, through a study of satyagrahis' attitudes:

(1) What satyagraha really means to the large number of people who constitute its rank and file; and to its leadership;
(2) which kinds of people participate in a nonviolent movement.
(3) what is the role of religion in a satyagraha;
(4) what is the effect of satyagraha on the participants as reflected in their attitudes.

This study is based on a survey of attitudes related to three satyagrahas, namely, Bardoli, (1928), Rajkot (1938-39), and Pardi (1953-65). We preferred a 'survey' for the study of this problem because, the big advantage of a survey is that the researcher is able to carry out his investigation in the natural environment. A survey is particularly useful where the research is exploratory. It allows the researcher to form a wholistic picture of the situation under study. The researcher is not bound by one method but can capitalize on any approach which might aid understanding of the 'unexplained' phenomena. Thus, in this case we were able to compile evidence and ideas and at the same time get a 'feel' of the people and the situation that we were trying to study.

Very little, if any, empirical work has been done on 'nonviolent direct action'. This work purports to be exploratory in nature. Several different methods were used, including use of documents, newspaper reports, questionnaires interviews, etc.

The main body of data was gathered in interviews with the leaders and the volunteers who participated in the three satyagrahas and in visits to the Gandhi Library at Sabarmati Ashrama, Gujerat Vidyapith Library in Ahmedabad, Swaraj Ashram in Bardoli, Rashtriya Shala Library in Rajkot, Delhi University Library, Praja Socialist Party Offices in Surat and Bombay and the personal records in the custody of certain leaders. The data collection was done in the months of July through December 1970, and subsequently in the summer of 1976.

A researcher usually seeks an optimal setting for his investigation so as to obtain the best results. Sometimes for the sake of convenience a survey research has to be concentrated on a single case or organization. This has a major weakness. There is the problem of 'typicality' or 'generalization'. The researcher always hopes to get results that can be 'generalized' to many situations. For this reason the survey analysts go to great lengths in trying to make their samples as 'random' and representative as possible. But the problem is that there is no guarantee that a case chosen for study is representative of other similar cases.

It is possible to get around this problem to some extent by selecting more than one case which are 'representative' of the researcher's interest and then subject them to a thorough invesgation. What we did in this case was that first we developed a model of satyagraha from writings by and about Gandhi; then, we looked closely at some of the non-violent movements which were waged in India during the period 1920 through 1960 to see how many of them were carried out in conformity with our model. From these we selected three, namely, Bardoli, Rajkot, and Pardi Satyagrahas for our study.

Our choice in selecting the three movements was influenced by the following considerations:

(1) All the three satyagrahas were carried out in accordance with our model.
(2) They were all waged in the state of Gujerat in India. This facilitated movement from one place to another for data collection. The Gujerati language Interview Schedule could be used for all three satyagrahas, since Gujerati is understood by all the people in the region.
(3) The three movements took place in different social settings thus providing an opportunity to investigate the 'typical' in attitudes on nonviolence. Bardoli is a movement in which the small land owners are the subordinate group; the officials of the revenue department, the police and the Government of Bombay are the dominant group. In Pardi the landless are the subordinate group; the landlords and, indirectly the responsible leaders of the Government of Bombay are the dominant group. In Rajkot the subordinate group is the people of Rajkot; the dominant group is the State Ruler and indirectly the British Resident. All the three were organized by different political parties.

INTERVIEWS

The first stage of the research was a series of fifteen interviews at Ahmedabad, Rajkot, and Surat with a variety of people who participated in various Gandhian campaigns. These included four leaders and eleven rank and file satyagrahis. The interviews were 'focused', that is, a definite set of relevant topics was chosen and brought up for consideration in some manner. No attempt was made to force a person to answer the questions in a particular sequence or in any special manner. The answers were open-ended with the respondent making whatever comments he liked to make, taking as long as he wanted or branching off into as many relevant side issues as he wanted. From these interviews, after several alterations and modifications, final interview guides for both rank and file and leaders of satyagraha were developed.

THE INTERVIEWERS

The interviews were conducted with the help of six socio-

Methodology

logy graduate students[2] of K.P. Commerce College, Surat and Saurashtra University, Rajkot. The interviewers were selected from Surat and Rajkot not only because of their facility with Gujerati language but also because of their familiarity with Surat, Bardoli, Pardi and Rajkot areas where most of our respondents were located. The interviewers met together with me at a ten day session in Surat where they where acquainted with the interview guide and the interview techniques with the objective of reducing interviewer bias to the minimum. We were ably assisted in this phase of work by Professor P.S. Jethwa, the Chairman of the Department of Sociology at Saurahtra University in Rajkot. Two sets of Interview Guides, one each for the leaders, and the rank and file satyagrahis were prepared. The original interview guides were prepared in the English language. Professor Babu Bhai of K.P. Commerce College helped in translating the interview guides for the satyagrahis into Gujerati language; he also personally assisted the interviewers in their interviewing work in Pardi. All the leaders were personally interviewed by me either in English or Hindi language.

THE INTERVIEW SCHEDULE

In an exploratory study, preparing an interview schedule poses a number of problems. If all the questions are 'closed' there is a possibility of losing a lot of useful information. On the other hand, if all the questions are kept 'open', the researcher is deluged with such a vast amount of information that it becomes extremely difficult to select that which is useful. In this case we kept about fifty per cent of the questions 'open-ended'. For the rest, although they were 'closed', the interviewers were instructed to take notes if there were additional comments from the respondents. That this arrangement worked very well is proved from the amount of notes that accumulated from these 'additional' comments. All the responses to 'open-ended' questions were content analyzed by carefully reading and recording the persistent, as well as exceptional patterns of responses. Even a cursory glance at the interview schedule would reveal that the categories of responses to a few questions do not seem to be mutually exclusive. Thus, for example, the categories of responses listed in the schedule to question "which two of the following best describe your feelings regarding why you participated in this satyagraha?" are Faith in the efficacy of nonviolence, faith in local leadership, faith in your religious principles and faith because of Gandhi's support and blessings. It could be argued that responses to the above question could be anything from just one category to any combination of and including all the four categories. While admitting that this is possible, the question has been framed in this manner so as to tap responses regarding the most influential sources of favorable attitudes to nonviolence. On the other hand, categories of responses to a few questions such as, "During the movement what did you consider nonviolence to be, a tactic, creed, or both?" do not seem to be exclusive at all; in fact, they are not. Here again the framing of the questions and responses is deliberate. Insofar as Gandhi claimed that preparations that precede the actual launching of the active phase of satyagraha are important for instilling faith in nonviolence as a creed, we wanted to find out how far this is true by tapping their spontaneous responses to the above question.

THE SAMPLE

The object of any sampling procedure is to secure a sample which will 'typically' represent the whole population. Having selected Bardoli, Rajkot, and Pardi as the three movements in conformity with our satyagraha model, as developed in the last chapter, the next problem was to secure a sample for interviewing from the three campaigns such that they will represent the characteristics of the population; the population in this case being the people who participated in the three satyagrahas. The simple way of doing this was to draw a random sample out of an available population. Originally, for Bardoli and Rajkot, we intended to draw random samples from the lists of names of all the persons who participated in these movements and were still living. Such lists were supposed to be in the custody of the District Congress Offices in Surat and Rajkot. On closer scrutiny, however, it was revealed that these lists were not up to date. A very large number of people included in the list were either dead or their whereabouts were not known. The District

Methodology

Commissioners were not able to help either. Under these circumstances the only course open to us was to include all those persons in our sample whose whereabouts could be located. Thus, we could locate forty-five participants for Bardoli and forty-four for Rajkot. They all were included in our sample. All these people lived in different areas of Gujerat State. But for the hard work of the interviewers, it would have been difficult to locate and interview them. In all forty-four interviews were taken for Rajkot but unfortunately thirty of the interview records were lost during unprecedented floods in the region where the interviews were being taken. Rail and road communications were completely disrupted in the region for almost two months following these floods and hence it became impossible to do the interviewing again.

We had, however, much better luck in the case of Pardi. One of the reasons why Pardi was included for the purposes of this study was the fact that this being more recent, we not only expected to be able to have a more reliable sample, but at the same time to have access to all the needed information. Originally the local branch of the Praja Socialist Party had promised to supply from their records a list of names of all the volunteers who participated in the Pardi Satyagraha. In the absence of such a list we prepared another list containing one thousand names from police records of all the persons who were arrested by the police during the satyagrahas for violation of local laws and ordinances. We were helped by Uttam Bhai, the local satyagraha leader, in the preparation of this list. Many names in the list were added from Uttam Bhai's own personal records. From this list of one thousand we drew a randam sample of 110. It should, thus, be kept in mind that the sample of 110 is not drawn from the total population of Pardi satyagrahis. It is likely that the sample is biased in favor of those who were more strongly committed to the goals of the movement than other participants. This is because one would expect that the satyagrahis courting arrest would also be the ones who are more strongly committed to the goals than the rest who do not court arrest.

As far as the leader interviews are concerned, we tried to get hold of as many as possible. It is unfortunate that we could not get hold of any leader for Bardoli but we did interview six leaders for Rajkot; and eight for Pardi. The six leaders for Rajkot include two, U.N. Dhebar and Jetha Lal Joshi, topmost and active leaders of the movement. The eight for Pardi constitute 90% of the most important and active leadership of that satyagraha.[3] The interview schedule used for leader-interviews was the same as for the rank and file satyagrahis except for the questions about the strategies adopted in recruiting, mobilizing, keeping up morale, the tactics in nonviolent action, bargaining with the opponent, etc. These were like depth 'interviews' where as much information about and from the leader was extracted as he was willing to give. Thus the interview with each leader lasted from three hours to eight hours. The interviews with leaders were conducted in either Hindi or the English language.

TABLE 1
THE SAMPLE

Name of satyagraha	No. of volunteers interviewed	No. of leaders interviewed	Total
Pardi	110	8	118
Rajkot	14	6	20
Bardoli	45	0	45
Total	169	14	183

A total of 183 respondents, as shown in the preceding table, were interviewed. It would be clear from the table that almost 66% of the rank and file respondents are from the Pardi satyagraha. The reasons for disproportionately small number of respondents for the 'Gandhi Sample'[4] have already been mentioned. One hundred sixty-nine (92.4%) of the respondents are males and only fourteen (7.6%) females. The reason for the large percentage of males in the sample is that in the case of the Gandhi Sample we could locate only eight (13.6% of the total Gandhi Sample) females who participated in the satyagrahas. In the case of Pardi, the number is still smaller, only three (2.7% of Pardi Sample), because our sample was drawn from the police records, where most of the individuals

Methodology

listed were males since comparatively few females were arrested. There is one female (out of fourteen) among the leaders. As regards the age distribution of the total sample in both Gandhi and Pardi Samples almost 68% of the volunteers are under twenty-five years of age; on the other hand, among the leaders eleven (76%) are above twenty-five years of age.

Most of the interviews were conducted in the morning or afternoon. Except in the case of the Pardi satyagrahis, a majority of the interviews were taken in the homes of the respondents. In Pardi, since most of the respondents (volunteers) were laborers and it was a busy time of the year with regard to the availability of work, they were interviewed wherever it was convenient for them. Thus in Pardi about sixty (54%) were interviewed at work or on the way to work. The rest were interviewed at home. Almost all of the leaders were interviewed at their homes.

DRAWBACKS OF THE STUDY

Before we proceed to a brief description of the three satyagrahas included in this study, we would like to draw attention to the weakness of such a study.

This survey relies on 'expost facto' analysis. For those who believe that a scientific theory can only be generated out of hypotheses which are empirically testable, such a study would seem to have a very limited value. In an expost facto analysis it is not possible to isolate the effects of various independent variable. Also, it is difficult for a survey to give definitive answer to problems because of their lack of control over causal relationships. On the other hand, it might be argued that where the goals of a research are to get a wholistic picture and arrive at 'generalizations', as in this case, survey is a useful tool. Another problem with expost facto analysis is that the attitudes recorded might be biased because of the intervening period between the actual occurrence of the event and the time of the interview. Thus, it might be argued that whatever their attitudes on nonviolence at the time of participation in the satyagrahas, the increasing eruption of violence all over India in the subsequent years is bound to bias the expression of their past attitudes. While admitting that this objection is valid, we contend that this can be minimized by proper interviewing. Thus, in this survey the interviewers were first made to thoroughly acquaint themselves with the history of the movements so that they could help the respondents recapitulate their memories by reminding them of major incidents, etc., if necessary. Also, the attitude expressed on one question could be double checked from his answers to other related questions. One problem, which is endemic to all studies involving interview data, is the problem of 'reactive measurement', i.e., the interviewer, by asking a question, might only create an attitude rather than measure it. Here again we believe that this kind of bias can be minimized by proper interviewing and double-checking the responses from answers to other questions.

Among the many problems that we faced during the interviewing phase of research, the most frustrating was the severity of the monsoon that particular year. Not only were thirty completed interview schedules lost in Rajkot floods, even elsewhere in cases where parts of certain interview schedules were left unfilled because the respondents demanded time to think so that they could articulate, the follow-up visits could not be made in many cases because of the difficulty of movement from one place to another. In the case of Pardi, where the reluctance to be interviewed was the greatest and articulation of attitudes the poorest, it was a frustrating experience to try to engage the respondents for a continuous period of even thirty to forty minutes. This time being the busiest time of the year for earning labor wages—and since most of the respondents in our Pardi sample of satyagrahis belonged to this class—it was almost impossible to catch hold of them a second time since they would seldom work at the same place again. It is for these reasons that the number of responses on various questions do not add up to the totals in all of the tables.

A brief reference to the problem of random sampling has already been made. The samples are not random in the strict sense of the term. Under these conditions, we believe that a researcher has to be extremely 'alert' before he draws any inference from the data, and even then the inferences have to be treated as 'suggestive' rather than 'conclusive'.

In spite of the shortcomings noted above, we believe that after due caution has been exercised, we can come up with

Methodology

valuable generalizations which can become a basis for further research into the problem. After all, as Hymen Levy observes, scientific truth is not an idealized truth to which the universe closely approximated, it is a first step in the process of finding out the truth about the universe by examining it in chips.[5]

A brief description of the three satyagrahas follows:

BARDOLI[6] (1928)

Bardoli 'satyagraha' took place in 1928. Bardoli, with a population of 87,000 was a Taluka—an administrative division of a district—of Surat District in Bombay Province. It consisted of 137 villages and covered an area of 222 square miles. About half the population consisted of the Kaliparaj[7] and the remaining comprised the Kanbis[8], Anavils[9], and Baniyas[10]. There was a sprinkling of Parsis (Zoroastrians) and Muslims.

Bombay, of which Bardoli Taluka was a part, was a Ryotwari Province, i.e., a province made up of numerous peasant proprietors holding land directly under Government and paying a fixed revenue levied on each proprietor. It was common practice for the Government of Bombay to revise the assessment of land every thirty years in each taluka. Each revision meant an increase in assessment. In 1927 the Government increased the assessment in Bardoli and Chorasi Taluka by about 30%. The Government increased its assessment on the basis that the population of the area had increased by about 3,800. There was also an increase in wealth as evidenced in the increase in the construction of new houses, number of milch cattle and carts. It was also claimed that improved communication, including the opening of Broad Gauge Railway line of the Tapti-Valley Railway, abnormal rise in the prices of the food grains and of cotton, doubling of the wages in the last thirty years and the increase in the prices of land clearly justified the 30% increase in assessment. And lastly, the consideration which weighed most in recommending the increase was that the price of the total products of the Taluka had gone up considerably over the price of the products during the previous settlement thirty years back.

Following protests by the peasantry, Mr. Anderson, the Settlement Commissioner, reduced the assessment to 22%. The peasants, however, were not satisfied. They claimed that their economic condition, far from improving, had only worsened. They also complained that the assessment of 1896, which was used as a base for the 1927 assessment, was in itself unjust. In this connection they also cited the remarks of the Settlement Commissioner who himself admitted that "the general conclusion from all the recorded statistics is that the taluka in 1896 was over assessed."[11] The peasants supported their claims with strong arguments and statistics, but the government refused to pay any heed. Through protests, petitions, public meetings, etc., the Congress Party Organization had also been trying to draw the attention of the government against the enhanced assessment. It prepared and published a critical report to show that the peasants could not sustain the increased assessment. In spite of the justice of their case, however, the peasants kept their demand to the minimum. All they wanted was the establishment of an impartial commission of inquiry to go into the problem of the fairness of assessment. Jurisdiction of the civil courts in the matters of land assessment had been excluded by a special Act of the Legislature and hence the use of the judiciary for redress of this grievance was out of the question.

Months of efforts by the satyagraha to convince the government of the justice of their demand finally come to nought as it totally spurned all their overtures. Satyagraha was the last resort. The peoble of Bardoli already had experience in satyagraha. Some of them had participated in the successful Kaira District satyagraha of 1918 against the enhanced assessment, where the government finally retraced its steps. Since 1921, Gandhi's program of constructive activities was in full swing in Bardoli. Inaugurated in April 1921, the Swarajya Ashram of Bardoli had become the hub of activity for the satyagrahis of the national movement. Thus, the people of Bardoli were in constant touch with the Gandhian satyagrahas. Some in Bardoli had also participated with Gandhi in the satyagrahas in South Africa. Thus, the Bardolians, generally, were more familiar with nonviolent action than any other people in the rest of India.

Having resolved among themselves that they were determined to launch a satyagraha, the people of Bardoli approached Sardar Patel to lead their movement. This satyagraha was

Methodology

unique in that the people first resolved among themselves and then requested Sardar Patel to be the leader. After satisfying himself that the people were ready for the sacrifice required of a nonviolent soldier, Sardar Patel accepted the leadership. Battle lines were drawn. On one side were the satyagrahi peasants of Bardoli under the command of Sardar Patel. Gandhi supported the campaign through his writings in the *Young India*, and after the satyagraha had been in progress for six months, he placed himself under the command of Sardar Patel. On the opposite side were the officials of the Revenue Department, the police and the Governor of Bombay who declared the issue to be: "whether the writ of His Majesty the King Emperor is to run in a portion of his Majesty's dominions, or whether the edict of some unofficial body of individuals is to be obeyed."[12]

The first shot in the struggle was the refusal of the peasants to pay the taxes. The real confrontation started in February 1928 when the government started to compel payment. It tried flattery, bribery, threats, imprisonments, forfeiture and lathi charges. It tried to create dissensions within the communities. Properties were attached on a large scale and sold for a song to outside buyers since no buyers came forward from the local populace. But all the repression was not able to break the morale of and the solidarity of the movement. K.M. Munshi, an eye-witness to the Bardoli satyagraha, describes in his book, *I Follow the Mahatma*, the conditions of the peasants.[13]

> There are 17,000 Khatedars[14] concerned in this matter. They had their families go to make about 40,000 buffaloes. which are loved by their owners with an affection, the strength of which can only be appreciated by a born cattle lover. Forty thousand men, women and children with these cattle have locked themselves up in small and unsanitary houses for over three months. As I passed through villages silent, empty and deserted with sentinels posted at different ends, as I saw women peeping through the barrel window to see whether it was the arrival of the Japti-officer,[15] as on being assured the doors were opended and I was taken inside, as I saw the darkness, the stench, the filth, and the men, women and children who had herded for months in

the same room with their beloved cattle, miserable, ulcerated, grown whitish by disease, and as I heard their determination to remain in that conditions for months rather than abandon their cattle to the tender mercies of the Japti-officer, I could not help thinking that the imagination which conceived the dire Japti-methods, the severity which had enforced them, and the policy which had sanctioned them were difficult to be found outside the pages of a history of medieval times.[16]

Tragedy was compounded and made more poignant in view of the fact that these people had to remain inside huddled together in Monsoon Season, when rain, stink, and wind added to their misery because of the siege.

In many cases the Pathans, especially employed by the government to break the back of the satyagraha, broke into several homes and attached cattle and other property. Mahadev Desai has reported dozens of such cases of attachment and brutal beating of the satyagrahis by the police.[17] In our interviewing alone 45% reported that their property was confiscated and 15% had experienced violence at the hands of the police.

All these repressive measures only strengthened the satyagrahis' resolve for justice. Public meetings and Prabhat Pheries—early morning processions—were regularly organized. Many village officers, Talatis[18] and Patels[19], resigned their jobs. A social boycott was established on all government representatives and those who had bought the attached property. However, care was taken that no physical necessities were denied the opponents who were performing their 'status roles'. Sardar Patel constantly reminded the satyagrahis that " In a struggle based essentially on truth and nonviolence" they "must not do anything in resentment and anger" and the opponents must not be denied the ordinary amenities of life. "They must get whatever they want at market rates."[20]

The satyagraha lasted five and a half months before the government showed any willingness to respond. The terms of an agreement were prepared by Gandhi and finally accepted by the government with minor adjustments:

(1) Pending the Inquiry the old assessment to be accepted.

(2) Satyagrahis to pay the old assessment and to call off the campaign on the inquiry being announced.

(3) Inquiry to be open judicial inquiry, by a Judicial Officer alone or assisted by a Revenue Officer with terms of reference as given below and under which the people will have a right to lead and test evidence with the help of counsel if necessary.

TERMS OF REFERENCE

Firstly:

To inquire into a report upon the complaint of the people of Bardoli and Valod (a) that the enhancement of revenue recently made is not warranted in terms of the Land Revenue Code; (b) that the report and the notifications accessible to the public do not contain sufficient data warranting the enhancement and that some of the data given are wrong;

And to find out, if the people's complaint is held to be justified, what enhancement or reduction, if any, there should be upon the old assessment.

And secondly:

To report upon the allegations made by or on behalf of the people about the coercive measures adopted by the government in order to collect the revenue.

(4) All lands to be restored.
(5) All satyagrahi prisoners to be released.
(6) All Talatis and Patels to be reinstated.

A judicial inquiry commission was established under the agreement. All the attached property was restored and the village officers reinstated. The Commission in its final report held that the claims of the satyagrahis were substantially correct and recommended an assessment of only $6\frac{1}{2}$%.

RAJKOT[21] (1938-39)

Most of the satyagrahas till the late 1930's had been limited to so-called British India, but none in Native States which were areas ruled by some 562 big and small semi-independent hereditary Indian Rulers bearing various titles, Rajas, Nabobs, Maharajas, Thakhores, etc., who owed their allegiance to the British Crown. To understand the Rajkot satyagraha, it would be helpful to delve briefly into the historical background of these 'native' or 'princely' Indian (variously called) states.

Just before India achieved independence in 1947, almost 40% of its land area was covered by the Indian states. These states varied vastly in size, population, revenue and the extent of the power they enjoyed.

Following the Act of 1858 and the Proclamation of Queen Victoria, the possessions of the East India Company, which comprised the remaining 60% of the land area of India, were transferred to the British Crown. Thus, we had the so-called British India where the British Crown was sovereign, and 562 states, big and small, which were ruled by the local rulers.[22] Twenty states out of 562 covered 66% of the total land area and 75% of the total population. Twenty-three states between them generated 77% of the total revenue.[23]

By the Act of 1858 and up to the granting of independence to India, one thing that was common, at least theoretically, to all the states was that their territory was not British and their people were not subject to the British Crown. British Indian courts had no jurisdiction inside even the smallest states and the laws passed by the Indian legislature in British India, except in certain cases in relation to the British subjects, did not extend to the states.

However, within three years of the passing of the Act of 1858, the States were already experiencing erosion of power as a result of the claim of suzerainty by the Crown over the States. Lord Canning, in his address to the Princes of Rajputana, declared in 1871:

> The Crown of England stands forward, the unquestioned ruler and 'paramount' power in all of India, and is for the first time brought face to face with its feudatories. There is a reality in the suzerainty of England which has never existed before and which is not only felt but eagerly acknowledged by the Chiefs.[24]

Methodology

The rulers were forced to accept the suzerainty of England in return for the promise of not annexing the states. By 1877 the paramount power put forward and enforced "claims to intervene in the affairs of the states and to depose, degrade, and otherwise take action against the rulers."[25] In the name of 'paramountcy' the British, in some cases, subjected States' administration to stricter supervision. Some states were required to submit their legislation for informal approval and some had limitations imposed on judicial powers by the British. While there was no legal basis for the exercise of such power, the claim to 'paramountcy' was established by usage. The paramountcy was defined as a "complex of Crown rights both general and particular which limit the sovereignty of the States."[26] In its particular aspects it was defined as the practice and usage which developed in regard to each state. Thus, for example, the Crown claimed the right to approve the appointment of Dewans—prime ministers—in regard to certain states.

The overall effect of all these developments was a serious erosion in the powers of the rulers. In return for conceding to the paramountcy of the British, the states' rulers received promise of protection of their thrones, protection from attacks by other states, and from annexation by the British themselves. Generally speaking, the states' rulers were free to raise and collect taxes and to administer their territory as they wished. A small fraction of the revenue had to be paid to the British, supposedly, in return for the protection the rulers received from the British. Most of the states were, for all practical purposes, absolute monarchies. The rulers carried on their administration with the help of a Dewan—prime minister—and the guidance and supervision of the unseen hand of paramountcy. In the medieval period of Indian History the rulers of the most powerful states such as Indore, Gwalior, Hyderabad, Baroda, Mysore, Jaipur, etc., distinguished themselves with their heroism and patriotism and gave stable and progressive regimes to their people. By the end of the 19th century, the glorious past was, however, only a fond memory. Most of the rulers, being under the protective umbrella of the British, had ceased to take active and personal interest in the welfare of their subjects. All they were interested in was the revenue from the people most of which was frittered away over the palaces, harems and the luxuries of the Maharajas.

Ironically, having been assured of protection by the British, the only dangers to their regime seemed to stem from outside their borders—from British India. By 1918 the leadership of the national movement for Indian independence was firmly in the hands of Gandhi. The whole country was in ferment and totally mobilized to Gandhi's clarion call of satyagraha. The rulers of the native states were afraid of the spillover of this movement for freedom into their borders. They had already lost much of their past glory and power to the British; they did not want further erosion, this time by the people. The rulers tightened their autocratic grip on their people. The British government lent them wholehearted support where it suited them. By 1930, the slogan "Representative Government" of the satyagrahis in British India had already penetrated the borders of these native states. There were small satyagrahas in Mysore, Udaipur, Nathadwara, Jaipur, etc., against their rulers demanding representation in the governance of the states.

The most significant satyagraha was, however, offered in Rajkot, a very small but an important state on the West Coast of India, with a population of 115,000. It soon became a 'test case' to see whether there would be 'representative' government in the states under the aegis of the ruling princes. In spite of its small size Rajkot State, including Rajkot City, was of strategic importance because it was also the center of the Agency for all the Native States in the Kathiawar region.[27] At one time, Gandhi's father, Karam Chand Gandhi, was Dewan of Rajkot; the former rulerLakhaji Raj, (entitled Thakore Saheb) regarded him as his father. He was a progressive ruler and he promised increased participation of the people in the affairs of the state. However, his son Dharmendra Singh, the Thakore, at the time of the satyagraha was a different kind of man. He was drowned in wine and women. The administration was steeped in corruption and public treasury was almost empty. In June 1938, the Thakore announced a series of measures to prop up the dwindling treasury. These included granting monopoly in the sale of matchboxes, sugar and ice to the cronies of the administration. There was, also, talk of mortgaging the state owned power station. Laborers in the state-owned textile mills were forced to work for fourteen hours a day; the leaders of protests were dismissed from jobs and driven out of Rajkot state. And finally, a carnival was invited into the state and granted license for gambling. For puritan-minded Rajkot population, this was more than they could take.

The scenario was, thus, complete for the launching of a satyagraha. In this case, the satyagraha was launched by Praja Mandal Party under the leadership of U.N. Dhebar and Jetha Lal Joshi, with the active guidance of Sardar Patel and blessings of Gandhi. On the opposition were Thakore Saheb, his ministry and indirectly the British Resident Gibson.

On August 15, 1938 a mammoth public meeting was held in Rajkot to protest the autocratic rule and demanded the abolition of monopoly in matches, sugar, ice, etc., and that steps be taken for the establishment of a responsible government.[28] The police brutally lathi-charged the people attending the meeting; hundreds were arrested. A period of negotiations followed without success. Finally, the satyagraha was launched in full fury in October 1938. It proved to be a long drawn out struggle. The satyagrahis organized processions, public meetings, strikes, picketing, etc. Rashtriya Shala (school) became the center of constructive activity preparing people for the discipline of ahimsa.

Thakore Saheb resorted to indiscriminate repression. Hundreds of satyagrahis were arrested, beaten and shot. Mounted police charged on the demonstrators and beat them with lathis. On November 1, 1938 after U.N. Dhebar, the satyagrahi leader was arrested, there were lathi charges on the satyagrahis eleven times.

By December 26, 1938 the ruler gave in. He removed his English Dewan—this was one of the demands—and he agreed to give the widest powers to the people "consistent with his obligation to the paramount power and with his prerogative as a Ruling Chief."[29] To this end it was agreed that "a committee of ten, consisting of three Officials of the state and seven popular leaders recommended by Sardar Patel be appointed."[30] All the satyagrahis were released from prison. The decision, hailed by the whole country as the beginning of 'representative government in states', was considered a danger signal by the rulers of other states. They and R.C. Gibson, the British Resident in Western India, brought pressure on the young

Thakore Saheb. The result was that the ruler, contrary to the terms of the agreement, rejected the seven members recommended by Sardar Patel on the pretext that the seven members did not give adequate representation to minority groups such as Moslems and backward classes.

Thus, began the second phase of the satyagraha. Thousands of people were on the streets, protesting, picketing and demonstrating. Kasturba, the wife of Gandhi, and Mani Ben Patel, the daughter of Sardar Patel, joined the satyagraha on February 3, 1939, and were promptly arrested. Soon thousands joined, and hundreds, including U.N. Dhebar and Jetha Lal Joshi, were arrested. Many were brutally beaten and some shot. The prisoners were subjected to humiliating treatment in jail.

Finally Gandhi himself entered the fray. First he wrote a letter to Thakore Dharmendra Singh addressing him as "My dear son" and impressed upon him the necessity of abiding by his earlier "generous decision" which was in accordance with Thakore's promise of a respresentative government.[31] He gave the Thakore until March 2, 1939 to fulfill his promise. Failing to get any response on March 3, 1939 exactly a month after his wife's arrest, Gandhi began 'fast unto death' to awaken the conscience of the ruler. In the meantime, he also wrote to the Marquess of Linlithgo, Viceroy of India to interfere. Sardar Patel warned the viceroy, "Parliamentary Policy will come to an end, if Viceroy does interfere in Rajkot."[32] Linlithgo, in a message sent through Gibson, proposed to Gandhi that the dispute on the interpretation of the agreement of December 26, 1938 between the Thakore and the satyagrahis be submitted for arbitration to the Chief Justice of India, Sir Maurice Gwyer. Finding the proposal reasonable and acceptable, Gandhi broke his fast on March 7, 1939. The award was announced on April 3 by Sir Gwyer in Delhi and it was in favor of the satyagrahis. On April 7, the Viceroy sent a letter to Gandhi assuring him of compliance by the Thakore.

PARDI[33] (1953-64)

If Bardoli satyagraha was launched to secure justice in regard to the assessment of land revenue for the small land-

Methodology

lords, Pardi was intended to secure justice to the landless Adivasis[34] in regard to their rights on land.

The movement was directed primarily against those members of the Congress party who occupied positions of prominence in the Bombay Government and against the land owners of the Taluka.

At the time of the Satyagraha, Pardi was a Taluka in Surat District in the state of Bombay[35] with an area of some 162 square miles with 82 villages and a population of 111,000.[36] There was no industrial development and no commercial center in the Taluka. The years preceding the satyagraha in September 1953, were periods of radical transition for Pardi Taluka. This period of radical tranisition began with India's independence from British rule in 1947. Among major reforms contemplated by the Congress party was reform of the agraian structure. The Congress program called for liquidation of a great variety of ancient and feudatory land tenures. Because of the proximity with Gandhian uplift Ashramas and Gandhian Workers in Surat District new ideas of social reforms brought new awareness. The establishment of the Indian Democratic Republic and the adoption of the new Constitution of India on January 26, 1950 raised new hopes, and promises, particularly for the low castes, tribes and backward classes of India. Article 46 of the Constitution directed that the

> state shall promote with special care the educational and economic interests of the weaker sections of the people and in particular the Scheduled Castes and the Scheduled Tribes and shall protect them from social injustice and all forms of exploitation.

Article 244 and Fifth Schedule empowered the President of India to declare any area as Scheduled Area and to make and administer arrangements to give effect to the provisions of Article 46.[37]

Since 1947, as the tribal people of Gujerat, and particularly of Pardi, sank into increasing depths of misery, poverty and despair, the promise of the new dawn following the independence of India and the establishment of the republic proved to be hollow.

The miserable condition of the peasants came to the notice of Ishverbhai, the most important leader of the satyagraha and a prominent leader of the Gujerat Praja Socialist Party[38] in connection with 1952 General Elections in India when he toured the area to compaign for the PSP candidate for State Assembly seat. Victory of their own candidate on the PSP ticket against a powerful Congress party rival created a new confidence and a revolution in expectations among the peasants. Also Ishverbhai continued to fan this fire of rising expectations by devoting the rest of his life almost wholly to the uplift of the poor peasantry in the area. He made Pardi almost his home establishing contacts and educating them about their rights.

The Praja Socialist Party, under the sponsorship of which the satyagraha was to be launched, claimed that in the densely populated area of Pardi, with a population of 682 persons per square mile, 34,000 of whom were dependent on agriculture were completely landless, and about 90 families owned 70% of all the land. Moreover a disproportionate amount of land was converted to pasture land which saved landlords from spending money on employing agriculture labor since grass grew naturally in rainy season without need of any labor. Some 40,000 acres had lapsed into wasteland in the past five years since 1953. Organizers of the satyagraha also claimed that the evictions of Adivasis from the land, taking advantage of their illiteracy, had been widespread since 1948 and that the food situation was serious and unemployment had reached serious proportions. PSP demanded setting up an enquiry committee to determine the number of evictions and the extent of agriculture land converted to pasture land.

Through the personal efforts of Ishverbhai the PSP had already become influential in the region. The victory of an Adivasi on a PSP ticket to a State Assembly seat added to the prestige of the party. Since June 1951 the Pardi Branch of the PSP had been sending petitions to the local Mamlatdar[39] and the state government to redress the growing distress in the area but without effect. Special complaint was registered against the conversion of 54,000 acres of land into pastures which rendered thousands unemployed. On September 1, 1952 Ishverbhai announced that unless steps were taken in the future a land satyagraha would be launched on September 1, 1953. Thus a period of one year was granted to the government in which to take action. In January 1953 a detailed representation was submitted to the authorities to take over the management of the land which had reverted to wasteland or had been converted to pastures.[40] In the meantime mass meetings were held to educate the Pardi people and also draw the attention of the authorities. A seven-point program of constructive activities to educate the peasants was also inaugurated. The activities included spinning, adult literacy, prohibition, cleanliness, marriage reforms, road construction, etc. In addition, efforts were made to solve the land problem through Bhoodan.[41] Jay Prakash Narain, the Bhoodan leader, inaugurated his campaign for the whole Gujerat state from Pardi. But the response in Pardi was poor. Most of the land gifts came from small landowners, who were themselves Adivasis, but little was donated by big landlords.[42] After a series of petitions and appeals at different periods to the authorities the final ultimatum was announced by the national PSP leader Asoka Mehta at a Press Conference in Bombay that 2,000 peasants would launch a satyagraha on September 1, 1953 since the Government had failed to take any action.

The demands of the satyagrahis were:

(1) that the state government take under its management 5,000 acres of land which had been converted into grasslands; and turn them over to peasants for food crop cultivation.
(2) that a Commission of Enquiry be set up to look into the grievances of Pardi peasants.

Another ultimatum was issued on August 22 that the satyagraha would be launched on September 1, 1953 by ploughing 1,000 acres of pasture lands in Pardi Taluka and that the campaign would proceed in a series of nonviolent invasions on pasture lands with the objective of ploughing them at every interval of five days. The actual satyagraha was inaugurated by Asoka Mehta when he, leading a group of 1,500 satyagrahis carrying pick axes and flags, began to break the soil at Dadri village.

The satyagraha underwent progressive phases of escalation. After September 25, it was intensified. Daily trespass on selected lands in several villages replaced trespass at five day intervals. Satyagrahis offered satyagraha until arrested and in the event of their release after arrest they would rejoin the movement.[43] In a further escalation the program of forcibly tilling the land was abandoned in favor on noncooperation with the landowners. In the new campaign peasants would refuse to work for landlords owning more than one hundred acres of land. Buyers of grass were urged to boycott the landowners. Laborers from outside the Taluka were requested not to work for the landlords. The satyagrahis charged that the state Government had openly sided with the landlords against the poor Adivasis in spite of the fact that the satyagraha was a "unique and inspiring example of discipline, peacefulness and nonviolence to the whole of India."[41]

Civil authorities took action according to law. However, hundreds were also arrested, detained and harassed indiscriminately. All the top leaders of the movement including Asoka Mehta, Ishverbhai were arrested in the early phase of the movement and were later awarded imprisonments for periods ranging from ten to twelve months on charges of "committing criminal trespass and inciting others to do the same."[45] The PSP charged that the land owners had hired 'Bhaiyas'[46] who beat up the unarmed satyagrahis in many cases. One of the leaders of the satyagraha reported the murder of one satyagrahi.[47]

In Bombay the Chief Minister, Morarji Desai, the leader of the ruling Congress Party in the state legislature denied charges of indiscriminate arrests and ill treatment[48] and charged that the satyagraha was politically motivated and a result of rash promises made to the Adivasis by the PSP during the election campaign.

On the other hand, the land owners charged the PSP was carrying on a "huge propaganda campaign" based on lies and intimidation. They were forcibly preventing laborers from outside the Taluka from working for the landlords.

The satyagraha leaders did an excellent job of conducting the satyagraha in a systematic Gandhian way. There was always a cadre of leaders and sub-leaders to take the place of

Methodology

other leaders when they were arrested by the police. The satyagrahis, the opponents and the public were constantly kept informed of any developments through public speeches, pamphlets, bulletins and press releases. Most of the major national newspapers covered the movement, not only because of the involvement of the top national socialist leaders, e.g., Asoka Mehta, Acharya Kripalani, Ishverbhai, etc., but also because of the manner in which the satyagraha was being carried out.

The state government was terribly embarrassed because the most important single reform promise of the Ruling Congress Party during the election was land reform. The Government, while expressing agreement with the general objectives for which satyagraha was launched, did not agree with the tactics of the satyagrahis. It claimed that the reforms could be introduced only gradually. However, the persistence of the satyagrahis and widespread support from the public and newspapers led to a small concession by the Government. It announced the setting up of ten man Enquiry Commission headed by Professor Driver of Poona to investigate the characteristics of the soil of the grasslands and to look into the question whether 'food crop cultivation was economical' in the Pardi area. The satyagraha leaders rejected the terms of enquiry and hence the commission on the basis that what the peasants demanded was whether, 'food crop cultivation was feasible'. At the same time the satyagraha leaders announced the formation of an impartial enquiry commission headed by Ravishankar Maharaj, a prominent and respected leader of Gujerat State, and other expert farmers and economists like Professor Dantwala. The Driver Commission in its findings concluded that 'food crop cultivation on Pardi lands was not profitable'.[49] On the other hand, Ravishankar Maharaj commission, in its report submitted that food crop cultivation was feasible. The report categorically stated that 90% of the grass lands were fit for paddy and other food cultivation.[50] The report of the Driver Commission was full of so many contradictions that it was not put into public circulation for five years. However, even this report declared that out of 55,000 acres of grasslands, 25,000 acres could be converted into food cultivation.

In a parallel development the satyagraha started to affect the course of the conflict by activating the forces of Bhoodan.

Congress leaders in Surat District and in the state capital started persuading the land owners to donate lands to Bhoodan generously. This would automatically solve the problem of the landless, once they have lands obtained as gifts from landlords, distributed to them. Thus the Bhoodan Movement became incorporated into the Pardi satyagraha in an indirect and subtle way. The pressures on the Government and the land owners were not only for utilization of pasture lands for food crops and increases in wages, but also for donating land to Bhoodan so that it could be distributed among the landless. The sentiment of the satyagrahis was well expressed by Asoka Mehta in a statement following his conviction, "our Satyagraha was only for work and wages, but if land distribution comes out of it none will be happier than ourselves."[51]

Another side effect of the satyagraha was an increase in agricultural wages which were raised from a scandalously low six to eight annas per day to twenty-four annas a day. While the satyagraha assumed its most vigorous form in 1953-54, it continued on a smaller scale[52] for a long time so as to give time to the government, the Congress leaders, etc., to fulfill their promises. By September 1956 the satyagrahis were once again ready to launch a full scale satyagraha, as a result of which the Government hastily passed the Land Tenancy Act of 1956 which secured the tenants, in this case the tribals, on one-third of the total lands of Pardi on the land they tilled as owners. Land records were set right. However, still a large number of the landless tribals, including Harijans, remained without any source of income.

From here on the satyagraha leaders intensified their satyagraha with occasional protest meetings and demonstrations, once again giving time to the Government to keep its promises. In 1959 the Bombay Government came out with a Land Ceiling Act which would limit land holdings by land owners to a particular maximum, the surplus land was to be confiscated by the state and distributed among the tribals. But the act failed in its objective as the landlords partitioned the land among the members of their families. On September 1, 1959 satyagraha was resumed with full fury. Thirty thousand peasants put down their sickles as a result of which most of the grass lands dried out and the landlords lost thousands of rupees. The satyagraha

Methodology

continued with varying degrees of intensity until 1964.

The satyagraha finally came to an end with the formal signing of a policy statement by Utsav Parikh on behalf of the State Government and Ishverbhai on behalf of the satyagrahis. The statement admitted that "most of the grass lands are capable of being used for agriculture purposes and are fit for the cultivation of rice."[53] The Government declared its intentions of confiscating about 18,000 acres of land which had been illegally converted into grass lands from agriculture lands and distribute them among the Adivasis for cultivation. The Government also expressed its intention to treat the "partitions of joint family lands made malafide in favor of minors and wives" as void. All the possible surplus land will be made available to the poor Adivasis and financial assistance provided. The Government proposed to undertake an integrated developmental program consisting of schemes of land development, minor irrigation, animal husbandry, dairy and cottage industries, etc. In 1967 Prime Minister Mrs. Indira Gandhi formally inaugurated the new scheme by signing away a piece of land to an Adivasi. So far about 14,000 acres have been given to the Adivasis.

CONCLUSION REGARDING THE THREE MOVEMENTS

It is doubtful if there is any movement which can be carried out exactly according to plan. This is also true of Satyagrahas including the above three. To a very large degree, however, they satisfy the conditions of satyagraha we mentioned above. Thus, we see that all three satyagrahas proceeded through the early steps of attempted negotiation, agitations, public protests through meetings and demonstrations and the issuing of ultimata. At each step the opponent was kept informed of the intention and the procedure.

There was a high degree of self-reliance in the conduct of the satyagrahas. Organized propaganda was published and distributed through newspapers, bulletins and the pamphlets for educating and informing satyagrahis, the opponents and the general public.

In all three satyagrahas the participants strictly abided by the tenets of nonviolence even in the face of violence from the opponent. Self-suffering was an important element of all three satyagrahas; this came in the form of jail-going, tribulations for the family, loss of jobs and property in many cases, etc.

Constructive activity was an important part of all three campaigns. Apart from organizing, adult literacy classes, spinning, prohibition, etc., the constructive activity was utilized for acquainting the participants with the teaching and discipline of nonviolence. This was done through prayers, the singing of hymns, speeches by organizational leaders and face-to-face contact with the participants.

NOTES and REFERENCES

[1] *War Without Violence* (New York: Harcourt, Brace and Company, 1957).

[2] Four men and two women. All men were from K.P. Commerce College, Surat, and women from Saurashtra University, Rajkot.

[3] Ishverbhai, the most important leader and chief architect of Pardi satyagraha, died in 1965. Asoka Mehta and Acharya Kripalani, PSP leaders of national stature participated only briefly.

[4] The term 'Gandhi sample' will henceforth be used to describe the Bardoli and Rajkot samples combined as opposed to Pardi sample. Although Rajkot and Bardoli Satyagrahas were launched for different purposes, they have some common characteristics which justifies our grouping them together. Both belong to the Gandhi era where all participants were subject to the constant 'charismatic' influence of Gandhi; they were all subject to the same kind of strict discipline, organization and ideology where the guiding voice was always Gandhi's. The respondents in the Gandhi sample are much more experienced in satyagraha participation, jail-going, and more educated as compared to respondents in the Pardi sample.

[5] Hymen Levy, *The Universe of Science*, 2nd ed. (London: Watta and Company, 1947), p. 11.

[6] For an excellent description of Bardoli satyagraha see Mahadev Desai, *The Story of Bardoli* (Nav Jivan Publishers, 1957).

[7] Kaliparaj literally means 'Kali' meaning 'dark', 'paraj' meaning 'people', contrasted from 'Ujaliparaj' meaning fair people.

[8] A subcaste among Brahmins.

[9] Another subcaste among Brahmins.

[10] A trading class, usually comes from Vaishya caste or Jains.

[11] Cited in Mahadev Desai, p. 9.

[12] Cited from Joan Bondurant, *Conquest of Violence* (Berkeley: University of California Press, 1965), p. 55.

Methodology

[13] Cited in Hiral Lal Seth, *The Iron Dictator* (Hero Publications, 1943), pp. 23-24.
[14] Occupants of land holding directly under the Government on payment of a fixed revenue.
[15] The attachment officer.
[16] Cited in Hiral Lal Seth, pp. 23-24.
[17] Op. cit., pp. 76-88.
[18] Subordinate Officer in charge of the collection of revenue of a village.
[19] Village headman.
[20] Cited in Mahadev Desai, p. 74.
[21] This description of the Rajkot Satyagraha is based on the interviews with the respondents and two excellent books on Sardar Patel which include chapters on Rajkot Satyagraha. Books are: Acharya Chandrashekhar Shastri, *Rashtra Nirmata Sardar Patel*, published by the Society for Parliamentary Studies, National Printing Works, 1963; and N.D. Parikh, *Sardar Vallabh Bhai Patel*, in Gujerati language, 2 vols. (Navjivan Publishing House, 1952). Also 'Rajkot Supplement' of the *States People*, 1, No. 1 (October 1938) and 'Rajkot Makes History' in *States People*, 1, No. 2 (November, 1938), pp. 7-8.
[22] The roots of some of these states, along with their Nabobs and Maharajas and dynasties, went back almost two to three thousand years. For a fascinating account of the history of these states and their eventual integration into a united India following independence, see V.P. Menon, *The Story of the Integration of Indian States* (New York: Arm Press, 1956).
[23] In 1941, the Indian states covered a total area of 598,138 square miles, with a population of 78,996,854 and a total revenue of Rs. 450 million. Most of the states were very small, almost tiny specks on the vast landscape. Four hundred twenty-seven between them had a population of only about 29,500.

These figures are taken from K.M. Panikkar, *Indian States* (London: Oxford University Press, 1944), pp. 3-4.
[24] Cited from Panikkar, ibid., p. 14.
[25] Ibid., p. 19.
[26] Ibid., p. 22.
[27] Kathiawar region was the name given to about twelve Native States which included Rajkot on the West Coast above Gujerat. The British had established administrative centers, called 'agencies', all over the country at strategic points to be able to oversee the administration in the Native states. These Agencies were headed by British Political Agents and were headquarters for British Indian troops to be used in the States if and when necessary. Thanks to the concession given by the Rajkot Ruler, or rather extracted by the British, the agency for the Kathiawar region was located almost in Rajkot City. The Railway line leading out of Rajkot was the dividing line between Rajkot City and the Agency. Thus, the Agency was literally within a stone's throw from the Rajkot City.

[28] See in this connection 'Rajkot Makes History' in *States People*, 1, No. 2 (November, 1936), p. 7.

[29] K.S. Shridharani, p. 107.

[30] The terms of the agreement were published in the *Rajkot State Gazette* dated December 26, 1938, cited in Acharya Chandrashekhar Shastri, *Rashtra Nirmata Sardar Patel* (Society for Parliamentary Studies, National Printing Works, 1963), p. 135.

[31] For text of the letter see N.D. Parikh, *Sardar Vallabh Bhai Patel*, p. 359.

[32] Cited from Hiral Lal Seth, p. 84.

[33] Most of the information for Pardi Satyagraha was culled from the personal records of the satyagraha leaders in Pardi, daily newspapers, the *Hindustan Times* and the *Times of India*, the *Weekly Janta* and *Indian Press Digests* of the period.

[34] Adivasis means 'tribes', a term used to describe the 'aboriginals' of India.

[35] Following the bifurcation of Bombay State into two viz., Maharashtra and Gujerat States, Pardi is a part of Bulsar District in Gujerat now.

[36] Figures taken from the *Janta*, September 20, 1953, p. 2.

[37] The Censes of India reports 2.7 million tribal population in Gujerat.

[38] Henceforth we will use the term PSP to denote Praja Socialist Party.

[39] The Local Civil Officer.

[40] Section 65 of the Bombay Tenancy and Agricultural Lands Act, 1948, provides that Government may assume management of land "lying uncultivated for any two cultivating seasons." PSP held that the Government should have taken over the land in question which had been lying uncultivated for more than two seasons. It was pointed out that the Government did, in fact, as early as 1949 serve notice to certain landlords asking them to "show cause" why land should not be taken over without compensation under Tenancy Act but "it did not pursue the matter." *Janta* (October 4, 1953), p. 6.

[41] Bhoodan literally means 'land gift'. The Bhoodan movement attempts the abolition of private ownership of land because its fundamental principle is 'all land belongs to God'. Man is only a trustee of land. Its modus operandi is voluntary. No force is used in obtaining land. It is 'loot by love'. In the first stage one sixth of land is demanded in donation from the land owner and distributed among the landless. In the second the idea that land should belong to the tiller is propagated; only that much land should be kept as can be cultivated personally by a land holder. The excess should be donated. In the 3rd stage all lands belong to village community to be managed by village Panchayats for efficient management.

[42] *Janta*, August 23, 1953.

[43] The *Times of India*, October 23, 1953.

[44] *Janta*, October 25, 1953, p. 20.

[45] The *Times of India*, November 1, 1953 1: 3.
[46] This was disclosed by one of the leaders in a personal interview with me.
[47] Here it refers to hired ruffians.
[48] The *Hindustan Times*, September 6, 1953, 9: 2.
[49] See P.N. Driver, *Survey of Grasslands in Pardi Taluka* (Government of Bombay, Agricultural Department, 1956).
[50] See *Report of Pardi Development Committee* in Gujerati language (Vedchi: Gujarat Bhoomidan Samiti, 1955).
[51] *Janta*, November 8, 1953, p. 1.
[52] Throughout this period public meetings, demonstrations, etc., were held at regular intervals.
[53] See *Policy Statement Regarding Grass Lands at Pardi* in Gujerat language (n.p., 1964).

4
Participation, Social Background and Goal Orientation of the Rank and File

The satyagrahis for the three movements were drawn from various walks of life. We have satyagrahis ranging from the illiterate to those having a college education, businessmen having high incomes, to the lowliest laborers and unemployed, people with an ideological goal orientation, (e.g., people participating in the movement with the long range objective of achieving independence for India, as in case of Rajkot and Bardoli or establishment of a socialist society) to a bread-and-butter goal orientation as in the case of Pardi satyagrahis.

PARTICIPATION

In spite of the fact that none of those in either the Gandhi sample or the Pardi sample reported having had any formal training in nonviolent action, one common denominator among all these people was that they were all heavily committed to satyagraha, devoting a very great amount of time and effort to the movement.

Thus, as the following table suggests 51.5% of the total sample have participated in nonviolent direct action at least once and 49.5% have participated at least two times or more. As we had expected, the satyagrahis in the Gandhi sample showed a greater degree of participation, than those in the Pardi sample. In the Gandhi sample almost 22% had participated in nonviolent direct action at least four times or more.

Table 2
AMOUNT OF PARTICIPATION IN THE SATYAGRAHAS
(Percentages in parentheses)

No of times Participated	Gandhi Sample	Pardi Sample	Total
1	30(50.8)	57(51.8)	87(51.5)
2	11(18.6)	30(27.3)	41(24.3)
3	5(8.5)	23(20.9)	28(16.6)
4	9(15.3)		9(5.3)
5 or more	4(6.8)		4(2.4)
Total	59(100)	110(104)	169(100)

We had expected a greater degree of experience of participation in the Gandhi sample for the obvious reason that while most of the satyagrahis in the Gandhi sample were in their twenty's, they had been under the spell of Gandhi since the Ahmedabad labor satyagraha of 1918 and the nationwide satyagraha against the Rowlatt Bills in 1919. Following these two satyagrahas the respondent in the Gandhi sample had plenty of opportunities to participate in numerous satyagrahas. The two most commonly named satyagrahas were the satyagraha against the Rowlatt Bills and the Salt satyagraha of 1930-31. In contrast, the experience of respondents in the Pardi sample was mostly limited to Pardi. Actually in the Pardi sample, most of the 48.2 who reported having participated in more than one satyagraha were actually referring to the number of times they had participated in Pardi satyagraha at various periods. Since it covered a span of almost ten years, most of them who participated a second time considered it as participation in a new satyagraha.

Another indication of heavy involvement is provided by the number of times the respondents courted jail in connection with the satyagrahas. Thus 25(42%) in the Gandhi sample and 64(58%) in the Pardi sample[1] reported having gone to jail ranging from once to ten times for the Gandhi sample and once to four times for the Pardi sample. Fifty-seven (82.6%) among the jail-goers in Pardi underwent imprisonment for periods ranging from a few days to six months, the rest spent from six to fifteen months. For the Gandhi sample, 50% spent from fifteen months to more than forty months in jail. Actually 20% of this group reported having spent more than forty months in jail. One respondent in the Gandhi sample who went to jail ten times (six times in connection with Bardoli alone) reported, his face beaming with pride, spending sixty-two months in jail in connection with various satyagraha activities.

Greater intensity of involvement of the respondents in the Gandhi sample as compared to the Pardi sample is indicated by the number of hours per week devoted to satyagraha. Thus in the Gandhi sample, we find that an overwhelming number 53(91.4%) devoted thirty hours or more per week to the satyagraha. The comparative figure for the Pardi satyagraha is 19(24.4%).

TABLE 3
NUMBER OF HOURS PER WEEK
DEVOTED TO SATYAGRHA ACTIVITIES
(Percentages in parentheses)

Hrs. per week	Gandhi Sample	Pardi Sample
30 or more	53(91.4)	19(24.4)
20-29	3(5.2)	15(19.2)
10-19	1(1.7)	25(32.1)
4-9	1(1.7)	15(19.2)
LT 4		4(5.1)
Total	58(100)	78(100)

SOCIAL BACKGROUND

Other important factors associated with satyagraha and emphasized by Gandhi have been a strict discipline and inculcation of purity in life on the part of the individual satyagrahi. The discipline calls forth a complete obedience to the satyagrahi leader. While a military strategy depends upon the tactics of the enemy, "the satyagrahi general has to obey his inner voice, far over and above the situation outside, he examines himself constantly and listens to the dictates of the inner self."[2] But the position of the satyagrahi is very nearly the same as that of the soldier in an army. He has to be under constant discipline and obey the general's command. Giving his own example, Gandhi suggests that the satyagrahi leader ought always "to try conviction with his co-workers, and to carry their hearts and their reason with him"[3] but where they cannot follow they will have to have faith. And Gandhi quotes in this connection Tennyson approvingly—"Theirs not to reason, why, theirs not to make reply, theirs but to do and die."[4] Purity, which is itself a part of the discipline, consists in leading an austere life. A satyagrahi should give up mill-made and foreign cloth and habitually use khadi. Khadi is symbolic of the people's power.[5] Satyagrahis must also give up drinking and eating meat. Drinking according to Gandhi "saps the moral well being of those who are given to the habit."[6] As far as vegetarianism is concerned, it has very often been associated, in India particularly, with the values of nonviolence. Thus in both Jainism and Hinduism, vegetarianism has been described as part of the social ethic of nonviolence. To the scientifically minded, the significance of these requirements for participation in a nonviolent direct action for conflict resolution may seem trivial or of dubious value. But the fact is that in the Indian context, on the social psychological level, these factors may not only indicate the degree of internalization of satyagraha ideology but at the same time underscore their role in fostering identity formation and imbue the participants with a new sense of superiority and self-esteem vis a vis the opponents. (The point will be discussed in greater detail in Chapter 8). In our sample we find that 54(91.5%) in the Gandhi sample and 34(30.0%) in the Pardi sample wore khadi. Similarly an overwhelming number 58(98.3%) in the Gandhi sample and 108(98.3%) in the Pardi sample reported that they did not drink. As regards eating meat only 2(3.4%) and 30(27.3%) in the Gandhi and Pardi samples, respectively, reported eating meat.

TABLE 4
VEGETARIAN OR NONVEGETARIAN SATAYGARHIS
(Percentages in parentheses)

Vegetarian or Nonvegetarian	Gandhi Sample	Pardi Sample
Vegetarian	57(96.6)	80(27.3)
Nonvegetarian	2(3.0)	30(27.3)
Total	59(100)	110(100)

Such a low percentage of drinkers and nonvegetarians in the Pardi sample was surprising since the Adivasis were known to be given to drinking and nonvegetarianism, traditionally. Acharya Chandrshekhar writing about 'Dhodias'—a subcaste among tribals, the kind we had in Pardi—reports that liquor had penetrated the very structure of their family life. It was a religious custom to put a drop of wine in the mouth of a newborn baby; it was considered a good omen. At death, the dead body, before cremation, was sprinkled with wine. All the Dhodias were extremely poor and because of widespread alcoholism were permanently crushed with the burden of debts to the local 'Savkar'—the money lender.[7] This basic change in their life style can undoubtedly be attributed to participation in satyagraha.

The satyagrahis represented a select group of the local population where the satyagrahas were held. An overwhelming majority 48(81.4%) in the Gandhi sample were Hindus, there were 10(16.9%) respondents who identified themselves as Jains and there was one Muslim. In the Pardi sample, all 110 identified their religion as Hinduism. It would seem that Muslims are a bit under-represented in the sample. As regards caste, 54(93.1%) in the Gandhi sample and only 2(1.8%) in the Pardi sample reported belonging to high caste.[8]

Such a high percentage of Hindus and the low caste is not surprising since there was a predominance of Adivasis in the area and all the Adivasis identified themselves as the low caste. Predominance of the Adivasis in the sample is explained by the fact that the Pardi satyagraha was wholly Adivasis'

TABLE 5
CASTE STATUS OF THE RESPONDENTS IN THE TWO SAMPLES
(Percentages in parentheses)

Caste Status	Gandhi Sample	Pardi Sample
High caste	54(93.1)	2(1.8)
Low caste	4(6.9)	108(98.2)
Total	59(100)	110(100)

satyagraha with limited objectives and confined only to them.

One of the most striking features about our satyagrahis was their educational level. A high 56(94.9%) and 46 (41.8%) reported themselves as literate. When contrasted against the literacy[9] level of only 16.6% (1951 census figures) this is indeed striking.[10] In the Gandhi sample among those who identified themselves as literate, 30(52.7%) had graduated from high school or college. Among the Pardi literates, 44(93.7%) had education up to the primary or middle level. This, once again must be considered a very high figure for the Adivasis.

TABLE 6
LEVEL OF EDUCATION IN GANDHI AND PARDI SAMPLES
(Percentages in parentheses)

Education Level	Gandhi sample	Pardi sample
Literate but no formal education	2(3.5)	3(6.4)
Primary	12(21.1)	42(89.4)
Middle	13(22.8)	2(4.3)
High school	16(28.1)	—
College	14(24.6)	—
Total	57(100)	47(100)

Occupationally those connected with agriculture represented the highest percentage in the two samples. Somewhat surprising was the number of businessmen in the Gandhi sample. Business class usually has a vested interest in the status quo and consequently keeps away from activities like satyagraha which involve the subversion of the eastablished order. Considering this, the number of businessmen in the sample, 9(16.4%) must be considered high. Also interesting was the number of students, 14(25.5%), eight of whom reported how during their college days, most of their time was taken up in recruiting, educating other students and people to the ideal and objectives of the satyagrahas.

TABLE 7
OCCUPATIONS OF SATYAGRAHIS
IN GANDHI AND PARDI SAMPLES
(Percentages in parentheses)

Occupation	Gandhi Sample	Pardi Sample
Unemployed	3(5.5)	67(60.9)
Agricultural labor	—	—
Other labor	1(1.8)	26(23.6)
Business	9(16.4)	3(2.7)
Own agriculture	17(30.9)	8(7.3)
Blue Collar	8(14.5)	1(0.9)
Student	14(25.5)	5(4.5)
Other	3(5.5)	—
Total	55(100)	110(100)

As far as the economic status is concerned, satyagrahis in Pardi were relatively poorer as compared to the participants in Bardoli and Rajkot. This was to be expected since the tribals, especially the low caste tribals as in Pardi, all over India were uniformly poor. Thus, as compared to 56.4% in the Gandhi sample 93.6% in the Pardi sample had incomes of less than Rs 1,000 per annum. However, even at this low level the economic condition of the Pardians was slightly better than that of the low caste tribals in the rest of the country, who were on the verge of starvation most of the time. The maximum annual income reported by one respondent in Pardi was Rs 10,000. In Gandhi sample, 11% said they had annual incomes exceeding Rs 15,000.

GOAL ORIENTATION

The leadership appeal to the rank and file usually comes in the form of an ideological rhetoric which covers a diversity of their needs and with frequent references to God. According to Hans Toch, "By and large the most important appeals of a social movement are contained in its ideology."[11] The term ideology here refers to a set of related beliefs which a group holds. It is a statement of the general objectives of the movement which the people are collectively trying to affirm and accomplish. Such a statement also specifies the principles underlying the objectives and the course of the collective action.

Thus during one of the speeches Sardar Vallabh Bhai Patel, the most important leader of Bardoli satyagraha, second only to Gandhi in his influence, thundered:

> I still ask you to think twice before you take the plunge. Do not derive comfort from the feeling that you have as your leader a fighter like myself. Forget me and forget my companions, fight if you feel that you must resist oppression and injustice. Do not take the plunge lightly. If you miserably fail, you will fail not to rise again for several years, but if you succeed you will have done much to lay the foundations of Swaraj (self-rule). Now I am going to ask you to take charge of the resolution, you will move it and you will second and support it. None of us will speak on it. It will be the expression of your own free will and choice.[12]

We see that although the immediate aim of Bardoli satyagraha was protest against enhanced land revenue, the appeal to the rank and file satyagrahis was couched in terms of oppression, injustice, swaraj, etc.

The same ideological tenor is noted in the songs which the satyagrahis sang as inspiration to themselves and as a display of an identity of goals to the enemy. A frequent song during

Bardoli satyagraha exhorts the satyagrahis in these words:

> With full knowledge take up your arms even like a Gnani (seer) . . .
> The tyrant has run amok and crushed the peasant under his heels. We slumbered so long, we have now found our Guru and are blessed with knowledge.
> With full knowledge take . . .
> He has taught us to fit righteousness and truth against oppression and injustice. God is sure to run to the rescue of right and vanquish the wrong.
> With full knowledge . . .[13]

In Pardi, the most favorite song during the satyagraha showed the same ideological appeal:

> We are the peasants of the earth . . .
> For ages she fed us. The more we work with her the more we get from her.
> We are the peasants . . .
> God gave land and earth to all
> But the deceitful landlord seized it all
> All our dreams are broken.
> We are the peasants . . .
> We will win back the land and give it back to all
> We will put up with heat, cold and rain and work hard
> To make the earth shower us with her rich bounties
> We will share those bounties with all
> So no one in Bharat (India) will have to go hungry
> We are the peasants . . .[14]

Similarly during Pardi satyagraha Hakumat Desai, a prominent leader declared in his speech to the Adivasis:

> This conquest-of-bread campaign you are carrying on is a remarkable nonviolent movement. This is a remarkable movement for what it seeks to achieve. It is a movement for the best utilization of land resources and idle man power, it is a movement for self-sufficiency in food, it is a movement against backwardness, unemployment and semi-starva-

tion. The final goal is the establishment of socialism.[15]

Here again we find that appeal to the immediate interest was punctuated with plenty of ideological rhetoric. The question is how do the satyagrahis perceive this appeal? In other words, what kind of goal orientation did they bring to their movement. To find this we asked our respondents what kinds of benefits, they thought, would accrue if the movement succeeded. The responses largely fell into three categories;

1. ideological orientation: where the respondents mentioned as benefits, establishment of swaraj, a socialistic society, justice, dignity of the individual, etc. 2. Bread and Butter orientation: where the respondent referred to personal material gains such as increased profits, acquisition of lost land, reduced land revenue, increased wages, etc. 3. and combination of ideological and bread and butter orientation. From the following table it is clear that the rank and file satyagrahis in the Gandhi sample were strongly motivated by ideological considerations. Here the most frequent statement regarding the goals of the movement was that it was a step in the establishment of 'Swaraj' (self-rule) or 'Pratinidhi Sarkar' (representative government). On the other hand, the most common theme with the Pardi satyagrahis was the betterment of their economic condition. As the following table indicates 52 (91.2%) of the respondents in the Gandhi sample saw the main benefit of the satyagraha in ideological terms. In case of Pardi, the bread and butter fared in the case of 103(96.3%), bread and butter socialism in the case of 23(21.5%) and ideology only in case of 4(3.7%). In the Gandhi sample, there was only one respondent from Bardoli satyagraha who saw it purely as a struggle for bread and butter.

The following are a few typical responses:

> The immediate goal of the (Bardoli) satyagraha was to get land revenues reduced. Personally, however, I was not interested in this aspect at all. I participated because I knew this satyagraha was going to awaken the people of India and the world to injustice and exploitation by the British Government. The British were more interested in their own

TABLE 8
RESPONDENTS' PERCEPTION
OF BENEFITS ACCRUING FROM SATYAGRAHA
(Percentages in parentheses)

Kinds of Benefit	Gandhi Sample	Pardi Sample
Ideological	52(91.2)	4(3.7)
Bread and Butter	1(1.8)	71(66.4)
BB and Welfare	——	9(8.4)
BB and Socialism	——	23(14.0)
Ideology and BB	2(3.5)	——
Other	1(1.8)	——
DK	1(1.8)	——
Total	57(100)	107(100)

welfare rather than the welfare of India. Thus to me the Bardoli satyagraha was only a part of the ongoing struggle for swaraj.

—*a rank and file Bardoli satyagrahi*

My participation in boycott and picketing at the carnival was only a symbolic act. While the rest of the country was in ferment and fighting for independence, here we were, we had our own king but he was only a tool of the British. The rest of the country was fighting for swaraj and an increasing role in Indian government. We were being ruled by arbitrary laws of a king who was a mere tool of the British. We wanted a voice in running Rajkot. I was in the satyagraha because I wanted a representative government in Rajkot. I participated in spite of the fact that my grocery business suffered heavy losses because of it.

—*a satyagrahi from Rajkot*

All I wanted was that the landlord for whom I had been working so hard for so many years would give me enough to bring up my children and feed my family. I knew it would be easy (to get enough and feed the family) if the landlord, instead of growing only wild grass, would only let me sow food crops. We know this land well. We toiled on it for generations. If we had the opportunity we could make this land yield enough for both the landlord and us.

—a satyagrahi from Pardi

Thus, our findings suggest that the appeal of a satyagraha or for that matter any movement for participants may consist in things like physical facilities or hope of personal and group gains, or it may simply consist in its ideology.

Not all those who join a satyagraha join it because they are well aware and convinced of the rightness of their goals. Also, like any other movement there is a constant turnover of membership at the periphery. The hardcore satyagrahis will start at the beginning of a satyagraha and continue until the end. On the other hand, at the periphery a few drop out and a few join as the movement progresses. A small percentage (2.4%) in our total sample reported that they joined the satyagrahas only midway. A small percentage (10.3%) for the Gandhi sample and (5.5%) for the Pardi sample indicated that they were not aware of the objectives when they joined the satyagrahas. Some joined the satyagrahas simply because their peer groups and friends had joined or because of exhortation by their respected leader. They became aware of the goals as the satyagrahas progressed. One adivasi from Pardi said, "I did not understand a thing. Uttam Bhai ordered me to come. I knew it must be for good (purpose)."

SUMMARY

The satyagrahis did not represent a cross section of the population. They were a 'vanguard' group who were actively devoted to and involved in the satyagrahas. Undoubtedly, there were innumerable more men and women who participated in these satyagrahas with varying degrees of commitment, but the satyagrahis were much more active and elite in relation to the rest. Also the satyagrahis show a relatively high educational and economic status. Another characteristic of these groups is their youth. As mentioned before almost 68% of the participants were in their twenty's. All these factors coupled with their deep commitment to the satyagraha as indicated by the figures on jail-going, number of hours per week devoted to the satyagraha, etc., made the three satyagrahas extremely forceful and full of life. The findings also suggest that the commitment of a nonviolent movement can be sustained either on ideological goals or goals involving economic, personal or group gains of the participants.

NOTES and REFERENCES

[1] A higher percentage of jail-going is indicated for the Pardi sample probably because our sample was drawn from Pardi police records which contained the names of all persons arrested (but not necessarily tried and convicted) by the police during the satyagraha.

[2] Gandhi, *Nonviolent Resistance*, p. 98; also, *Harijan*, 10th June, 1939.

[3] Ibid., p. 98.

[4] Ibid., p. 98.

[5] Ibid., p. 70.

[6] Ibid., p. 326.

[7] *Rashtra Nirmata Sardar Patel* (Society for Parliamentary Studies National Printing Works, 1963), p. 25.

[8] High caste comprises three castes namely, Brahmin, Kshatriya and Vaishya and the low caste comprises the shudras and the untouchables whom Gandhi described as Harijans, meaning servants of God.

[9] Any person who can at least sign his name is categorized as literate by the Indian Census Bureau.

[10] 41.8% literacy level for the Adivasis must also be considered very high since the all India literacy level for the Adivasis was much below 16.5%.

[11] Hans Toch, *Social Psychology of Social Movements* (Indianapolis: Bobbs and Merrill Company, 1965), p. 21.

[12] Mahadev Desai, *The Story of Bardoli* (Ahmedabad: Navjivan Press, 1957), p. 34.

[13] Quoted from Mahadev Desai, p. 107.

[14] Translated from Gujerati language.

[15] Quoted from the pamphlet supplied by Professor Hakumat Desai.

5
Meanings of Nonviolence for the Rank and File

In elaborating the theory of satyagraha we have seen that a heavy emphasis is placed on the fundamental unity of the universe, where all human beings are viewed as basically "good" and endowed with divine powers. True satyagraha can ignite that divine spark which leads to the moral persuasion of the opponent by awakening his conscience. However, this is possible only when the satyagrahi confronts the opponent with nonviolence by conviction rather than nonviolence by expediency. This is the distinction that Gandhi made between what he calls the "nonviolence of the strong" and "nonviolence of the weak". By the former is meant a belief system of nonviolence which would be replaced by violence if the means for violent action were available or if nonviolence did not achieve the desired results. It would seem, then, what is involved in a satyagraha is the internalization of the norms of nonviolence to such an extent that they are perceived as valid in a large variety of circumstances, if not in an absolute way.

In this section we plan to analyze and understand the cognition and perception of nonviolence among the satyagrahis. We want to do this at two levels, namely, at the level of the rank and file and at the level of the secondary leadership. Perception is defined by sociologists and psychologists as an intermediate range of conceptualization which lies between the raw sensations on the one hand and the crystallized cognitive processes known as 'concepts' on the other. Nonviolence is not something which can be understood or analysed as a single concept. It is a system of interrelated beliefs and norms. In order to get a total picture of cognition and perception of nonviolence at the individual level, we still have to examine the whole spectrum of interrelated attitudes and beliefs. Here the analysis of the cognition and perception of nonviolence, mainly based on the attitudinal data collected from extensive interview, is being undertaken at two levels, at the level of the rank and file and at the level of the secondary leadership.

SATYAGRAHA A 'CREED' OR A 'TACTIC'?

In the previous chapter we saw that one thing the satyagrahis in the three movements did not lack was commitment to the movement. This was evident from the sacrifices they made, time devoted to the movement, the time spent in jail, etc. This, however, did not say much about their commitment to nonviolence on the action level or in other words their commitment to satyagraha as a method of conflict resolution. To find this we asked our respondents whether satyagraha for them was a 'creed' or a 'tactic'. Where satyagraha was described as a moral imperative and nonviolence as an absolute principle under all circumstances we coded the response under 'creed'. Where the respondents said that the satyagraha was one of the several methods available or that satyagraha was the best under the existing circumstances, etc., we coded it under 'tactics'. If the respondents said satyagraha was a way of life, however, to the extent that it was able to bring about conversion of the opponent and hence it was both a 'creed' and a 'tactic', we coded under 'creed'.

As the table below indicates, an overwhelming number 39(67.2%) in the Gandhi sample and 102(92.7%) in the Pardi sample said that satyagraha was a creed.

The fact that a greater percentage in the Pardi sample as compared to the Gandhi sample said that satyagraha was a 'creed' was a bit surprising. In the light of the greater experience and deeper commitment of the Gandhi satyagraha and higher level of education as compared to the Pardi satyagrahis, as indicated by the data, we might expect a higher percentage of the former giving 'creed' as their response.[1] But it was not so.

TABLE 9
PROJECTIVE RESPONSES ON WHETHER NONVIOLENCE WAS A TACTIC OR A CREED
(Percentages in parentheses)

Response	Gandhi Sample	Pardi Sample
Tactic	15(25.2)	5(4.5)
Creed	89(67.2)	102(92.7)
Other	4(6.9)	3(217)
Total	58(100)	110(100)

Crosstabulation of education by attitude whether nonviolence was a tactic or a creed further strengthens our argument. The following table indicates that 86.5% of the satyagrahis with low education said that nonviolence was a creed. On the other hand 67.3% of those who had high education reported that it was a tactic; although this percentage is still high, the difference is statistically significant.

TABLE 10
TABLE SHOWING THE PROJECTIVE RESPONSES ON EDUCATION BY WHETHER NONVIOLENCE WAS A TACTIC OR A CREED
(Percentages in parentheses)

*Education Level	Political Tactic	Creed	Other	Total
Low	9(8.7)	91(86.5)	5(4.8)	105(100)
High	8(33.3)	16(67.3)	—	24(100)
Total	17(13.2)	107(82.9)	5(3.9)	129(100)

$Chi^2 = 11.46$, $P \angle .01$

*Low Education refers to elementary and middle level, high education to high school and over.

INTELLECTUAL GRASP OF NONVIOLENCE

How much intellectual grasp and conviction did the satyagrahis have of nonviolence? In Gandhi's theory of satyagraha, nonviolence is interpreted in traditional religico-cultural terms. Since then most of the writers, Indian and foreign, have followed suit in their interpretation of the Indian satyagrahas as conforming to those religious traditions. In our study we found that only one respondent in the Gandhi sample said that his familiarity with nonviolence was because of his religion; none in the Pardi sample attributed his knowledge of nonviolence to religion. The name of Gandhi and or of the local leaders figured in most of the responses when asked how they first became familiar with nonviolence. In Pardi the names of Ishver Bhai and Uttam Bhai figured in the responses of all the 110(100%) satyagrahis. Of those in Pardi 6(5.5%) who also mentioned having been exposed to nonviolence through reading, five had not read anything beyond the pamphlets circulated by the PSP during the movement. Three respondents said they had read a few chapters describing Gandhi's contribution to Indian independence, during their years in school. One said he had read Gandhi's autobiography. The works that had been read in the Gandhi sample were the speeches of Gandhi which appeared in the *Young India* and elsewhere; two mentioned Gandhi's autobiography. By far, the largest number in both the samples was exposed to nonviolence through the speeches of its leaders.

Besides Gandhi, the name of the leader most often mentioned by the Bardoli satyagrahis as their source of information on nonviolence was that of Sardar Patel by the Rajkot satyagrahis and that of U.N. Dhebar by the Bardoli satyagrahis. The most frequently mentioned leaders by Pardi satyagrahis were Ishver Bhai and Uttam Bhai. All these men were prominent leaders in their respective movement.

From interviews it was also evident that for some satyagrahis the introduction and conversion to nonviolence was simultaneous and instantaneous. A respondent from the Gandhi sample observed thus;

Mahatma Gandhi had taken the country by storm. Everywhere, talk about nonviolence was in the air. Frankly, I did not understand too much of it then. I had the first chance to hear and see him in person at Bhavnagar. As I saw him,

TABLE 11
PROJECTIVE RESPONSES SHOWING THE SOURCE OF FAMILIARITY WITH NONVIOLENCE
(Percentages in parentheses)

Source	Gandhi Sample	Pardi Sample
Reading and local leaders	3(5.1)	6(5.5)
Gandhi speech and local leaders	15(25.4)	1(0.9)
Local leaders and constructive activity	5(8.5)	74(67.3)
Gandhi speech and reading	16(27.1)	———
Gandhi speech and constructive activity	10(16.9)	———
Local leaders plus others	1(1.7)	29(26.4)
Reading and Religion	1(1.7)	———
Gandhi speeches and other	8(13.6)	———
Total	59(100)	110(100)

standing on the dias, I was struck by his appearance. He was incredibly lean and thin, wearing only a dhoti and carrying a stick in his hand, there was something about him that told me that he was one of us and yet he represented the best in us. He explained to us the meaning of ahimsa and why an 'ahimsak'—nonviolent—person was close to God and hence superior to the 'himsak' (violent) person. It was then, that I was introduced to systematic nonviolence. It filled me with pride to know that this nonviolence was part of that great religious and cultural heritage of which I was a part. Subsequently, I had more opportunities to listen to Gandhi, Sardar Patel and others and my faith in nonviolence was only strengthened.

—*A Bardoli satyagrahi*

The only respondent out of the total sample who mentioned religion as the source of his familiarity with nonviolence provided an interesting study. At seventy he looked relaxed and confident. He had spent the last fifty years of his life in Gandhi Ashramas and other institutions engaged in promoting

Gandhian principles and ideals. He came under the spell of Gandhi at twenty during the Bardoli satyagraha but, he attributed his intellectual grasp of nonviolence first to his religion then to Gandhi. He came from a deeply religious Jain family where "living a jain life was considered as important as understanding it." And indeed this respondent surprised us with his depth of knowledge and undoubtedly was the most articulate of all the respondents on the subject of nonviolence. He said,

> No religion in the world is so emphatic on nonviolence as Jainism. The Jains are the most rigorous practitioners of daily ahimsa. They are prohibited from indulging in 'himsa' (violence) either by word or deed. In most contexts 'dharma' for a jain is the universal rule of nonviolence. The *Book of Good Conduct* makes it clear that no living being whatsoever should be slain or treated with violence or insulted or tortured.

However, the most interesting points made by this absolutist on nonviolence was that while, to him, nonviolence was a creed, he believed "for most of the satyagrahis, including the leaders, it was nothing more than a tactic." This was so disappointing to him that instead of participating in the 'direct action' projects such as sit-ins, picketing, etc., he concentrated on constructive activities only where he "could practice pure ahimsa." And indeed true to his conviction, this man had dedicated his whole life to social service in Gandhian Ashramas.

Another typical example of the source of familiarity with or conversion to nonviolence was provided by this female respondent whose father was lawyer but she herself never had any education. Apart from participating in Bardoli satyagraha at 25 years of age she participated in various satyagrahas in 1930, 32 and 40 and finally the Quit India movement in 1942. She said she grew with the belief that violence was the only way against the British.

> When I was 15 years old my husband had a job in Baroda city. At that time I had no faith in Gandhi's nonviolence. I was convinced in my own mind that nonviolence was not a suitable weapon at all particularly against the British; you

have to fight the devil with fire. At that age I even used to dream of violent revolution against the British. The dedication displayed by violent revolutionaries in Bengal had the greatest impact on me. Since then I had a keen desire to participate in violent revolutionary acts against the British. Then I came to know the existence of a revolutionary group, in the town of Billimora. The members of this group made bombs and indulged in terrorist activities. I approached this group and expressed my desire to joint it and learn to make bombs. Before I could completely get into it, the existence of the group became known to the Government. All of the members of the group were arrested and prosecuted. I managed to escape and was underground for quite some time.

It was only as a result of my personal contacts with Gandhiji and Sardar Patel and their speeches that my ideas started to change. However my complete conversion to nonviolence as a suitable technique came only after I saw how numerous satyagrahis were sacrificing their homes and comforts of life so as to participate in the Bardoli satyagraha. Another factor in my conversion was the distinct change I noticed in the Government's policy in favour of the satyagrahis.

This respondent, unlike our Rajkot respondent, stated that nonviolence for her was no more than a tactic. However she said, like him, that "not all who participated believed in nonviolence. They had to go along only because Gandhiji said so and they all knew that the real source of pressure on the British, the masses, was with him."

From the above data, it is clear that the most important source of knowledge about nonviolence to the satyagrahis was the leadership and particularly the topmost leadership, Gandhi, in case of Bardoli and Rajkot, and Ishver Bhai and Uttam Bhai, in case of Pardi.

And at least for some of them the cognition of nonviolence was deeply intertwined in their consciousness with the image of their leadership. Thus a Rajkot satyagrahi observed:

I believe that Ahimsa is both a tactic and creed, depending

upon the situation. I don't think we common satyagrahis, are people so sublime and pure that we can translate nonviolence totally as a creed in our lives. However, when nonviolent means are adopted under the influence of a leader in a particular situation, it can, for that time, become a creed.

Another indication that faith in the topmost leadership and faith in ahimsa, and in that order, were the two most important ingredients of the satyagrahas came in response to the question whether the respondents participated in the satyagraha because of faith in Gandhi or Ishver Bhai or faith in nonviolence or because of their religious beliefs, etc. Seventy-six and three tenths percent (45) of the satyagrahis mentioned the name of Gandhi in the Gandhi sample as the determining factor for their participation. In Pardi all 100% (110) said they participated because of faith in Ishver Bhai and nonviolence. Surprisingly only one mentioned his religious principles as a reason for participation.

NONVIOLENCE AS A FAITH

Although a larger percentage of the satyagrahis in the Pardi sample as against the Gandhi sample identified nonviolence as a 'creed', it is clear that the percentage of Gandhians who identified it as a 'creed' is large enough for us to infer that nonviolence was a creed, to the overwhelming number of satyagrahis. To probe their cognitive understanding of nonviolence further we asked them, "In what ways do you think ahimsa is effective during conflict"?

In spite of the fact that such an overwhelming number identified nonviolence as a 'creed', most of the satyagrahis had great difficulty in articulating themselves. Pardi satyagrahis were the least articulate; this can be explained by their relatively low level of education. Thus, against only one in the Gandhi sample, 35(32.1%) in the Pardi sample responded with 'DK'. Among those who did respond, a very large number in both samples, 42(70%) in Gandhian and 65(58%) in Pardi considered nonviolence to be purely based on faith. According to one respondent,

TABLE 12

PROJECTIVE RESPONSES ON HOW NONVIOLENCE WORKS

(Percentages in parentheses)

How Nonviolence works	Gandhi Sample	Pardi Sample
Works through faith	33(55.0)	41(36.6)
Works through love and conversion	9(15.3)	24(22.0)
Through compromise	2(3.4)	—
Through coercion	—	3(2.8)
Through compromise and coercion	1(1.7)	5(4.6)
Other	13(22.0)	1(0.9)
Don't know	1(1.7)	35(36.1)
Total	59(1.00)	1.10(1.00)

Satyagrahi's faith makes him so strong that the opponent has no alternative but to listen to the voice of the truth which resides in the satyagrahi. Ahimsa is effective and supreme power; this faith itself is what makes it powerful.

Other respondents who emphasized the element of 'faith' simply asserted, nonviolence can never fail; still others said it can never fail when you have a Gandhi or an Ishver Bhai on your side. "How could Pandavas have lost the war against the Kauravas, when Arjuna had Lord Krishna as his charioteer?"[2], asked one respondent in the Pardi sample. The implication is clear. Lord Krishna was the incarnation of God and he was on the side of the truth. Similarly with the truth on the side of the satyagrahis, God is on their side and there is no way they can lose. The difference between this and Gandhi's position in this regard should be noted. While for Gandhi the satyagraha was only a process for the discovery of the truth by both sides, here the respondents obviously participated in the satyagraha convinced that they not only had a hold on the truth but that it was also on their side. One Bardoli respondent who said nonviolence was a 'creed' expressed his faith almost paraphrasing Gandhi in these words:

> Through nonviolence, you can win against any power. In Bardoli, the opponent had to bend in spite of all the power at his command. Also, ahimsa not only blesses the whole life of the satyagrahi but also of the opponent. Even God cannot resist the call of the satyagrahi. From my experiences with the ahimsa and the effect I have seen it making on the opponent, I have unshakeable faith in the efficacy of ahimsa.

A small number 9 (15.3%) in Gandhi sample and 24 (22%) in Pardi sample emphasized that nonviolence works through love and conversion of the opponent. They expressed a belief in some kind of basic unity of all living beings. Nonviolent action helped the opponent realize the potential within him. The suffering by the satyagrahi awakened him to the sense of truth and justice within him. This shows that at least some satyagrahis had internalized the norms of nonviolence deeply enough to believe with Gandhi that "an implicit trust in human nature is the very essence of his (satyagrahi's) creed."[3] Their belief was based on an optimistic view of human nature, and the compatibility of nonviolence with it. One Bardoli respondent believed that nonviolence was especially suited to Indian conditions. "There is ahimsa in the very blood, culture and atmosphere of India. Indian cannot take up arms without extreme feelings of guilt. This guilt complex does not occur in nonviolence."

The following are a few sample responses;

> Violence may have more visibility but the fact is world lives due to nonviolence. Only through nonviolence can we spread love among fellow beings and develop respect for life. Father-son, mother-son, brother-sister, husband-wife, etc., are all bound together by mutuality and love. The true nonviolence leads to unselfish and loving life. Violence only reduces us to the level of brutes.
> —*A Bardoli satyagrahi*

> What you achieve by violence is not permanent. Violence creates polarization and everlasting ill-will and sorrow. On

the other hand ahimsa gives spiritual satisfaction.

—*A Rajkot satyagrahi*

One respondent from Pardi, the only one to have had college education since the Pardi satyagraha, said:

The success obtained by Christ, Buddha, Socrates and Gandhi convinced me that ahimsa humanizes the oppressor. Violence is based on disrespect toward life and hence is self-defeating.

Another respondent from Bardoli said:

Ahimsa is an instrument which results in spiritual uplift. The spiritual strength is a 'must' in a nonviolent struggle since it refuses to hurt and invokes the humanity in the opponent by challenging him to hurt.

Among those who said nonviolence was a tactic some believed that satyagraha as a technique was adopted in the first place because the aggrieved party, in the absence of any access to arms and weapons, was too weak to be able to resort to violent tactics.

It was the power generated by sheer numbers, rather than nonviolence that affected the opponent. I do not believe that one man's nonviolence can accomplish anything.

—*A Bardoli satyagrahi*

Another gave a utilitarian argument:

During conflict nonviolence is the best means of communicating with the opponent because there is much less polarization than in a violent conflict. Nonviolence is also best in that it results in the least loss of life and property to the parties in conflict.

—*A Bardoli satyagrahi*

A sizeable number of satyagrahis, 13 (22%), in the Gandhi sample—in the 'other' category—gave various reasons for the success of a satyagraha. A few said that nonviolent action works because it causes so much confusion in the opponent's camp that he is left with no alternative but to surrender. One respondent from Rajkot said, "When the other side (the opponent) is too strong, satyagraha can work only if the oppressor takes pity on the suffering satyagrahis." Still others, including one from Pardi, said that the success of satyagraha was attributable to its novelty as a method.

The above observations adequately bring out the degree of cognition of nonviolence along one dimension namely, whether nonviolence is a tactic or a creed. The data suggests that an overwhelming number of satyagrahis considered nonviolence to be a 'creed'.

SATYAGRAHA AND VIOLENCE

Another factor related to the cognition of nonviolence may be to see how the satyagrahis' perception of nonviolence as a creed (or tactic) affects their perception of the possibilities of eruption of violence during a satyagraha. To find this we asked our respondents "If a protracted nonviolent action over a particular period of time does not produce the desired result, do you think that the satyagrahis are bound to turn violent?" We expected that those who considered nonviolence to be a creed would also believe that a satyagraha was not likely to turn violent even if it showed no meaningful progress or was threatened with total failure, in spite of a prolonged struggle.

As the tables 13 and 13a indicate this, in fact, was found to be the case. Ninety-one and seven tenths per cent of the satyagrahis who said nonviolence was a creed also said that a satyagraha could not turn violent. Of those who said it was a tactic 78.9% said that satyagraha is not bound to turn violent. Although the latter figure also seems high, the difference between the two categories regarding the likelihood of violence is significant. Also, it should be noted that among those who considered nonviolence to be a tactic, 21.4% reported that nonviolence was bound to turn violent. On the other hand, of those who reported nonviolence to be a creed only 2.9% said it could turn violent. This suggests that an overwhelming majority did not expect violence during a satyagraha even if it

TABLE 13
PROJECTIVE RESPONSES ON PERCEPTION OF NONVIOLENCE AS A TACTIC OR CREED BY POSSIBILITY OF VIOLENCE IN CASE OF FAILURE
(Percentages in parentheses)

Attitude to Nonviolence at participation	Gandhi Satyagraha Possibility of violence		
	Yes	No	Total
Political Tactic	2(14.3)	12(85.7)	14(100)
Creed	3(7.7)	36(92.3)	39(100)
Other	2(50.0)	2(50.0)	4(100)
Total	7(12.3)	50(87.7)	57(100)

Chi^2 = 6.0973 $P < .02$
Cramer's V = 0.3138

TABLE 13a
PROJECTIVE RESPONSES ON PERCEPTION OF NONVIOLENCE AS A TACTIC OR CREED BY POSSIBILITY OF VIOLENCE IN CASE OF FAILURE
(Percentages in parentheses)

Attitude to Nonviolence at participation	Pardi Satyagraha Possibility of violence		
	Yes	No	Total
Political Tactic	2(40.0)	3(60.0)	5(100)
Creed	1(1.0)	101(99.0)	102(100)
Other	—	3(100)	3(100)
Total	3(2.7)	107(97.3)	110(100)

Chi^2 = 27.4411 $P < .001$
Cramer's V = .49946

failed. By the same token we can also conclude that majority of them also disapproved of violence, under most of the circumstances if not absolutely. Among those who said nonviolence was a creed and yet said that satyagraha could turn violent, two attributed it to faulty leadership.

There are a few leaders who are not as strong in their power of suffering as they should be. If at any time it seems satyagraha is not making progress or is heading toward a failure, frustration may be wide spread. If, at this time the leaders do not have and display good morale, violence is the result.

Two satyagrahis attributed eruption of violence to human nature. "Failure or anticipation of failure causes frustration and anger. In anger man forgets everything and commits violence."

Interestingly, almost half of those who reported nonviolence was a tactic and also said it could turn violent also attributed it to bad leadership and loose discipline.

IMPACT ON OPPONENTS

Another question related to the perception and cognition of nonviolence that we were interested in was, how the satyagrahis perceived the effect of nonviolence on the opponent. Gandhi was never tired of reminding his followers that satyagrahi's appeal is to the heart of the opponent. The opponent is won by conversion rather than coercion. Ishver Bhai, the main leader of the Pardi satyagraha also repeatedly impressed this aspect of their movement upon the satyagrahis. How far is this aspect reflected in the attitudes of the satyagrahis?

To find this, we asked our respondents; "Knowing that your movement succeeded in its objective to a considerable extent, did you think the opponent was forced into submission, persuaded or converted?" Major categories were listed under three heads namely, (1) coerced (2) persuaded and (3) converted. Projective responses where respondent said that the opponent gave in because of adverse public opinion, financial loss, etc., were coded 'coerced'. If the respondent stated that the opponent conceded because he was genuinely convinced of satyagrahis' demands, or because of justice etc., the response was coded 'converted'. Where the respondent reported that the opponent only relented so as to stop the satyagraha 'nuisance' or to get them 'off his back', or the conflict resolution, was the result of 'accommodation' or 'adjustment' between the conflicting positions of the two parties without any change in the opponent's views regarding satyagrahi demands, the response was coded 'persuaded'.

Responses to this question would be important information to have not only because it would indicate a further degree of internalization of satyagraha norms but also because of the underlying psychological association with the behavior of the satyagrahis during the movement. One would expect that where a satyagrahi perceived the opponent 'converted' by the satyagraha, he (the satyagrahi) was much more likely to avoid indulging in coercive behavior than where he perceived the opponent giving in due to coercion.

TABLE 14

ATTITUDE TO NONVIOLENCE AT
PARTICIPATION BY EFFECT ON OPPONENT
(Percentages in parentheses)

Attitude to nonviolence at participation			Gandhi Sample		
			Effect on Opponent		
	Coerced	Persuaded	Converted	DK	Total
Political Tactic	3(75.0)	1(25.0)	—	—	4(100)
Creed	11(40.7)	9(33.3)	6(22.2)	1(3.7)	27(100)
Other	2(66.7)	—	1(33.3)	—	3(100)
Total	16(47.1)	10(29.4)	7(20.6)	1(2.9)	34(100)

Chi^2 = 3.5422   P $\angle$ .8
Cramer's V = 0.22824

The data (Table 14 and 14a) indicate that a surprisingly small number of satyagrahis 20.6% (7) for the Gandhi sample and only 2(2.0%) from the Pardi sample believed that the opponent was 'converted.' The fact that the number reporting conversion

TABLE 14a
ATTITUDE TO NONVIOLENCE AT PARTICIPATION BY EFFECT ON OPPONENT
(Percentages in parentheses)

Attitude to nonviolence at participation	Pardi Sample Effect on Opponent				
	Coerced	Persuaded	Converted	DK	Total
Political Tactic	——	5(100)	——	——	5(100)
Creed	3(2.9)	77(75.5)	2(2.10)	20(19.6)	102(100)
Other	1(33.3)	2(66.7)	——	——	3(100)
Total	4(3.6)	84(76.4)	2(1.8)	20(18.2)	110(100)

$Chi^2 = 9.7315$ $P < .2$
Cramer's V $= 0.2103$

is much smaller in the Pardi sample than in the Gandhi sample may be because the opponent in the case of Pardi, the landlord, was much more visible, hence real. After the satyagraha, two satyagrahis might have come to this conclusion as a result of working with and for him. In contrast, the opponent for the two Gandhi satyagrahas was in the long run the British Goverment and hence distant and impersonal. Therefore, in the absence of any first hand contact with the opponent, it was easier for the Gandhi satyagrahis to subscribe to the 'abstract' notion that the opponent was 'converted'.

How is the satyagrahis' perception of the effect of nonviolence on the opponent related to his belief in nonviolence as a 'creed' or 'tactic'? The data does not indicate any significant association. Seventy-five and five tenths percent of those who reported nonviolence to be a 'creed' in the Pardi sample reported that the opponent was 'persuaded'. On the other hand in the Gandhi sample the largest plurality 11 (40.7%) in the same category reported that the opponent was 'coerced'. Thus, the data does not suggest any specific direction in the relationship between the perception of nonviolence as a 'creed' or 'tactic' and the effect of nonviolence on the opponent whether he was 'converted', 'persuaded' or 'coerced'. Does the degree of experience in satyagraha participation affect this relationship? For example, is it possible that among those satyagrahis who considered nonviolence to be a 'creed' and who participated in satyagrahas a greater number of times than the others in the 'creed' category, might perceive the opponent to be 'converted'? We might expect such a perception because of greater participation and consequently, greater chance for the internalization of Gandhian norms. However, controlling for 'the number of times the respondent participated in satyagrahas' we still do not find any significant association between the perception of nonviolence as a 'creed' or 'tactic' and the effect on the opponent.[4]

One possible explanation for this overwhelming 'persuaded' response in spite of heavy insistence on 'conversion' by satyagraha leaders might also be that the rank and file satyagrahis did not consider 'persuasion' any less acceptable and honorable than 'conversion'. In an honorable tradition dating back to antiquity, the Indians have placed great emphasis on conflict resolution through a frank discussion and compromise between the contending parties. In the Western 'adversary' tradition the conflict is believed to be best resolved through the frank confrontation of alternatives, their clash and finally, the victory of one alternative over the other. Studies of village governmental processes in India amply document the opposition to the 'adversary' process.[5] Traditional Indian ideas of conflict management tend to stress arbitration, 'consensus', etc., and downplay overt hostility, defeat and victory. According to Rudolf and Rudolf,

> Resistance to the notion of conflict arises partly from the romance and reality that surround the image of the village in the minds of many Indians. When the council of five, the Panchayat, spoke as one it was said to be the voice of God; it gave expression to the consensus of the traditional moral order.[6]

To sum up, the affective component of attitude toward nonviolence was strong. An overwhelming majority of the satyagrahis passionately believed in nonviolence as a creed without necessarily understanding it. Few showed familiarity with the religious or philosophical aspects of nonviolence, and fewer still with its eschatological underpinnings. For most of the satyagrahis nonviolence was a faith which commanded the unquestioning following by the devotee. The faith in nonviolence in turn was derived from faith in the topmost leadership, Gandhi in the case of Rajkot and Bardoli satyagrahas and Ishver Bhai in the case of Pardi satyagraha.

The lack of philosophical understanding of nonviolence, however was no bar to the internalization of nonviolence on the action level. For those who considered nonviolence a creed, its requirements in the context of the satyagrahas were simple and straight forward enough to understand—no physical violence under any circumstances. Beyond this we find a wide spectrum of attitudes regarding other related aspects of nonviolence.

Thus, very few satyagrahis believed that the opponent was converted to their point of view as a result of the satyagraha. A fairly large percentage believed that the successful conclusion of the satyagraha was the result of accommodation between the contending parties rather than conversion of the opponent. These perceptions regarding the effect of nonviolence on the opponent did not seem to be related to satyagrahis' belief in nonviolence as a creed or tactic.

NOTES and REFERENCES

[1] Inge Bell in her study of the CORE found that members of the CORE with high educational and occupational level were more likely to accept nonviolence as a moral commitment. *CORE and The Strategy of Nonviolence* (New York: Random House, 1960), pp. 64-81.

[2] The incident refers to the great Hindu religious epic *The Mahabharata* which describes the great war between the Pandavas and Kauravas. The five 'Pandava' brothers led by Arjuna, related to one hundred Kaurava brothers as cousins asserted their right to ancestral home and land after they returned from a five year exile in forest. War was the result after Duryodhana, one of the 100 Kauravas refused to yield land equivalent of even the 'point of a needle'. Before the war began, Lord Krishna gave Arjuna the choice of taking him or hundreds of thousands of soldiers he had. Arjuna opted for Lord Krishna; the soldiers went to Kauravas. The Kauravas had many times more soldiers than Pandavas. On Pandavas' side was Lord Krishna who

became a charioteer for Arjuna, the ace archer. The war was finally won by the Pandavas, and right and justice established.

[3] Gandhi, *Satyagraha in South Africa*, 1928, trans. V.G. Desai (Ahmedabad: Nav Jivan, 1950), p. 332.

[4] (Chi. sq.$=4.150$ and $P \angle .7$).

[5] See e.g., W.H. Morris-Jones, "India's Political Idioms," in C.H. Philips, ed., *Politics and Society in India* (London: 1963). Among the modern proponents of ideas about 'compromise' and 'consensus' as opposed to the 'adversary' mode, for conflict resolution is Jay Prakash Narayan. See his "Reconstruction of Indian Polity" in Bimla Prasad, ed., *Socialism, Sarvodaya and Democracy* (London: 1964). A vigorous critique and defense of the essay may be found in W.H Morris-Jones, "The Unhappy Utopia, J.P. in Wonderland, *Economic Weekly*, June 25, 1960. Also, William Carpenter, "Reconstruction of Indian Polity: Defense of J.P.," *Economic Weekly*, Feb. 4, 1961.

[6] Lloyd I. and Susanne Hoeber Rudolph, *The Modernity of Tradition, Political Development in India* (Chicago: University of Chicago Press, 1967), p. 187. For an extended discussion of traditional Indian approach to conflict resolution see also Susanne Rudolph "Conflict and Consensus in Indian Politics," in *World Politics*, 13 (April, 1961).

6
Participation, Social Background and Attitudes of the Leaders

As mentioned earlier the number of leaders interviewed in Pardi comprises almost 90% of the total leadership of Pardi satyagraha and the leaders interviewed for the Gandhi sample include the two most prominent leaders of Rajkot satyagraha.

SOCIAL BACKGROUND

If the rank and file satyagrahis were a vanguard group in relation to the rest of the peple, the subleaders selected for this study reflected more of the same but to a higher degree. Apart from being entrusted with the responsibility of initiating, organizing specific nonviolent action projects under the overall leadership of the main leader (Ishver Bhai or Gandhi), the subleaders were young—all were below 35 at the time of participation—highly educated and also had a greater degree of experience in satyagraha participation. Actually three of the fourteen leaders, U.N. Dhebar and Jetha Lal Joshi in the Gandhi satyagrahas and Uttam Bhai in the Pardi satyagraha, were the most influential leaders in terms of organization and the conduct of the satyagrahas. This was evident from the responses of the rank and file satyagrahis. A large percentage of the satyagrahis in the Gandhi sample mentioned the name of Dhebar and Jetha Lal Joshi, along with that of Gandhi, when asked about their source of familiarity with nonviolence and the reason for their participation in the satyagraha. Similarly, the Pardi satyagrahis mentioned the name of Uttam Bhai along with that of Ishver Bhai.

Thus our data indicates that of the fourteen subleaders interviewed, nine had participated in three or more satyagrahas, four in two or three and one in one satyagraha. One leader had participated in more than nine satyagrahas. Here again a greater degree of participation is indicated by Gandhi leaders as compared to Pardi leaders, because most of them had been involved with Gandhi's satyagrahas since the late 1910. As expected all the leaders except two, had spent time in jail in connection with their movements. The two who indicated they did not go to jail were involved in organizational activities such as recruitment, fund raising and constructive activities. As regards Gandhi's insistence on purity and austerity in the life of a satyagrahi, we found all the fourteen leaders to be wearing khadi. They took to khadi since they became satyagrahis. All the leaders of Pardi were already using only khadi under the influence of Gandhi. Similarly all fourteen said they were vegetarians. This was particularly surprising in case of two leaders, one of them a Kshatriya by caste and the other a Muslim by religion. In these cases, the vegetarianism can, undoubtedly be attributed to Gandhi. In both cases meat-eating is common and approved by religion. Another surprise was regarding drinking. There were two leaders, one each from Rajkot and Pardi who said they were drinkers. This was surprising not only because they were part of the leadership structure but also because Gandhi was most uncompromising in regard to drinking. He considered it the worst kind of evil physically, morally and economically. One of the two explaining his reasons for drinking said,

> I drink because I can afford it.
> I do it in moderation. I drink
> also because I do not believe it
> affects my commitment to being
> nonviolent as long as I want to.

It would be apt to point out here that the same leader considered nonviolence to be a tactic rather than a creed.

All the leaders reflect a high level of education. Ten leaders had college level education and four, two each from Pardi and Gandhi samples, had elementary or middle school education. But more striking was the caste and occupational structure of the leadership.

TABLE 15
CASTE STATUS OF LEADERS
IN
PARDI AND GANDHI SATYAGRAHAS

Caste	Pardi	Gandhi	Total
Brahmin	5	3	8
Kshatriya	0	1	1
Shudra	2	0	2
Jain	1	1	2
Muslim	0	1	1
Total	8	6	14

TABLE 16
OCCUPATION OF LEADERS
IN
PARDI AND GANDHI SATYAGRAHAS

Occupation	Pardi	Gandhi	Total
Lawyer	3	3	6
Professor-Teacher	2	0	2
Student	0	1	1
Medical Dr.	1	0	1
Agriculture	2	2	4
Total	8	6	14

As the above tables indicate the leadership was dominated by high castes, namely, Brahmins. Eight out of fourteen leaders were Brahmins. The number of Brahmins, five out of eight, in Pardi is particularly high. Dr. Amul Desai, one of the Pardi leaders interviewed, made an interesting observation.

Attitudes of the Leaders

There is a parallel here with the Negro movement for civil rights in the United States. As it was started by whites there, the movement for the rights of the adivasis was started by Desais here.

Similarly, by profession, the number of lawyers was also high. There were six lawyers, two professors and one doctor. These figures seem to be typical. Many studies have pointed out that in the twenties and later, the Congress party, which had been the main vehicle of satyagraha movements, and other parties have been dominated to a very great extent by upper caste and that the composition has not basically altered.[1]

These aspects are reflected also in tha goal orientations of the leaders. Twelve out of fourteen indicated the goals of the satyagrahas in ideological terms. All the six leaders in the Gandhi satyagrahas reported that they only had the long range goal of independence of India from British rule in view. Six out of eight in the Pardi satyagraha said that their ultimate goal was the establishment of socialism in India. All the leaders who viewed the goals of the movement in ideological terms also reported, however, that their appeals to the rank and file were always geared to the local grievances as far as possible. Interestingly, the only two leaders in the Pardi satyagraha who expressed the goals of the movement purely in terms of local issues had the least education, up to the elementary level. We believe, however, that the role of caste is overstated. The more important factors lending homogeneity to the leadership structure, in our opinion, were their profession and education, rather than caste.[2] Under the influence of liberal western education the leaders were generally more secular in their understanding of the world, more egalitarian in their outlook, more accepting of science and technology for progress and had developed a national outlook for the future of Indian society. They were also less sectional, less regional, less communal and less caste-minded, as compared to the rest of the people. Through their experiences with and struggle against British colonialism, they were all anti-imperialist and anti-capitalist and hence by implication socialist. So strong was their bias in favor of socialism that not only was it reflected in the Constitution of India and the policy planning in India but a whole generation or two was brought up into the belief that socialism was the panacea for all of India's ills. In spite of the influence of these ideas, some leaders managed to stay embedded in their traditional familial institutions and retained indigenous elements in their style of life. Some who could not make the compromise between western liberal ideas and indigenous elements found themselves in strain and conflict and alienated from society.[3]

MEANING OF NONVIOLENCE FOR THE LEADERS

We need not overemphasize the significance of leaders in a satyagraha. Satyagrahas do not just happen. Whether a satyagraha is spontaneous or planned, leadership in one form or another is always implied. Thus, even in a spontaneous movement someone will have to propose or initiate a particular course of action to bring homogeneity and effectiveness to the movement. Even where the movements are led by charismatic figures, a string of leaders will be needed to organize and implement the charismatic leader's plan. In the medium-sized satyagrahas, that we have under study here, several subleaders are needed. Nonviolent action may have to be carried on simultaneously at several places separated by long distance. These actions at various levels and places may give rise to unusual or emergency situations where the leaders may have to use their own initiative and knowledge to solve the problems. Even in the presence of a charismatic leadership, a string of leaders will be required to help in working out general strategy and tactics for action, promoting discipline, negotiating with the opponent, evolving counter strategies in case of failure, etc.

The functions described above are common to all kinds of movements, including a satyagraha. However, more important and crucial from the point of view of a satyagraha, is the responsibility the leaders face in ensuring that the movement is nonviolent under all circumstances. The responsibility is even greater where the knowledge and understanding of the principles and practice of nonviolent action are not widespread and deep among the rank and file. We would expect, though, that the leaders will be able to discharge their responsibility, provided they have themselves understood and internalized the norms of satyagraha. Gandhi, himself, stressed the significance of strong leaders and volunteers

> who thoroughly understood the strict conditions of satyagraha. . . . could explain these to the people, and by sleepless vigilance keep them on the right path.[4]

Since a satyagraha might have to undergo several stages of development before it is brought to a conclusion, it is obvious there will be occasions and incidents where satyagrahis might feel terribly depressed or might be tempted to indulge in violence. There might be incidents where the leaders and the satyagrahis, both, will be the targets of violence by the opponent; or in spite of all the deprivations and the suffering engendered by the satyagraha, it might be perceived by satyagrahis as threatened with failure. In such crisis situations not only the satyagrahis, even the leaders without the proper internalization of satyagraha norms, might get so frustrated as to lose all the grip on the course of the satyagraha. Gandhi argued that to save a satyagraha from lapsing into violence or taking actions which might lead to violence, in crisis situations it was essential that the leadership should be in the hands of those who believed in ahimsa as a moral principle.

The belief system of the leadership structure is important from still another point of view. Even where a movement is led by charismatic leaders, as in the case of Pardi and Gandhi satyagrahas, most of the satyagrahis are bound to be in a situation of greater interaction with the leaders and sub-leaders than with the charismatic leader.

Also at the various levels and phases of the satyagraha, and activities related to the satyagraha, such as recruitment, fund raising, constructive activities or during the initiating, organizing and carrying-on stage of an actual nonviolent project —say picketing or a sit-in—it is the leaders who are in face-to-face interaction with the satyagrahis. The message of nonviolence filters through to the satyagrahis in the numerous pep talks and strategy sessions that the leaders hold, and by the examples of sacrifice and fearlessness which they themselves place before the satyagrahis.

NONVIOLENCE A 'CREED' OR 'TACTIC'?

In our earlier analysis, we saw that an overwhelming percentage of the rank and file satyagrahis considered nonviolence as a 'creed'. In the light of the above we were interested in knowing the leader's cognition and perception of nonviolence.

Interviewing the leaders it became evident that all the leaders were, as expected, much more knowledgeable about the norms of satyagraha than the rank and file. What we did not expect, however, was the number of leaders who would say they considered nonviolence to be a tactic rather than a way of life.

TABLE 17
PROJECTIVE RESPONSES OF
LEADERS ON WHETHER SATYAGRAHA
WAS A TACTIC OR A CREED

Response	Pardi satyagraha	Gandhi satyagraha	Total
Poltactic	2	5	7
Creed	6	1	7
Total	8	6	14

As the table above indicates, half the leaders interviewed said they considered nonviolence only a tactic, which to us was a surprise. Even more surprising was the number of leaders from the Gandhi satyagrahas, who said nonviolence was a tactic. Five out of six leaders from the Gandhi satyagrahas said nonviolence was no more than a tactic; only two out of eight from the Pardi sample said it was a tactic. Thus the pattern was similar to the one we found in the case of the rank and file satyagrahis where a greater percentage in the Gandhi sample— though, not as great as in the leaders' case—as compared to the Pardi sample, said that they considered nonviolence to be a tactic.

We chose the three satyagrahas for our study because we considered them, at least externally, more or less conforming to our satyagraha model. We can infer from the above data that for the successful conduct of a nonviolent satyagraha, it is not essential for all the leaders to believe in nonviolence as a moral principle. The important question then is what kind of intellectual grasp and conviction did the leaders bring to the movement?

Another factor of similarity that one found between the rank and file satyagrahis and the leaders was in regard to the source of their familiarity with nonviolence. The name of Gandhi figured in the answers of ten leaders, two mentioned their readings as the source of nonviolence. One leader from Rajkot attributed his knowledge to his religion and his own readings. Uttam Bhai, the adivasi leader and the most prominent leader after Ishver Bhai and in a way charismatic in his own right, imputed his familiarity and training in ahimsa to Ishver Bhai.

One common thread running through the attitudes of the leaders who considered ahimsa to be a tactic was that they all viewed conflict as basically a contest for power.

The subordinate group, lacking power to affect decision through the institutional means and also lacking control over the use of force, find in satyagraha a possible avenue for the redress of grievances. However, the nature of nonviolent action to be taken will depend upon the nature of the issue in question and the characteristics of the dominant group itself. Where the leadership of the subordinate group views the opponents to be so well entrenched in their power as to be not amenable to reason at all or too reluctant to part with a part of their power, the nonviolent action will have to be increasingly vigorous and militant. This also leaves open the possibility that if the nonviolent action does not have the desired effect on the opponent, the only alternative may be to resort to violence.

In this context, our interviews with the two topmost leaders of the Rajkot satyagraha, Jetha Lal Joshi and U.N. Dhebar were instructive. Both Brahmins, about 35 years old at the time of the Rajkot satyagraha, lawyers and highly intellectual, were initiators, organizers and conductors of the Rajkot satyagraha right up to its conclusion. Both held the most important offices, suffered jail sentences and were party to negotiations at all stages of the satyagraha. Both regarded Gandhi as a God and claimed their spiritual ancestry to him. Both claimed that they applied all the principles of Gandhian satyagraha in

Rajkot to the full. Yet, both considered nonviolence to be a tactic rather than a creed.

Jetha Lal Joshi, in particular, narrated his version of Rajkot satyagraha in terms of a 'battle'. The more powerful, unjust and deceitful the enemy the harder and more militant the battle.

In a successful battle the army fighting for the cause of justice has to match the enemy's strategy with a superior counter strategy. The only difference between what we ordinarily understand by a battle and a satyagraha is that the satyagrahis are pledged to using only nonviolent means.

It was evident from this interview that the leader believed, by implication, that given certain characteristics of the opponent, nonviolent tactics may not work thus necessitating the use of other means, including violent means. If the opponent is easily amenable to reason, the conflict may be resolved before the subordinate group takes to more militant nonviolent measures. Thus in a labor conflict, the conflict between the labor and management may be resolved by simple negotiations or increasingly by threat of a strike or an actual one day strike and so on. Of course, it was obvious from Jetha Lal Joshi's interview that the Rajkot satyagraha was a battle because he considered the opponent to be not amenable to reason, since he was also a tool of the British Government.

This raises another question. If nonviolence is a tactic, what does the leader perceive his role to be in relation to the satyagrahis? The answer is once again in the framework of a 'battle'.

First and foremost requirement is a deep commitment to the goals of the movement on the part of the leaders as well as the followers. In a satyagraha, however, the participants need to have 'high morals' if the satyagraha has to be nonviolent and effective. It was quite obvious though, that 'high morals' that Jetha Lal Joshi was talking about was not used in the same sense as Gandhi talked about when he elevated ahimsa to a high moral principle. For Jetha Lal Joshi connotation by 'high morals' was simply the willingness to abide by a strict discipline.

A band of dedicated and disciplined volunteers are necessary and sufficient for waging a nonviolent struggle, under an accepted commander. Gandhi was, for us and the rank and file, the undisputed commander who would not have the movement by any but the nonviolent means.

Another of the leaders Brahm Kumar Bhatt from Pardi who considered nonviolence to be a tactic, flatly declared.'

I never had any faith and still have no faith in nonviolence. The only reason I was in the movement was because only Ishver Bhai could tap the massive power of the people. He insisted on nonviolence and I had to go along with that.

We spent almost eight hours interviewing U.N. Dhebar. He was, during and as a consequence of the Rajkot satyagraha, the undisputed leader in that part of the country. He went on later following the independence of India and reorganization of Indian states to become the chief minister of Saurashtra State. At the time of the interview he was chairman of the powerful Khadi and Village Industries Commission. But more importantly from the viewpoint of our interview, he was a highly respected leader because of his association with Gandhi. He had written a book and several articles on Gandhi.

As we asked him the question whether 'ahimsa' was a creed or a tactic, he seemed to agonize for some time before giving his final response. He was certain it was not a creed, but he was not quite certain if it was a tactic either. "I am inclined to say that my position lies somewhere between creed and tactic." Then he paused a few moments and said that it was certainly not a creed for him in the sense that Gandhi used the term. He finally made up his mind that his correct response should be 'tactic'.

There were some arguments which seemed to be common to all the leaders who considered nonviolence to be a tactic. All the leaders seemed to be saying that a satyagraha needed participants with a high sense of morality and discipline with unflinching devotion to the leadership. Nonviolence was a tactic because there was no guarantee that the enemy will view the issues in conflict in the same moral terms as the subordinate group does.

This moral opaqueness on the part of the opponent might make the operation of a successful satyagraha too difficult or even impossible. The only alternative, then, was to resort to violence. The interview with Dhebar was typical.

Ahimsa is a moral weapon and therefore it generates a stronger and deeper response, especially in the masses. Violent action may generate a stronger response but it is temporary and can never be so deep. Once the response is deep enough, human personality becomes effective in the deeper sense. On the moral level, this produces an impact upon the opponents and nonparticipants.

I must admit, however, that for nonviolence to be effective the nature of the opponent is also important. As Carl Jasper put it, as British needed a Gandhi against them; so Gandhi also needed British against him.

At the time of Rajkot satyagraha, I was in exploratory stage and still am. Under the impact of Mahatma Gandhi, we saw to it that the Rajkot struggle was nonviolent. We prepared a water-tight case on a moral basis and we believed that the other side was open to the voice of reason and morality. But on two different occasions, I failed to find nonviolent answers and I, myself, was responsible for suggesting violent remedies. This was 1. at the time of the accession of Junagadh to Pakistan. 2. at the time of Goa. On both the occasions, I was convinced that the opponent was totally insensitive to the moral issues. This insensitivity occurs when the holders of power become so intoxicated with their power that nothing, beyond their own narrow personal interests, matters any more.

Among the leaders who considered nonviolence to be a creed, some of the responses were remarkably similar to those of the rank and file.

Their belief in nonviolence as a creed was based either as a matter of faith or upon their belief in the basic goodness of human nature. Thus Uttam Bhai declared. "If the means are pure the results are bound to be good."[5] Another leader, Govindji Vakil said,

Attitudes of the Leaders

in violence; the innocent suffer while those indulging in violence go scot free. But in nonviolence the suffering is only for the sacrificer. Violence can only arouse mobs. But to arouse the masses you need nonviolence.

Vaju Bhai Shah, the only leader from Rajkot satyagraha who said he considered nonviolence to be a 'creed' declared:

> It (nonviolence) is mightier than the mightiest force. Nonviolence only brings out the best, not only in the religious or spiritual sense but in the material sense. This is my innermost conviction.

The other leaders pleaded the basic goodness of human being in support of their unflinching faith in nonviolence. Man may be bestial in origin, but he is still human because he is potentially good. The sight of a suffering satyagrahi who refuses to hurt in spite of his own pain provides in the behavior of the satyagrahi a mirror image of what he, the opponent, might himself be. Vaju Bhai Shah, in this connection, approvingly quoted a favorite Mohommedan saying of Gandhi.

> adam Kuda Nahin, Lekin Khuda Ke Nur Se Juda Nahin— Man is not God; but neither is he different from the spark of God.

Hakumat Desai, professor of sociology at the local college and a prominent organization leader of Pardi emphasized the role of nonviolence in bringing out the 'best' in man. He declared:

> Ahimsa is a broad principle of life. We talk of human values, humanism, fellowship, etc. No creed except nonviolence can bring it. We have seen it in Pardi. It is a philosophy of life. If law and 'Karuna'—compassion—go together violence will be wiped out. Nonviolence, like democracy is slow. But just as the legitimacy obtained through democratic processes is much stronger and lasting, gains made through nonviolence are permanent, be it politics or personal life.

None of the leaders, not even those who passionately defended nonvoilence as a creed, said that the opponent was converted. Out of fourteen nine said the opponent was persuaded; five said he was coerced. Actually two out of five who said the opponent was coerced into submission belonged to the category which believed nonviolence to be a creed. Thus, Kumud Ben Desai—professor of sociology, wife of Ishver Bhai, and the only woman leader in Pardi satyagraha said,

> Coercion is always there. Satyagrahis undergo a period of socialization and learning nonviolence through speeches and constant guidance of their leaders. The opponents have no comparable exposure to the virtues involved in a Satyagraha. It is, therefore, not surprising that they feel coerced when they have to give in to the satyagrahis.

Jetha Lal Joshi, the Rajkot leader who said nonviolence was a tactic bluntly declared,

> There is no doubt that Thakore Saheb was forced into surrendering. This is indicated by the fact that he continued to block or dilute the agreement reached between us and him for ten years. I believe conversion in a satyagraha is more an exception rather than a rule.

It is the leaders who are deeply involved in negotiations and 'haggling' with the opponent. The fact that all of them believed that the opponent was coerced or persuaded would seem to indicate that they saw the satyagraha in the final analysis boil down to a mere contest for power with each side trying to wrest the most from the other. Also, the overwhelming 'persuaded' response (from nine leaders) might also indicate their bias for the response, because all of them, endeavoring to be Gandhian but finding themselves without proof of conversion of the opponent found themselves much more comfortable in reporting 'persuaded' response, since 'persuasion' comprises at least some semblance of approval of the final result on the part of the opponent. The bias for 'persuasion' has strong roots in Indian tradition, as pointed out elsewhere.

SATYAGRAHA AND RELIGION

Finally, our long interviews with the leaders revealed a total absence of religious orientation in their understanding and elaboration of nonviolence. It was expected that the leaders who believed nonviolence to be a tactic would lack religious orientation in their belief system of nonviolence. But even among the leaders who considered nonviolence to be a creed, there was no reference to God or religion. The two adivasi leaders, Uttam Bhai and Ramabhai Devabhai Patel who expressed their passionate belief in nonviolence simply identified it with their faith in Ishver Bhai. Only, in so far as some of the leaders both in Rajkot and Pardi considered Gandhi and Ishver Bhai, respectively, Gods, was any reference made to God in our interviews with the leaders. This shows that the beliefs of the leaders regarding nonviolence were based on pragmatism and humanism rather than on religion. They also showed less affectivity as compared to the rank and file.

Joan Bondurant and other writers on Gandhi also arrived at the conclusion that most of the

> Indian leaders accepted satyagraha even when they had little faith in the religious elements which appeared to infuse it.[6]

The leaders accepted the technique because it was Gandhi alone who was able to awaken the masses. As the technique started to succeed, more leaders came to believe in it.

Elsewhere, Bondurant points out that most of the satyagraha participants did not believe in nonviolence as a creed[7] but the campaign could be run even with people who did not believe in nonviolence because they followed the strict discipline imposed by leaders who were themselves wedded to unadulterated nonviolence.[8] Our data in contrast to the above suggests that many satyagrahis did in fact believe in nonviolence as a creed while many leaders did not. The fact is all the leaders as well as satyagrahis, were closely knit together as a result of tight discipline under the charismatic leaders.

NONVIOLENCE AS COMMUNICATION

Given the pragmatic orientation of the leaders toward nonviolence, the question is, how did the three satyagrahas remain models of true satyagraha at least externally?

We believe the answer to this question lies in the content of communication from the leaders to the satyagrahis and the nature of the appeal of the topmost leadership to the rank and file. As the above data suggests, the subleaders do not always approach and participate in a movement with a total identification with the system of behavioral norms as established by the main leader.

Where the sustaining force of a movement, however, derives from a charismatic leader, the subleaders can discipline themselves enough to act as communicators of the norms in a way which may lead the followers into believing that the subleaders fully subscribe to the main leader's norms. The subleaders can establish credibility through their verbal communications and actions. Thus, in their numerous pamphlets, speeches, peptalks and other occasions of interaction, the subleaders constantly reiterated their adherence to the basic norms and demanded the same from the followers. In crisis situations the leaders can show by action that they also live those norms, although personally they might be doing it only as part of satyagraha discipline.

In the three satyagrahas we studied, we found that all the leaders were pledged to strict adherence to the discipline laid down by the charismatic leader. In their interaction with the rank and file satyagrahis we did not find any wavering from satyagraha rules either in speech or action. All the leaders, regardless of the fact whether nonviolence was a creed or a tactic for them personally, communicated with the followers in terms of norms and symbols established by Gandhi and Ishverbhai. The content analysis of the speeches by the subleaders clearly reveals that their speeches were generously punctuated with references to the power and infallibility of the weapon of nonviolence. The pledges of the nonviolence were frequently given and taken. Names of Gandhi and Ishverbhai and grace of God on the side of the satyagrahis were continually invoked.

Bell, in her study of the CORE attributes the switch of the CORE from nonviolent ideology to violent ideology to differentiation between exoteric and esoteric communication.[9] The dual nature of communication, one exoteric, geared to outsiders and potential supporters emphasized the purely nonviolent nature of their efforts to gain equality for the Negro. The emphasis on nonviolence was essential so as to gain legitimacy for their claims of equality from potential supporters. Second, the esoteric, directed only to the membership of the CORE, freely referred to the use of coercion to achieve equality. The members of the CORE being already convinced of the legitimacy of their claim to equality, were much more receptive to the idea of using coercion to gain that end.

We did not find this differentiation between 'exoteric' and 'esoteric' communication in any of the three movements. This was attributable to the nature of the topmost leadership and strict discipline imposed by Gandhi and Ishverbhai and the realization by the subleaders that without the support of the main leader, the movement will collapse. Only on rare occasions would the leaders express their dissatisfaction with nonviolent action. But this expression would be strictly limited to the close and small circle of friends. All care was taken that it did not spill over to the rank and file. Brahm Kumar, the only Pardi leader who flatly declared he had no faith in nonviolence said:

> Ishverlal was able to mobilize the satyagrahis in a way that no one else could. At times I would get extremely frustrated and impatient because the progress of the satyagraha was so slow that it seemed as if it would go on until eternity. . . .I would let off steam in discussions with my close friends. It was because of my impatience and skepticism regarding the effectiveness for nonviolent tactics that I kept myself also from direct action projects. I concentrated only on constructive activity.

An important question to ask here is, given the situation where such a large number of subleaders considered nonviolence to be a tactic how did these leaders help the satyagrahis sustain faith in nonviolent behavior? It seems fair to assume that in the absence of internalization of the norms of nonviolence they, the subleaders, would be more likely to feel intense frustration and resentment regarding the nonviolent method itself, if the satyagraha resulted in increased deprivation for the satyagrahis or failure. The frustration of the subleaders would not be lost on the rank and file since it is the subleaders with whom they are in direct and prolonged contact. The frustration and resentment of the leaders might show in their decreased enthusiasm or questioning the efficacy of nonviolence or even dropping subtle hints that violence was the only way to succeed.

The answer to this question, once again, has to be in terms of the nature of the topmost leadership and its linkages with the rank and file. The latter derived their faith in nonviolent behavior only from their faith in their main leader with whom they had a highly emotional identification. If a subleader had strong enough reservations about nonviolence to voice them openly he could do so only at the risk of being repudiated not only by the main leader but also by the rank and file under him. Thus, throughout the Gandhian satyagrahas dozens of influential leaders were skeptical of nonviolent tactics but they had to go along with Gandhi because if they did not, they risked rejection by their own followers. We asked Brahm Kumar Bhatt, the Pardi leader who flatly indicated he had no faith in nonviolence, if there was any frustration or propensity for violence among the satyagrahis as a result of violence from the enemy or increased deprivation. He replied:

> Pardi satyagraha was remarkable in many ways. The adivasis were well trained and prepared for nonviolence. There was no frustration that I know of. And believe it or not, whatever frustration there was, it was only for the leaders (subleaders). Guided by their faith in Ishver Bhai, it was the adivasis who helped the leaders keep hope and faith in nonviolence.

The above analysis suggests that so strongly were the rank and file cathected on the personality of the topmost leaders (Gandhi and Ishver Bhai) and through them to the norms of nonviolent behavior that their own perception of nonviolence as a creed caused them to percieve their subleaders also in the same light. The subleaders, through the content of their communication, only reinforced the nonviolent image of themselves. Thus, when we asked the satyagrahis what they thought of their subleaders, whether nonviolence for them was a tactic or a creed, an overwhelming percentage of 92.7% (102) of the Pardi satyagrahis and 59.3% (35) of the Gandhi satyagrahis said they believed that nonviolence was a creed for their subleaders. Only 5.5% (6) in the Pardi sample and 28.8% (17) in the Gandhi sample believed it was a tactic for the leaders.

How does the satyagrahis' perception of their leaders perception of commitment to nonviolence affect their own commitment to nonviolence? The cross tabulation of the satyagrahis, attitude to nonviolence at the time of satyagraha participation with their perception of leaders, commitment to nonviolence indicates a significant association.

TABLE 18

PROJECTIVE RESPONSES SHOWING SATYAGRAHIS, ATTITUDE TO NONVIOLENCE BY SATYAGRAHIS, PERCEPTION OF LEADERS, COMMITMENT TO NONVIOLENCE

(Percentages in parentheses)

Satyagrahis, attitude to nonviolence	Satyagrahis, perception of leaders' attitude to nonviolence			
			Gandhi Satyagraha	
	Tactic	Creed	Others	Total
Tactic	11 (73.3)	4 (26.7)	—	15 (100)
Creed	4 (10.3)	31 (79.5)	4 (10.3)	39 (100)
Other	1 (25.0)	—	3 (75.0)	4 (100)
Total	16 (27.6)	35 (60.3)	7 (21.1)	58 (100)

$Chi^2 = 38.2784$ $P < .001$
Cramer's $V = 0.57444$

TABLE 18a
PROJECTIVE RESPONSES SHOWING SATYAGRAHIS,
ATTITUDE TO NONVIOLENCE BY SATYAGRAHIS,
PERCEPTION OF LEADERS, COMMITMENT TO
NONVIOLENCE

(Percentages in parentheses)

Satyagrahis, attitude to nonviolence	Satyagrahis, perception of leaders' attitude to nonviolence			
	Pardi Satyagraha			
	Tactic	Creed	Other	Total
Tactic	5 (100)	—	—	5 (100)
Creed	1 (1.0)	101 (99.0)	—	102 (100)
Other	—	1 (33.7)	2 (66.7)	3 (100)
Total	6 (5.5)	102 (92.7)	2 (1.8)	110 (100)

Chi^2 = 163.3927 P $\angle$ .001
Cramer's V = 0.86.0

As the above table suggests, 101 (99%) in the Pardi satyagraha who said nonviolence was a creed for them also believed it was a creed for their leaders; all 5(100%) who said it was a tactic for themselves also believed it was a tactic for their leaders. Similarly, in the Gandhi satyagrahas 31 (79.5%) who said nonviolence was a creed also believed it was a creed for the leaders; 11(73.3%) said it was a tactic for themselves as well as the leaders. The above analysis suggests that where a movement is led by a strong charismatic leader, it is not essential that the subleaders must also have internalized his system of norms. They can still play a useful part in the movement through a disciplined leadership where they spell out and enforce only the main leader's norms without letting their own disagreements be known to the followers. In other words it is enough for the subleaders to appear resplendent and dazzling in the acceptance of the main leader's norms but they (the norms) need not be necessarily their skin.

Summarizing, the leadership of the satyagrahas was dominated by people who were young, highly educated and had greater degree of experience in satyagraha participation. High caste brahmins, particularly in the Pardi Satyagraha seem to predominate. However, factors lending homogeneity to the satyagrahas were the leaders' occupation and education rather than their caste. Under influence of liberal Western education they were more secular and egalitarian in their outlook toward the world. The leaders participating in the satyagrahas had larger ideological goals in mind rather than the immediate issues. In their attitudes towards nonviolence, the leaders reflected pragmatism and humanism and total absence of religious orientation.

Many of the leaders had not internalized the norms of nonviolence. But all the leaders accepted the authority of the main leader and consequently propagated his doctrine and abided by the discipline imposed by him. Coupled with the charisma of the main leader this was necessary and sufficient to train and entrench the satyagrahis into belief in nonviolence at least on the action level.

NOTES and REFERENCES

[1]See e.g., Lloyd I. Rudolph and Susanne Hoeber Rudolph who suggest that the core of national leadership derived from the twice-born castes, Brahmin, Vaishyas, and Kayasthas. *Modernity of Tradition: Political Development in India* (Chicago: University of Chicago Press, 1967), p. 185.

Rudolph and Rudolph also point to the domination by Brahmins, Vaishyas and Kayasthas through the 40's in Praja Mandals, Lok Parishads, and Harijan Sevak Sanghs (all Congress connected political and social service organizations in Rajasthan). Ibid., p. 186.

Also see Rajendra Prasad, *Satyagraha in Champaran* (Ahmedabad: Navjivan, 1949). For the nature of Gandhi's appeal to these men, also see his *At the Feet of the Mahatma* (Bombay: Hind Kitabs, 1955).

For the dominance of Congress politics by Brahmins, see Eugene Irschick, "Politics and Social Conflict in South India: A Study of Tamil Separation and the non-Brahman Movement", *Ph. D. Thesis* (Chicago: Department of History, University of Chicago, 1964).

[2]For this view also see Andre Beteille, "Elites, Status groups and Caste in Modern India" in Philip Mason, *India and Ceylon: Unity and Diversity* (Oxford University Press, 1967), p. 239.

Rudolph and Rudolph also emphasize the role of Western education. Op. cit., p. 185.

[3] For impact of western education on Indian intellectuals see Edward Shills, *The Intellectual Between Tradition and Modernity: The Indian Situation* (The Hague: Mouton, 1961).

[4] M.K. Gandhi, *An Autobiography or The Story of My Experiments with Truth* (Ahmedabad: Navjivan, 1956), pp. 470-471.

[5] At least three leaders, including Uttam Bhai made it a point to mention a movement in nearby Thana District which was being carried on at the same time as Pardi satyagraha by the local communist party under the leadership of one Godavari. Issues in conflict were exactly the same as in Pardi, namely, justice to the adivasis vis a vis the landlords. The adivasis, under the guidance of Godavari and the communist party, took to terrorist activities against the landlords. Many landlords and adivasis had been killed in the skirmishes. Uttam Bhai and other leaders of Pardi pointed out that the movement in Thana District had been a total failure because they used 'impure', meaning, violent means.

[6] *Conquest of Violence*, p 127.

[7] *Ibid.*, p. 103.

[8] *Ibid.*, p. 104.

[9] Bell takes the terms 'exoteric' and 'esoteric' from Gabriel Almond, *The Appeals of Communism* (Princeton: Princeton University Press, 1954). In his analysis of the communist party communications, Almond used these terms to describe the differentiation in the content of communications geared to the outsiders and those directed toward the insiders. See Inge Powell Bell, *CORE and the Strategy of Nonviolence* (New York: Random House, 1968), pp. 38-39.

7
Religion, Charisma and Nonviolence

One interesting feature of our findings regarding the perception and cognition of nonviolence was the almost total absence of any reference to religion in the subleaders' and satyagrahis' responses. In fact, the content analysis of the responses indicates that references to God or religion figured in the responses of only 7% (12) of the the satyagrahis. This was indeed surprising considering that there was barely a speech by Gandhi which did not involve the name of God in talking about a satyagraha, or a speech by Ishver Bhai which did not invoke either the name of Gandhi or God. Speehes by the subleaders were also punctuated with generous references to God during the satyagraha. However, none of them referred to God and religion during our interviewing.

In the light of the above, this lack of reference to religion needs deeper probing. Gandhi repeatedly reminded his followers that God is their only "help". "The grand theory of satyagraha is built upon a belief in that truth. Hindu religious literature...indeed all religious literature is full of illustrations to prove that truth."[1] Similarly Ishver Bhai, the leader of the Adivasis, reminded his followers of the "Guru Mantra" —the master key—of ahimsa given them by Gandhi which assured them of God's grace and victory.

Neither the subleaders nor the stayagrahis, however, claimed inspiration from God for themsleves, nor did they claim any kind of intervention by God on their behalf because of their creed of nonviolence. Rationalization of the satyagraha and its goals are largely in secular and ethical terms, both by the subleaders and the followers.[2] How do we explain this apparent incompatibility in the cognition of nonviolence between the topmost leader and his followers? Does it mean that we can write off religion as inconsequential to a satyagraha

WEBER AND THE CONCEPT OF CHARISMA

To answer these questions, we have to know not only the nature of the satyagraha but also the nature of the society in which the satyagraha is being attempted. India is a predominantly agrarian society and has been so since ancient times. According to Max Weber, "The more agrarian the essential social pattern of a culture." e.g., India, "the more likely it is that the agrarian element of the population will fall into a pattern of traditionalism and that religion, at least of the masses, will lack ethical rationalization."[3] It is in the context of this deep rooted traditionalism that we have to understand the processes of conflict and the change, or what Weber called the "breakthrough".

Gandhi attempted the rationalization of ethics in terms of religion to the extent that he hardly made a distinction between practical ehics and pure religious beliefs and practices. Thus, both the ethic of goals, viz., change in the name of justice, and the ethic of means, the nonviolent behavior, were rationalized in terms of religion. With reference to the question of "breakthrough", both Gandhi for the Bardoli and Rajkot satyagrahas and Ishver Bhai for the Pardi satyagraha in their specific contexts, can be considered no less than prophets, who according to Weber, are the agents of the process of change to a higher, in the sense of a more rationalized and systematized cultural order, an order at the level of religious ethics which in turn has implications for the nature of society in which it becomes institutionalized. This is Weber's much discussed concept of charisma. The role of the two leaders may further be understood in terms of two kinds of prophets as distinguished by Weber, namely, "exemplary prophet and the ethical prophet."[4] Gandhi can be considered an 'exemplary prophet' who provided a "model for a way of life which can be followed by others, embodying in a religious sense what is defined as a higher level of personal virtue."[5] On the other hand, the 'ethical prophet' "imposes demands on certain categories of men in such a way that not only do they have an opportunity but it is rather their duty, to follow his precepts."[6] Gandhi's and Ishver Bhai's life, to an extent, in the context of Pardi are examples of exemplary prophets of self-dedication and of motivational commitment to a set of normataive ideals.

Although the role of religious prophet for Weber was the prototype, it was not the only example of "charismatic leadership". In its more general sense, charisma was defined by Weber as

> a certain quality of an individual personality by virtue of which he is set apart from ordinary men and treated as endowed with supernatural, superhuman, or at least specifically exceptonal qualities.[7]

From this point of view, irrespective of the fact of whether qualities attributed to the leader are real or imaginary, the validity of his charisma rests on the recognition on the part of those who are subject to his authority.

That all the satyagrahas during Gandhi time were organized and held together by his charismatic influence, needs little documentation here. Literally, hundreds of books and articles have appeared about Gandhi's role in the satyagrahas. The belief that this role was overstressed to the total neglect of the role of satyagrahis, was one of the reasons that led this researcher to focus this study on the rank and file rather than on the topmost leadership. However, throughout our field study the evidence of the charismatic influence of Gandhi and Ishver Bhai had been so overwhelming that we were convinced that the almost exclusive focus on Gandhi by the analysts of satyagraha was not over done. To us the conclusion was inescapable that the presence of a charismatic leader was an important variable in satyagraha. This was true not only about Bardoli and Rajkot, but also about Pardi. At the time of interviews with the Adivasis, Ishver Bhai had long been dead. Yet, his impact was written all over the face of Pardian society. Uttam Bhai, the local Adivasi leader and probably the most important leader of the Pardi satyagraha, next only to Ishver Bhai, reminisced about Ishver Bhai with feeling.

> Ishver Bhai did not burst upon the Pardi scene suddenly. Our faith in him was built gradually over a long period of time. We, Adivasis, under the influence of the Gandhians, have been idealistic people. To us the promise of socialism, economic justice, etc., by the government and leaders held out great hopes for the future. But as our condition went from bad to worse our hopes changed to despair. Then came Ishver Bhai. Giving up living in his comfortable home in the Surat City, he cast his lot with us, the poor people of Pardi. He forged us into an organized group. Whatever we have achieved is all because of his leadership and initiative.[8]

This is not the place to analyze the concept of 'charisma' whether charisma consists in some actual inherent charismatic qualities in the personality of an individual or whether its validity is purely a function of 'recognition' of charisma on the part of the followers.

Weber, in fact, seems to take both the positions. Thus he points out that the basis of legitimacy of a "genuine" charisma is not so much the total trust of the followers as the conception by the leader that "it is the duty of those who have been called to a charismatic mission to recognize its quality and to act accordingly."[9] From this point of view, Gandhi cannot be considered a genuine charismatic leader since he repeatedly denied any charismatic qualities and warned his followers against following him blindly. He would often admonish his admirers whenever their admiration for him outran their common sense. B.R. Nanda narrates an incident in which during one of his tours the inhabitants of a village told him that his auspicious presence in their village miraculously made the village well filled with water. Gandhi reproved them,

> You are fools, beyond a doubt it was an accident. I have no more influence with God than you have. Suppose a crow sits on a palm tree at the moment when the tree falls to the ground, will you imagine that the weight of the bird brought down the tree?[10]

GANDHI AS A CHARISMATIC LEADER

We take the position with Parsons here that "charisma is a strictly empirical observable quality of men and things in relation to human acts and attitudes."[11] To this extent we consider both Gandhi and Ishver Bhai to be examples of genuine charismatic leadership. Its impact is clearly reflected in the acts and attitudes of their followers. It may seem a little odd to put the name of Ishver Bhai, an almost totally obscure figure, with Gandhi, in talking about charisma. We believe that what we observed in Pardi satyagraha was a true microcosm of Gandhian satyagrahas, at least in terms of the attitudes and acts of the satyagrahis. Much more than Uttam Bhai, the adivasi leader, it was the adivasis themselves who displayed their abiding faith in Ishver Bhai. Throughout our stay we did not find a single adivasi who did not bow his head with reverence at his name. Being used to associating such big names as Gandhi, Churchill, Hitler, etc., with 'charisma' to us the magnitude of Ishver Bhai's impact on adivasis was quite unexpected. Almost every adivasi home that we visited had a portrait of Ishver Bhai hung on the wall. Some pictures had garlands (leis) made of fresh flowers hung around them and some would burn incense in front of the portrait as a mark of respect and worship. Indeed, Ishver Bhai to most of the adivasis was no less than a God. A few did, in fact, refer to him as 'Bhagwan', meaning God, during our interviews with them.

The main difference between Gandhi and Ishver Bhai, in relation to their followers was not so much in the attitudes of the followers towards their two leaders—they were remarkably similar—as in the difference between the contents of their appeals. Here we found Gandhi to be more in accordance with Weber's description of a "prophet'. Gandhi not only laid down the blueprint for a new normative order that will replace the old outdated one, but he also rationalized into an integrated system in terms of religion. Although we found Ishver Bhai frequently invoking the name of God in his interaction with and speeches to the adivasis as he spurred them on to nonviolent action, we did not find any efforts by him to charter new paths to a changed normative order, nor did we find any attempt toward providing "meaning" of the terms of religion to the same extent as Gandhi did. Ishver Bhai's concern with nonviolence and God was only incidental to his main ideological commitment, namely, the establishment of socialism. Even as he exhorted the adivasis to participate in "satyagraha for bread and butter" or "satyagraha for emancipation", his own doubts regarding the meaning and efficacy of satyagraha surfaced from time to time. During a conversation with Vinoba Bhave, probably the greatest living disciple of Gandhi today, Ishver Bhai expressed his doubts thus :

> You seem to believe that truth has an inner potency to assert itself. That it needs no personal or mass effort to establish truth or good thought in life. Here I must point out that the ideals of truth, love, and compassion had been integral parts of out cultural heritage since the days of Buddha and even much before. And yet even after ages only Gandhiji could successfully introduce them in our social life for the first time in history through the application of his active dynamic weapon of satyagraha on individual or mass basis.[12]

Then Ishver Bhai went on to assert that "truth and nonviolence need the positive sanction of active soul force based on self suffering," implying that it was a difficult thing to achieve. He added further that when all democratic means failed and the nonviolence resistance also failed, violence and rowdysm "remain the only alternative for ventilation of people's grievances."[13]

Vinoba's reply was purely in Gandhian terms. After discounting the possibilities of failure of a satyagraha, he took Ishver Bhai through the fundamentals of satyagraha.

> We must rise from the plane of mind to the plane of intellect. As such, satyagraha must not create agitation or tension in the minds of opponents; satyagraha must avoid collision of minds and seek harmony of thought...mind of the opponent refuses to change and thinks of retaliating under condition of compulsions or conflicts. Our nonviolence should rise on psychical plane in this atomic age. For asserting truth we must rely on the power of persuasion and love till death. I know of only one power, the power

of love and one weapon, the weapon of thought or 'Dnyan."[14]

In the epilogue, Ishver Bhai concedes that all of Vinoba's "ideas originate from his basic philosophical attitude toward nonviolence" and that "he has a world perspective and his vision has a vast horizon." However, Ishver Bhai makes it clear, he cannot "accept all the implications of the suggestions made by Vinobaji." He remained "unconvinced, particularly in regard to his interpretation of the technique of satyagraha."[15]

In spite of his uncertainties regarding the place of satyagraha in his normative order, Ishver Bhai did not, as we said earlier., attempt to formulate his own "meaning". Of course to some extent all charismatic leaders do have some concept of 'order', since what a movement seeks to achieve presupposes the existence of some notion of 'order' that it either seeks to preserve, create, or destroy. Particularly during the period of social and institutional disorganization which accompanies a movement, people become much more sensitive and receptive to symbols which can give "meaning' to their new experience in terms of a fundamental cosmic, social or political order. A leader is able to establish his charismatic influence insofar as he can supply these symbols and who can, as Einstadt observes, also "prescribe the proper norms of behavior, to relate the individual to collective indentification, and to reassure him of his status and of his place in a given collectivity."[16] On the other hand, a salient feature is the establishment of Ishver Bhai's charisma and in the propagation of satyagraha as a way of life and of conflict resolution, was a generous sprinkling of the names and ideals of Vinobaji and Jaya Prakash Narain, both topmost disciples of Gandhi, and Gandhi himself.

INSTITUTIONALIZATION OF CHARISMA

This brings us to another aspect of charisma. An over emphasis on individualistic charisma obscures the fact that charisma is not simply the quality of the individual person, but it is also a characteristic of the normative order,[17] the leader is trying to destroy, preserve, or create. By the same token, the legitimacy accorded a charismatic leadership is also due to the norms of his 'order' which comprise all the prescribed institutions, rules, and regulations and proper modes of behavior. To this extent, "legitimacy is thus the institutional application of charisma."[18] Since by the very nature of the case charisma is a temporary phenomenon, institutionalization ensures, or is the only way that the message of the charismatic leader can be embodied in a permanent structure after he is removed from the scene.

This institutionalization may take either of two routes. One is traditionalization. In this mode the system of norms established by the charismatic leader becomes traditionalized and carries the same quality of sanctity as the person of the charismatic leader himself. The alternative route to institutionalization is where the norms established by the charismatic leader are divorced from him and are followed because they are rationalized and believed to be good and useful by objective considerations. Here the charismatic qualities may be transferred to a new leader where he is identified by followers as possessing the initial vision of the originator, and who also displays a capability to reinterpret and implement the norms in accordance with changed conditions. In another variation of this mode, the charismatic qualities may simply pass on into an office as in the case of a bureaucratic organization.

The mode of institutionalization mentioned above is 'ideal' type. It is doubtful if the real world ever conforms to the ideal. In practice the succeeding leadership will usually reflect a combination of both the 'traditional' and 'rational' in varying degrees, depending upon circumstances.

Pardi is a good case in point. Throughout the Gandhian satyagrahas great stress was placed on the inculcation of a way of life which among other things included external practices such as wearing of Khadi, vegetarianism, nondrinking, etc. Of course Gandhi had rationalized these in terms of religion as well as utilitarian advantages. Thus Khadi was recommended for "developing the power of the people,[19] through the boycott of foreign cloth and reliance on hand-spun cloth. More importantly, the appeal for Khadi was meant to instill a new sense of pride and identity among the satyagrahis which was lacking among them before. The spread of Khadi-wear was effected by Gandhi through appeal to utility as well as emotion. "From

Religion, Charisma and Nonviolence

their compliance with the Khadi test I shall infer that they have shed untouchability, and that they have nothing but brotherly feelings towards all without distinction of race, color, or creed,"[20] wrote Gandhi in the *Harijan*. The appeal for boycott of drinking was made in economic terms: "Prohibition of intoxicating drinks means loss of 25 Crores of revenue"[21] to the government and gain to the people. And the appeal for vegetarianism was made in the name of Hinduism. The overall appeal for Khadi, vegetarianism, and nondrinking was also made in terms of purity and simplicity of life which were essential for a person to be a good Hindu.

Within a few years after Gandhi appeared upon the Indian scene, literally hundreds of thousands of Indians had discarded wearing foreign and mill-made cloth and had taken to Khadi. It had not only become a symbol in the cause of India's freedom from the British, but also a symbol of dedication and acceptance of satyagraha as a way of achieving it. Nondrinking and vegetarianism, among other things, also became part of the dedication and discipline of a satyagrahi. But most important, in wearing Khadi, giving up drinking, and adopting vegetarianism, the followers were getting the satisfaction of identifying with the power of Gandhi.

It was, however, easier to comply with the Khadi test than to shed untouchability and "have nothing but brotherly feelings toward all" without distinction of caste, creed, and color. Increasingly, the outer trappings of Gandhian norms overshadowed the real norms. To be a Satyagrahi was to always wear Khadi, boycott drinking, and adopt vegetarianism. With the passing of Gandhi the outer trappings became traditionalized. For every person claiming to be a satyagrahi, wearing of Khadi became a ritual devoid of its original rationale. We should not then be surprised to see, as reported earlier, almost all the satyagrahis wearing Khadi and reporting themselves to be vegetarians and nondrinkers.

TRANSFERENCE OF CHARISMA

The inculcation of the outer trappings, however, are imporant from another point of view. At least symbolically. they indicate the continuing hold of the original charismatic leader's system of norms. Insofar as a new person can reiterate and reinterpret the original leader's norms to fit new conditions and to the extent this person can set an example in living up to these norms, a transference of charismatic authority from the original charismatic leader to this person is possible. It is obvious that in this case the route to institutionalization of charisma is through divorcing the norms from the holder of the charisma and transferring the charisma to another person who objectively displays a command of those norms. The new charismatic leader acquires his charisma through his own efforts. His efforts consist of first, displaying his total identity with the original charismatic leader by display of external symbols already familiar to the people, such as wearing Khadi, giving up comforts of life, participating in and leading in the regular singing of hymns with the people and constantly invoking the name of the charismatic leader, and God in communicating with the people. The latter, namely, invoking the name of God and the charismatic leader, saves this new leader from having to deal with the questions of "meaning" and to explain his normative order for the changed conditions in terms of religion.

In one of his speeches to the Pardi adivasis, Ishver Bhai exhorted them in these words:

> We are all children of God. God gave the land, the rivers, the mountains for all to share, but a few selfish people deceitfully appropriated to themselves what rightfully belongs to you. The government has been feeding you on empty promises for a long time. The time to act is now. There is a continual struggle between the truth and injustice. But in the end, 'satyamev jayate'—Truth must prevail. Everytime the world is threatened by the forces of injustice or untruth, God makes His appearance on the side of the truth. When the injustice and enslavement by the British people became intolerable, God sent the potent weapon of 'ahimsa' through Gandhi, and the powerful empire was brought to its knees. Today, you have the same mighty weapon of 'ahimsa'. With the spirit of Gandhiji with you and the truth on your side, you have the very God on your side. You cannot lose.[22]

However, the acquisition of a charismatic following by the new leader requires more than a simple demonstration of his identification with the original charismatic leader. The new leader articulates and gives expression to the inchoate sentiments deeply held by the people. Where the people are afraid to openly express their grievances and frustrations for fear of punishment from the dominant group, the leader boldly comes forward, expresses his views and bravely faces punishment which may range anywhere from a simple reprimand, economic deprivation or severe beating to jail-going and death itself. It is the fearlessness in the face of what the followers consider hazardous that fascinates them and makes them a charismatic following. Gandhi himself was well aware of this aspect of the role of a strong leader. He wrote in 1930: "Whilst the masses know what they want, they often do not know how to express their wants and, less often, how to get what they want. Herein comes the use of leadership."[23]

At another time he declared:

We must first come in living touch with them by working for them and in their midst. We must share their sorrows, understand their difficulties, and anticipate their wants.... We must see how we like being in the boxes, miscalled houses, of the labourers of Bombay. We must identify ourselves with the villagers who toil under the hot sun beating on their bent backs and see how we would like to drink water from the pool in which the villagers bathe, wash their clothes and pots, in which their cattle drink and roll. Then and not till then, shall we truly represent the masses and they will as surely as I am writing this respond to every call.[24]

This spirit of complete dedication by Ishver Bhai was obvious in our interviewing. Thus, Uttam Bhai, the adivasi leader, described the faith he and the adivasis had in Ishver Bhai :

They had great faith in Ishver Bhai. He was actively involved with them. Even in rain and storm he would keep his engagements. Where the adivasis would be hesitant to go, Ishver Bhai would lead the way.

A Pardi satyagrahi described his feelings thus :

> I never even imagined, I would be, one day, challenging the landlord. We were aware of our injustices but we did not know what to do about it. We were weak. We were afraid of the landlord, the police and the government. But Ishver Bhai showed us the way. He gave us courage by speaking up against the landlord. He went to jail for us. By his example, we were free of fear.

Our research in Pardi clearly brought before us the total dedication of Ishver Bhai to the adivasis cause and the genuine charisma he exercised over them. Whatever his larger ideological goal—for he was a prominent leader and one time president of the prestigious Praja Socialist Party of India—the adivasis perceived him as totally dedicated to their uplift. It was he who created an awakening among the adivasis by giving bold expression to their hopes and frustrations. He almost completely gave up living in his comfortable home at Surat and took quarters with the poorest and the lowliest. He spent days and months living in huts with the poor adivasis. He rejoiced as they rejoiced, and he suffered as they suffered. Finally, he had won them over. Here was a man they could trust. So completely was he identified with the adivasis that, to them, he was the bone of their bone, the flesh of their flesh. When Ishver Bhai spoke, they listened to him as to a prophet. Many considered him their 'Gandhi' and some called him their 'Bhagvan'.

Like Gandhi, Ishver Bhai had become a 'father figure' to the followers. He was the kind of person they would like their fathers to be, strong and fearless, who would take cudgels against repression and injustice. He also became a superego of the followers, an ideal object for identification. By identifying with him they saw themselves vicariously sharing in the power exercised by the leader.

Krech and Crutchfield, pointing out that a leader may become a 'father figure' commented:

> The leader serves as a perfect focus for the positive emotional feelings of the individual; he is the ideal object for

identification, for transference, for feelings of submissiveness.[25]

According to Bernard Bass,

> Turning to 'father figures' who will satisfy all wants is part of modern man's effort to gain security. It is a pseudo solution satisfying the need for security as well as providing opportunity through identification for vicarious experience in the personal power granted the leader.[26]

However, identification with a charismatic leader need not always be an 'escape from freedom'.[27] At the stage where the identification takes place, it may be a 'pseudo-solution' and an escape from freedom', but the experience gained in the actual exercise of power at the behest of the leader may only prove to be a stepping stone for progress toward responsible exercise of power. This is where the quality and the motives of the charismatic leader distinguishes him from a demagogue. The identification with a Hitler or a Mussolini, may prove to be an 'escape from freedom' while with a Gandhi it may prove, in the final analysis, to be a liberating experience. In fact the long term impact of both Gandhi and Ishver Bhai cannot be considered anything but positive, from the point of view of the followers.

RELIGION AND NONVIOLENCE

Coming back once again to the issue of the relationship of religion with satyagrahis' faith in nonviolence, it is true that as we interviewed the satyagrahis, all references to God and religion were missing. However, it would be wrong to conclude that the satyagrahis' perception and cognition of nonviolence were, in fact, devoid of religious considerations. We believe that the question of relationship of religion to nonviolence in the context of our satyagrahas is inextricably intertwined in the consciousness of the satyagrahis with the personality of their charismatic leader.

Dr. S. Radhakrishnan, a reputed scholar of Hinduism, points out that Hinduism is hardly a religion in the sense the Western people understand it. Hinduism is a way of life.

Little does an average Hindu know of the eschatological underpinnings of his religion; to him his religion consists in abiding by a certain code of conduct prescribed for everyday life. The code of conduct, which comprises respect for certain norms at the individual level and adherence to a network of social obligations at the societal level, is passed on by family traditions and established social practices. These moral and social teachings of Hinduism are originally set out in the *Dharmshastras*, the *Upanishads*, and other scriptures.

Perhaps no other religion places such high premium upon individual moral conduct as Hinduism. Apart from prescribing certain external ritual practices, such as performing certain worships in a certain way as, for instance getting a Brahmin to consummate a wedding in accordance with vedik rites, placing on the ground some food for dogs, outcasts, and sick, thus daily honoring all beings, and dozens of other practices, it is the individual moral character that is the main focus of attention. The foremost goal is attainment of 'Moksha' (salvation); and the individual can attain it only by strict adherence to the prescribed code of conduct.

The major thrust of this code of moral conduct is toward 'conquest of self'. Men are exhorted to conquer their 'Kama, Krodha, Mada, Moha, and Lobha'—sexual desire, anger, vanity, attachment, and greed. The Laws of Manu exhort individuals to "patiently bear hard words...against an angry man let him not show anger; let him bless when he is cursed."[28] In a similar vein the Mahabharata exhorts to conquer the anger of others by non-anger; conquer the evil-doers by saintliness; conquer the miser by gifts; conquer falsehood by truth.[29] The Kathopanishad also states that "When free from all desires which had root in his heart—the mortal even here becomes immortal and reaches Brahmo."[30]

Manu's summary of the laws of conduct for the four castes comprises "abstention from injury, veracity, abstention from unlawfully appropriating the goods of others, purity, and control of the organs."[31]

Similar moral imperatives for the conquest of 'self' are prescribed for public men, holders of power. The implied assumption is that a ruler who has conquered 'self' could be relied upon to follow 'Rajadharma'—ruler's duty by the people. A King "who is voluptuous, partial and deceitful will be destroyed even through the unjust punishment which he inflicts. ... Punishment cannot be inflicted justly by one... addicted to sensual pleasures."[32] In contrast to the Western tradition which stressed external restraints on holders of power—e.g., checks and balances in the American Constitution—the Indian religion and culture have emphasized inner restraints as necessary and sufficient condition for the ruler to be committed to 'Rajdharma'.

Even a cursory glance through Gandhi's autobiography[33] reveals clearly that the code of ethic that Gandhi lived by was evolved out of his experiment in the spiritual field. Similarly the code of conduct for the satyagrahis, including nonviolent action, was fashioned out of the scriptural writings; and the hallmark of this conduct is self-restraint, 'the conquest of self'. The Gita categorically states, "Purity, uprightness, continence, and nonviolence are the penance of the body"; and again "nonviolence, truth, freedom from anger, renunciation, tranquility, aversion to fault finding, compassions to living beings" and so on "are the endowments of him who is born with the divine nature."[34]

Perhaps the strictest test of the conquest of self was the conquest of 'Kama'—sexual desire. The most dangerous culprit distracting an individual off the path of virtue was the uncontrolable desire for sex. This assumption rested on the belief that every individual was endowed with a certain amount of 'vital energy' which if dissipated in sexual self-indulgence was not available for higher purposes. The Laws of Manu clearly state, "When one among all the organs slips away from control, thereby a man's wisdom slips away from him, even as the water flows through the one open foot of a water-carriers skin."[35]

Anyone closely familiar with the social life in India will subscribe to the fact that beliefs regarding sex have widespread acceptance. The result has been an inordinate emphasis on 'Brahmcharya'[36] for a true satyagrahi.[37] The vital energy is "the richest capital man can ever possess. ... He who uses it up, consciously or unconsciously, will ultimately be impotent. .. He who lusts with the thought will ever remain unsated and will end his life a moral wreck and burden on the earth."[38] Elsewhere he writes, "The sexual act divorced from the deliberate purpose of generation is a typical and gross form of dissipation. ..."[39]

Now it may be justifiably argued that the ethical code analysed above has been honored more in violation than actual subscription. The behavior of the rulers of Native States drowned in luxury and the tresses of their numerous mistresses, acting as parasites upon their people by draining the public treasury, can hardly be called a shining example of 'rajadharma'. Similarly the average Indian has found the ethical ideal to be remote and too difficult to translate into practice in real life. Psychologically, it may be argued that the excessive emphasis on self-restraint is too demanding and unnatural. In spite of these difficulties, the fact remains that the ideal of self-restraint finds widespread acceptance, if not in practice, at least in principle. What this means, however, in real life is that being incapable of abiding by the stiff ethical requirements, the average man has been guiltridden and in conflict. The higher one's familiarity and belief in these ethical requirements, more intense the conflict and the guilt. Self-restraint especially in regard to sexual passion has widespread acceptance.[40] The conflict and the guilt faced by Gandhi[41], particularly in regard to sexual matters, are very well protrayed in his autobiography; he resolved the conflict for himself by sublimation to 'satyagraha'.

The fact that the strict moral code requiring the 'conquest of self' has been found unrealizable by the average person does not, however, signify that it has lost all its meaning. It still remains an ideal. And

> if someone appears who can enact the ideal, he may fall heir to all the pent-up hopes that have survived the experience of repeated disillusionment; he may indeed command the more respect, and inspire the more reverence, because the standard has remained unrealized.[42]

It is therefore, in this context that we have to understand the role of Gandhi vis a vis the satyagrahis. Gandhi was a living example of purity, uprightness, continence, tranquility, freedom from anger, renunciation, compassion to all living beings, truth and nonviolence. To the satyagrahis, he was the very incarnation of virtues which they aspired to realize but found themselves wanting. They found relief from anxiety and tension resulting from their failure, by identifying with Gandhi. The Gita itself sanctions such identification by exhorting the common people to copy from the example of virtuous men. "Good men set standards of conduct for others."[43] The satyagrahis sought this identification by adopting certain external symbols such as taking to Khadi wear, vegetarianism, nondrinking and above all pledging unquestioning allegiance to nonviolent behavior under all circumstances.

To summarize, in spite of lack of references to religion in our interviews with the satyagrahis, we believe religion was an important aspect of their commitment to nonviolent action. By identifying with the charismatic leader, they not only vicariously experienced the power of the leader by adopting the nonviolent norms as established by the leader and interpreted in terms of their religion, but also they had the satisfaction of living the life of virtue that their religion prescribed. In fact, the capacity of a leader in providing his followers with an opportunity for vicarious satisfaction and participation in a virtuous life by credible interpretation of the recommended behavioral norms in terms of religion must, in itself, be considered a contributing factor in the uniqueness and charisma of a leader. Thus, even as the satyagrahis in our three movements identified with their charismatic leaders and emotionally committed themselves to nonviolence, the echo of their religion constantly resounded in the back of their minds.

NOTES and REFERENCES

[1] Extract from Gandhi's reply to a letter from a Vykom satyagrahi in M K. Gandhi, *Nonviolent Resistance*, p. 189.

[2] We should like to point out here that our references to the subleaders regarding the total absence of religious references relates only to our long interviews we had with them. As pointed out, their public speeches during the satyagrahas were full of references to religion. What we are implying here is that these references to religion during public speeches were only for public consumption. The only people continually exposed to the flood of information of nonviolence and religion from both the topmost leaders and the subleaders, were the rank and file satyagrahis.

[3] Max Weber, *On Charisma and Institution Building*. (Chicago: University of Chicago Press, 1968), p. 285.

[4] Max Weber, *Sociology of Religion*. (Boston: Beacon Press, 1964), pp. XXXV—XXXVI.
[5] *ibid.*, p. XXXV
[6] *ibid.* p. XXXV
[7] Max Weber, *On Charisma and Institution Building*, p. 48.
[8] Uttam Bhai.
[9] *ibid.*, p. 49.
[10] Cited in Nanda, *Mahatma Gandhi: A Biography* (London: George Allen and Unwin Ltd., 1959), p. 518.
[11] Talcott Parsons, *Structure of Social Action* (The Free Press Paper Back, 1968) p. 668.
[12] Ishverlal Desai, *Satyagraha, Democracy, and Gramdan* (Surat: Published by V.M. Dalal, February 1, 1959), p. 4.
[13] *ibid.*, p.4.
[14] *ibid.*, p. 5.
[15] *ibid.*, p. 12.
[16] Max Weber, *On Charisma and Institution Building*, p. XXVIII.
[17] This was used by Weber, as the basis for developing the concept of charisma of office. For elaboration of the concept along these lines see Talcott Parsons, *The Structure of Social Action*, especially chapter XVII, pp. 640-694.
[18] Parsons, *ibid.*, p. 669.
[19] M.K. Gandhi. *Nonviolent Resistance*, p. 70.
[20] April 27, 1940. Also *Nonviolent Resistance*, p. 307.
[21] *ibid.*, p. 327.
[22] Ishver Bhai.
[23] *Young India*. November 1930.
[24] *Young India*, September 1924.
[25] D. Krech and Crutchfield, *Theory and Problems of Social Psychology* (New York: Mcgraw Hill 1948), p. 421.
[26] *Leadership, Psychology, and Organization Behavior* (New York: Harper and Brothers, 1960) p. 224. See also Eric Fromm, *Escape From Freedom* (New York: Rinehart and Company, Inc., 1941), especially "Mechanisms of Escape", pp. 136-206.
[27] Such an implication has been made by others about Gandhi. He has been accused of being a Hitler and Mussolini. M.N. Roy, the Indian Marxist, who had read Fromm's *Escape From Freedom*, considered Gandhi a Hitler and Congress a Nazi Party. M.N. Roy, *The Problems of Freedom* (Calcutta: Renaissance Publishers 1945). See also L.A. Gordon, *Bengal's Gandhi: A Study in Modren Indian Regionalism, Politics, and Thought in Bengal Regional Identity*, David Kopf, ed., (East Lansing: Asian Studies Center, Michigan State University, January, 1969) p. 110.
[28] George Buehler, *The Laws of Manu* (Oxford: 1886), verses 92 and 47.
[29] The Mahabharata, verses 38,73, 74.
[30] II-iii-14. Cited in C. Rajgopalachari, *Hinduism, Doctrine and Way of Life* (Bombay: Bhartiya Vidya Bhavan, 1964), pp. 116. The same

work goes on to say. "Know the soul to be the rider in the chariot which is the body. The intellect is the charioteer and the mind the reins. The senses are the horses and the desirable things of the world are thorough fares on which they career. If the charioteer is unwise, and does not vigilantly restrain the mind, then the senses do bolt uncontorllably like wicked horses. If, on the contary, he is wise and keeps a firm hand on his mind, then the senses are in perfect control as good horses with a competent charioteer." IV-1, C Rajgopalachari, ibid., p. 117.

[31] *The Laws of Manu*, Verse 10.

[32] *The Laws of Manu*, Verses 27 and 30.

[33] *The Autobiography of Mohandas K. Gandhi* (Boston: Beacon Press, 1957).

[34] *The Gita*, 17, 14 and 16.

[35] *The Laws of Manu*, verse 99.

[36] Gandhi defined it as "Conservation of vital energy brought about by sexual restraint. *Nonviolent Resistance*, p. 95.

[37] It should be obvious that the word 'satyagrahis' used for our respondents is based on a much diluted version of satyagrahi than Gandhi uses it. In the strictest sense, by his own definition, only Gandhi was a true "satyagrahi.'

[38] M.K. Gandhi, *Nonviolent Resistance* pp. 95-96.

[39] *Ibid.*, p. 97.

[40] Erik Erikson ("In Search of Gandhi" in Dankwart A. Rustow, ed., *Philosophers and Kings*: *Studies in Leadership*, (New York: George Braziller, 1970), pp. 33-68) speaks of the ancient "Indian preoccupation with semen as a substance which pervades the whole body and which therefore, is released only at the expense of vitality, acuity and spiritual power. . . " Morris Carstairs (in his *The Twice Born*: *A Study of a Community of High Caste Hindus* (London, 1957), p. 86) talks about the belief that the villagers had about vital energy. It was a kind of thick viscous fluid that was stored in the head and is diminished as a result of lustful thought or lustful activity including sexual intercourse.

[41] Erik Erikson in his psycho historical study of Gandhi talks about the "confusing consequences" of his obsessive anti-sexual preoccupations and how he resolved the problem. See his "Psychoanalysis and Ongoing History: Problems of Identity, Hatred and Nonviolence in *The American Journal of Psychiatary*, (September 1965) p. 243. See also his "In Search of Gandhi" in Dankwart A. Rustow, ed., 33-68, especially pp. 56-60.

Morris Carstairs reports symptoms of "anxiety neurosis among the Hindu communities of Rajasthan, and perhaps elsewhere as well" as a result of disparity between the ideal and its fulfilment specially in regard to sex. Op. cit., p. 87.

[42] Lloyd and Susanne Rudolph, *The Modernity of Tradition*: *Political Development in India* (Chicago and London: University of Chicago Press, 1967), p. 196.

[43] Quoted in C. Rajgopalachari, op. cit., p. 102.

8
Impact of Satyagraha on The Rank and File

Operation of a successful satyagraha presupposes a long period of training and practice in the satyagraha system of norms. In a conflict situation it not only seeks to convert the dominant group to the satyagrahis' point of view but, as it does so, it has a continuing impact on the lives of the satyagrahis. When asked, whom do you think satyagraha affects the most, 37.5% (63) of the satyagrahis said that its greatest impact was on the satyagrahis themselves. Nine out of fourteen leaders also said the same thing. Dr. Amul Desai, a Pardi leader declared,

> Satyagraha is a unique weapon. Even when used in the context of a conflict, its incidental effects are more far reaching. It, not only, brings the opponent to the viewpoint of the satyagrahis, but more importantly it creates a new man out of the satyagrahi himself. I do not believe you will find a single adivasi in Pardi, whose life has not been changed or at least touched by satyagraha.

To understand the impact of satyagraha, as it emerges through the attitudes of the satyagrahis and our observations, we have to first understand their psychosocial background preceding the satyagrahas. We will devote the first section of this chapter to analysing the background of the satyagrahis and subsequently, we will discuss the impact of satyagraha.

Satyagraha and the Rank and File

PSYCHOSOCIAL BACKGROUND

The three movements were held at different times, spread over a period of almost forty years; they were led and organized by different leaders and under different political parties. In the previous chapters we noted the features in the social background which were common to all the satyagrahis. On the psychosocial level, a very important denominator common to all the satyagrahis was that they suffered from an increasing sense of inferiority complex. This inferiority complex in the case of the Pardi satyagrahis was the inevitable consequence of their being categorized as 'low caste'. In the case of Bardoli and Rajkot satyagrahis it was the result of British colonialism. In an incisive analysis of the problem Lloyd I. and Susanne Hoeber Rudolph point out that the long period of British domination and the doubts expressed by many British that the Indians lacked basic components of moral worth such as, 'courage' and 'manliness' had created a genuine crisis of confidence among most Indians.[1] Theories of British imperialism developed in the latter part of the 19th century and early part of the 20th century, emphasized the 'manliness' of the British people in contrast to the Indians who were depicted 'weak', 'passive' and even 'effiminate'. Widespread acceptance and prevalence of virtues such as 'humility' and 'compassion', stressed in Hindu religion and culture were cited in support of their views. Among the twice-born castes,[2] the brahmins and vaishyas, who were predominant in Gujerat and particularly the areas covered by Bardoli and Rajkot satyagrahas, were described as 'weak' and 'cowardly'.

Ironically, those sections of the Indian population who were more militant and violent were specially singled out to be pronounced weak and cowardly. Thus, the Chitpavan Brahmins of Maharashtra, who engaged the British in many a battle were characterized as weak and stupid. The Bengalis who had been in the forefront of violent terrorist activities throughout the period of the struggle for independence in Bengal were described as 'effiminate' and 'impotent'. Lord Macaulay's characterization of the Bengalis is an illustration of the length to which the British went in creating a distorted image of the Indians.

The physical organization of the Bengali is feeble even to effiminacy. He lives in constant vapor bath. His pursuits are sedentary, his limbs delicate, his movements languid. During many ages he has been trampled upon by men of bolder and more hardy breeds . . .[3]

Although the distinction between the twice-born castes as nonmartial and non-twice-born, such as Rajputs and Sikhs as martial class was built to some extent, in the caste structure itself, the British emphasized this point as much for its instrumental utility in the imperialistic theory as for its academic interest in the Indian caste structure. The Rajputs and Sikhs had already been long subjugated and put under the protective umbrella of the British in the form of hundreds of princely states. Having taken care of their menace by a combination of diplomacy and force, the British referred to them as the brave, hardy and masculine class of Indians. In contrast, the twice-born castes in Maharashtra and Bengal, who continued their violent militancy against the British, and the other twice-born castes, Brahmins, Vaishyas, Baniyas from Gujerat, Uttar Pradesh, Madhya Pradesh, etc., who were subsequently to be the main leaders in the satyagrahas for independence, were all portrayed as weak and lacking in courage. Interestingly, the twice-born castes considered the princes and Rajas "debauched and effiminate gentlemen, who had yielded to the British without a fight."[4]

Nor was the situation of the Western educated Indians any different. While the exposure to western education with its emphasis on egalitarianism, freedom, etc , whetted their appetite for proving their capabilities and assertiveness, they found themselves occupying only minor bureaucratic positions under the British bosses, completely powerless and at their behest in the name of 'On His Majesty's Service.' With the British generously reminding them, the feminine implications of this powerlessness were not lost on these educated Indians. In addition, many Indians who failed to emulate the Englishmen in manner, thought, speech and dress were castigated as typical Indians, weak-kneed and weak-willed who did not want to improve their lives on the other hand, those Indians who tried to model themselves after them were ridiculed for trying to be what they 'really' were not. Either way they lost.

How successful this psychological onslaught was in creating the stereotype image of an Indian, can be guaged from the fact that not only the common man but many leaders in India acquiesced in that judgment. For others it meant loss of self-esteem and serious doubts about their self-worth. As a young man of twenty-two years Gandhi wrote, "It must be at the outset admitted that the Hindus as a rule are notoriously weak."[5] As if, to proclaim to the British, but in fact more to assert for their own satisfaction, that the British were wrong about their assessment of the Indians, one constant theme running through the writings and speeches of the Indian leaders preceding and during the national movement was devoted to appeals to courage and fearlessness.

During Bardoli satyagraha Sardar Vallabh Bhai Patel again and again reminded the satyagrahis of the hazards and suffering they were likely to face and challenged them to steel their hearts and be prepared to make sacrifices for their cause.

According to the Rudolphs, "This state of mind—a sense of impotence combined with the fear of moral unworthiness arising from impotence—was one of the most degrading consequences of colonialism."[6]

The state of mind that the Rudolphs talk about was not peculiar to the satyagrahis of Bardoli only. Perhaps even more than in the case of Bardoli, the people of Rajkot were cowed down with feelings of inferiority complex for they did not even have the partial mitigation that the chance to participate in the national movement provided for the people of Bardoli[7] and the rest of British India. Gandhi strictly limited his satyagrahas for Indian independence to British India only. If the people in the native states wanted the establishment of self-rule or constitutional monarchy, they had to wage their own struggle and technically this struggle would be against the local rulers only, because they, rather than the British government, were directly responsible for ruling their territories. The fact was, however, as pointed out earlier, that the local rulers owed ultimate allegiance to the Paramount power, namely the king of Great Britain, who controlled them through the British Political Agents. Thus, the people of Rajkot were as much subject to the demoralizing judgment about themselves from the British, as the Indians in the rest of the country. In addition, they were subject to the autocratic rule of their ruler, the Thakore Saheb, who was no more than a puppet in the hands of the British Political Agent. Thus, the feelings of inferiority complex and frustration were more intense because not until the Rajkot Satyagraha could the people do any thing about it.

PARDI TRIBALS AS LOW CASTE

Finally the tribals of Pardi had their own axe to grind. Almost 5% of the Indian population are tribal people yet they have been, next only to the 'untouchables', perhaps, the most neglected class of the Indian people. In 1942 Gandhi declared:

> The adivasis are the original inhabitants whose material position is perhaps no better than that of the Harijans and who have long been victims of neglect on the part of the so called high castes.[8]

There are hundreds of kinds of tribes all over India; their origins, social and religious practices are still matters of enigmatic debate among sociologists and anthropologists. Originally, the tribes inhabited the hills and forests of India, practiced some kind of 'animism' and were nonvegetarians. It is not known definitely how, when and why they left their original abodes and sought assimilation with the Hindu social structure.

TRIBALS AND SANSKRITIZATION

Even today, there is no single and accepted criterion by which to distinguish a tribe from a caste.[9] Most tribals believe that they came to their present territories from somewhere else, their economic status is uniformly bad, most particularly lower castes, contain Hindu Gods and practices and are abhorred by high caste Hindus. Many of them are still isolated in hills and forests of India. In cases where they have been integrated into the widespread caste structure, they have only been accepted as lower castes. Thus, in a society resting on strict division of population into caste and rules governing eating, drinking, touching, etc., and social distance prescribed by tradition, any effort by the tribals to assimilate with the general stream of Hindu culture is fraught with threatening consequences. In spite of their serious efforts at sanskritization,[10] it is only in exceptional cases that the tribals have been able to pass and establish themselves as higher castes.[11] Most often they ended up as low castes. It is, therefore, not unusual today for tribes which are still not assimilated in the caste structure, to resist such assimilation. This is because, the once proud, free and innocent forest dwellers in their search for improved economic conditions and a new identity with the Hindu society ended up achieving only a negative identity.[12] David G. Mandelbaum states that many tribesmen avoid change to caste because "they feel that any gain in material benefits and social resources is offset by losses of firm identity, close solidarity, religious satisfaction and emotional security. They do not want to slip from a proud tribe to an inferior Jati (caste)."[13] Uttambhai, the adivasi leader from Pardi, said as much when he stated,

> We have lived on these lands for ages. Our forefathers were proud, hardy but simple people. But these people stripped us of our lands and our self-respect and reduced us to abject poverty and subjection.[14]

As we mentioned before, all the satyagrahis of Pardi not only reported themselves to be Hindus but also as 'low castes'. The fact that they were all vegetarians, nondrinkers and teetotallers might have been as much due to sanskritization. Sanskritization, however, is not a mere symbolic change in behavior. It is a means to an end. At worst it is an effort to compensate for loss of self-esteem by a partial identification with high caste values; at best it is an effort toward vertical mobility, greater acceptance and respect from the high castes in an effort to rid oneself of the negative identity. When it fails to perform this function—as it invariably does—as in the case of Pardi adivasins—the consequence is often a feeling of deep resentment and hatred against the upper castes. Resentment is further compounded by the fact that the upper castes are also the privileged class, holders of all the power and wealth in the community. This attitude of resentment is more marked among the younger generations who have been exposed to the ideas of secularism and democracy through participation in national, state and local elections. We see that 70% of the satyagrahis in Pardi were below 25 years of age. The failure of sanskritization led to search for new identity through increased participation in political process. The tribals, in some cases, have pressed their demands by formation of parties representing their exclusive interests[15] or they have done so by joining parties committed to integration and unity as in the case of Pardi where the tribals enbloc joined the Praja Socialist Party. It was easy for the Praja Socialist Party to mobilize the Pardians under the party flag and channelize their resentment into political participation. So great was their enthusiasm that they were able to defeat a very powerful opponent from the Congress party in 1952 state election, their very first political contest.

Thus, the shift in emphasis from a ritual idiom of sanskritization to one which relies more on organized politics is common to tribal societies. According to Vidyarthi, the modern leaders represent

> the tribal people to an outside political world. They are not concerned primarily with raising social status of the tribals by making ritual practices more closely resemble those of the Hindus. Their chief task is to improve the material condition of the tribals and to obtain funds and services. Their activities then, are more within the realm of the civil and political and less within the realm of the religious and social.[16]

While political participation itself might give slight and temporary relief from frustration, its failure to improve their material condition in spite of the promises of the national leaders and the constitution is bound to make, as in the case of Pardi, the original frustration worse. And add to this the regress from their original status as hardy and proud people, to the ranks of the low caste the psychological disaster is complete. Severely limited by the upper caste stereotype branding them as inferior, weak and even child-like compounded by abject poverty and total subjection to the landlord, the Pardians had no avenues open to express the normal aggressive and masculine strivings. The emphasis on healthy, assertive and aggressive masculinity is not peculiar to Western culture only. In Latin America it is 'Machismo'; in India it is 'Mardangi'. S.C. Dube, an internationally known scholar on Indian villages, emphasizes that ' "Manliness' and 'defending the honour' play a significant part...within the community.[17] However, as Rudolph points out, it differs from the definition of masculinity in the West which emphasizes 'masterful aggressiveness based on the classical military model of the soldier willing and eager to charge a numerically superior enemy bayonet in hand, in a heroic act of self-assertion."[18] Within the framework of the community affairs in India, the first thing that comes to an Indian mind in order to assert his masculinity and courage is resisting by self-sacrifice and suffering. Obviously such a model of behavior is based on the assumption of 'community' between the resister and the resisted where the former believes that the latter is amenable to moral influence and pressure. On the other hand, where a subordinate group becomes convinced of its inferiority, as in the case of our satyagrahis and particularly the Pardians, depths of frustration and degradation are total[19] since the familiar avenues for the expression of 'manliness' are now blocked.

Mrs. Kumud Ben, a professor of Sociology, and the only woman leader in Pardi said,

> Both my husband and I knew the adivasis of Pardi very well much before the satyagraha was launched. A long period of economic and social exploitation by the landlords and the upper castes had made them acquiesce to their stereotyping as low caste and hence inferior people.[20] They would only talk to you with bowed heads and lowered eyes. They would never speak without the proper form of address, such as 'Ji Hajoor', 'Mai Baap', 'an data'—'Sir', 'mother-father', 'provider of food'—etc. However, I do not know a single adivasi who did not nurture an intense feeling of anger and resentment against their exploiter. And you know, it is out of this, the satyagraha was born.

IMPACT OF SATYAGRAHA

Thus, we see from the above discussion that the satyagrahis in all three movements were weighed down by a deep sense of inferiority and powerlessness. Moreover, they had to suppress and disguise the feelings of hostility that were engendered by their sense of inferiority and powerlessness. This role of passivity and acceptance of the dominant group's stereotype was enhanced through the internalization of certain of the brahminical norms which emphasized nonviolence. Culturally and traditionally certain castes, such as the Rajputs and other Kshatriyas had acquired a martial orientation; and others such as Brahmins, Vaishyas, Shudras, etc., a nonmartial one and hence a nonviolent perspective. Branding by the British of Indians as lacking in 'masculinity' and 'courage' only strengthened the appearance and reality of nonviolence. Regardless of the fact whether the subordinate groups were able to fathom the eschatological horizons of ahimsa—and most were not—it acted at least partially as a compensatory mechanism for their feeling of impotence because it was in accordance with their religious norms. This nonviolence, however, being passive and hence unrelated to the resolution of conflicts within the subordinate group, was inadequate to heal the psychic wound caused by the dominant group's questioning of his moral worth. The impact of satyagraha, therefore, needs to be judged not only in terms of the immediate goals they sought to achieve—and which they did achieve to a considerable extent—but in terms also of the momentous changes they brought about in the life of the satyagrahis and their social character.

The main problem, of course, was to first extricate themselves from the self-deprecating image as weak and cowardly before they could take up fighting for their cause. The problem could be resolved by nothing less than a sensational and heroic display of courage. However, if one had to avoid developing new forms of anxiety and guilt in trying to overcome the original problem, one had to display courage in a way that would not conflict with one's religious and traditional norms and roles. Gandhian satyagraha, through its emphasis on militant nonviolence provided the ideal solution. The passive-cowardly implications of nonviolence were overcome by linking it with courage, sacrifice and discipline of the highest order. Susanne Rudolph writing about the effect of nonviolence on the satyagrahis, stated that Gandhi

> resurrected an old and familiar path to courage, one that had always been significant to twice-born castes, but had fallen into disrepute. By giving it new toughness and discipline in action, by stressing the sacrifice and self-control which it required, by making it an effective device of mass action, by involving millions in it, he reasserted its worth with an effectiveness that convinced his countrymen.[21]

In the same vein, Jawahar Lal Nehru observed:
The essence of his teaching was fearlessness and truth and action allied to these...so suddenly as it were that black pall of fear was lifted from the people's shoulders, not wholly, of course, but to an amazing degree it was a psychological change, almost as if some expert in psychoanlytical method had probed deep into the patient's past found out the origins of his complexes, exposed them to his view and thus rid him of that burden.[22]

The impact of the satyagrahas on the self-estimation of the participants needs little documentation here. Through the display of their fearlessness and courage they became the torch bearers of the newly rediscovered identity, an identity which continued to be rooted in their religion and tradition. Many of the participants established themselves as leaders in subsequent years in the lives of their communities and the nation.[23]

IMPACT ON PARDI SATYAGRAHIS

It may be argued that the above observation relating the establishment of a new identity with satyagraha is too far flung considering that many other variables, including experience in participation in provincial governments in British India and independence of India, etc., might have intervened in developing this new identity. From this point of view, our findings in Pardi may be more relevant to the observations made earlier. When we interviewed the Pardians, the satyagraha was the biggest 'happening' in their lives and still fresh in their memories. In a way, the satyagraha was still continuing insofar as the 'Bhoodan' volunteers were still carrying on their movement to persuade landlords in the area to donate more lands for the landless in the region. Similarly, adult literacy campaigns and programs promoting cottage industries—originally started during the Pardi satyagraha as part of 'constructive activity'— were also continuing.

While, the portrait of the tribals presented earlier—abject poverty, illiteracy, low self-estimation, extreme submissiveness, frustration and resentment—continues to be true for tribals in most of the country, the Pardi tribals bore clear signs of the effect of the satyagraha. The very first visit of this researcher to Pardi was a refreshing experience. The adivasis were still visibly economically poor but a new awakening was in evidence. As we interviewed them, a sense of pride beamed on each face. Before, one could not except a low caste to raise his head in talking to a high caste or an outsider let alone look at him straight in the eyes. Still a bit shy, and extremely polite—a general cultural trait among Indians—the Pardian tribals that we interviewed exuded a confidence that was nothing short of remarkable. Only someone familiar with social conditions of the tribals and other low castes can realize the significance of this change. These tribals, in spite of their low education, tried to answer each of our questions as they could and as they talked they were no more afraid or hesitant to look straight at their interviewers.

To a greater degree than the Gandhi satyagrahis, the Pardi satyagrahis' psychological history was characterized by a need to suppress their hostility toward the dominant group. Like the American Negroes, they were forced to assume a manifest role of submission and passivity. The role was further accentuated because of their total economic and social dependence on the dominant group. In nonviolent action, the satyagrahis found the formula for the adequate expression of the feelings of hostility that the above role engendered. The phenomena may be characterized as what the social psychologists call, 'passive aggression'. It allowed them to challenge the dominant group and at the same time preserve their traditional passivity by not being overtly violent. The linking of nonviolent action with courage and heroism provided relief from the feelings of impotence, inadequacy and depression. This aspect of the satyagraha was brought before us in bold relief in our interviewing. When asked to describe what they considered to be the most important experience of the satyagraha, the answers invariably revolved around examples of events and incidents stressing self-sacrifice, courage, determination, and the fact of participation itself. The following account from a Pardi satyagrahi indicates his fears and frustrations and the subsequent release from them as a result of his participation in the satyagraha.

The satyagraha seemed long in coming. All of us in our village seemed to have steeled our hearts and were bracing for action. I had volunteered myself to be among the first group of satyagrahis who would trespass the landlords' grassland in order to plough it. A part of me could not even wait for the day to arrive when a satyagraha was to be launched; another part of me, however, was afraid. What was going to happen to me? Who will look after my family if something happened to me? I am a small (weak) person; I will be beaten up and put in jail where I might languish forever and no one will care about it. All kinds of thoughts passed through my mind. And yet as the day drew nearer my fears began receding. Two days before the satyagraha, when Ishver Bhai put his hand on my shoulder and said with a smile, 'Are you ready for the sacrifice?', the last trace of fear had vanished and I boldly said, 'Yes'. I will never forget the first day. As we were getting ready to enter this grassland, there were hundreds of people and dozens of policemen around. I was surprised at myself; the police did not frighten me any more. No sacrifice was too great for I almost wished that the police should come and hurt or arrest me before anyone else and I would show them my mettle. As we entered the farms and started to dig the earth the police immediately started arresting the satyagrahis. Two policemen caught Uttam Bhai by the arm and took him away. I pretended not to notice. Another policeman came from behind and angrily snatched my 'Kudari' (hoe) and pushed me so hard that I fell flat on my face. Even before I could get up, two policemen started dragging me bodily away from the field. My feet and legs were getting bruised and bloodied as they dragged me. But I never uttered a cry of pain. Even though I was in pain I had a smile on my face as the policemen carried me away through the assembled crowd. I was then put in a police van and sent to jail. I will never forget this experience.

Like the Pardi satyagrahis, the Gandhi satyagrahis also stressed the satisfaction they felt in the display of courage, sacrifice and determination. They also experienced a new sense of power born out of discipline and united action.[24] Most of the satyagrahis expressed their sense of pride and satisfaction in simply being arrested and put in jail. Thus one Gandhi satyagrahi said:

The best experience of the satyagraha came when I was jailed. The degree of awakening that came about as a result of the exchange of ideas was amazing.

Courage and heroism involved in inflicting suffering upon oneself rather than others was emphasized in the following account:

Two incidents are stamped on my memory. First was when police insulted the satyagrahis. In protest I, along with four other satyagrahis fasted for six days.
The second incident was when police, after arresting me with others, carried us through a jungle path to detain us in Kuwadiya jail. On the way, the police beat me up mercilessly with a stick. However, I bore it bravely and courageously without getting least bit hateful against the policemen.
—*A Rajkot Satyagrahi*

The following female satyagrahi from Bardoli, like others expressed her sense of satisfaction at the courage she displayed in facing up to the enemy nonviolently. But she rationalized her nonviolence and capacity for suffering by identifying a woman's power with Great Goddess Kali—incarnation of strength and power:

During one of the several demonstrations and protests, Sardar Patel had asked me and other women not to join picketing lines on this occasion because of high tension and fear that the police will resort to lathi-charge or even firing against the satyagrahis. I was not deterred. Woman in India has been a symbol of self-sacrifice, suffering and tolerance for ages. Her power is a gift of Great Goddess Kali which enables her to carry the heavy burdens of the family with a smile. Her power of endurance is matchless as compared to that of man.

Undeterred by the warning given by Sardar Patel, I led a group of fifty sisters in spite of promulgation of the article under Section 144[25], broke the police cordon and joined the picket lines. I was arrested along with twenty-four of my sisters. This was my most unforgettable experience of of the satyagraha.

SATYAGRAHA AND 'SELF-SUFFERING'

One of the most discussed and least understood aspects of satyagraha has been the insistence on 'self-suffering' by the satyagarahis. Some analysts of satyagraha have argued that nonviolent action encouraged unnecessary masochism. Thus, M.N. Roy suggests that Gandhi himself had a masochistic personality and that he led other satyagrahis into unnecessary masochism.[26] Leo Kuper suggests the same when he points out that if the opponents perceive the satyagrahis to be taking self-suffering upon themselves as part of the masochistic tendency, then it does not bother them too much because they are doing it for their own pleasure. He also argues that in the Gandhian satyagrahas, suffering is "positively desired" and that the resister seeks it as an end rather then a means, once again strongly suggesting the presence of masochistic tendencies among the satyagrahis.[27]

Throughout our interviewing most of the satyagrahis not only described their experiences in 'suffering' with a sense of pride but also, as the accounts above indicate, as the most important experience of the satyagraha. From some of the interviews, it is easy to conclude that some satyagrahis actually looked forward to taking 'self-suffering' upon themsleves. The following account by Ashgar Ali Gandhi, one of the subleaders of the Rajkot satyagrahis is reflective of at least some of the satyagrahis' feelings toward 'suffering' in an exaggerated way:

> During the course of the satyagraha, I was arrested along with the others. We were detained in dingy basement of a building in a nearby village. The conditions within this detention center were really intolerable. The top leaders were detained at different locations and treated well. But, for satyagrahis it was a living hell. Food was bad, water filthy and there were no beds to sleep on. One hundred and sixty-eight satyagrahis were huddled together in this dark, dingy and unventilated basement. Many satyagrahis got sick and some vomited adding to the stench and suffocation. The suffering was taking a heavy toll of the morale of the detainees. I felt sorry for satyagrahis. Personally, to me this was a test of the satyagraha and only the beginning. I knew, the satyagrahis would have to steel their hearts and be ready for more sacrifices. But I was ready. In fact I strongly hoped that I would be the one chosen for the final 'Agni Pariksha'.[28] Even if death were to come what could be better then to die in the service of the people?
>
> In order to protest the living conditions, satyagrahis constantly shouted slogans; some went on fast. Information about the deplorable living conditions inside the detention centers trickled out regularly through the visitors who came to see the detained satyagrahis and also through some of the policemen who were increasingly drawn to the side of the satyagrahis. Leaders all over the country including Gandhi strongly protested the treatment of the satyagrahis. Newspapers carried stories about the brutal treatment meted out to the satygarahis. The government denied the allegation. Finally Gandhi, on his insistence, was permitted to visit the dentention centers and see the conditions for himself.
>
> Two hours before Gandhi was to visit our center, a group of policemen along with the Inspector of the Police came to warn us that if any of us complained when Gandhi was there, he would get the punishment of his life. When, fin-

ally Gandhi arrived, each of the satyagrahis forgot his suffering. There were smiles all around, but no one dared to complain of the mistreatment. As Gandhiji passed by me, I described in detail what was going on. Following my complaint the conditions inside the center improved considerably. However, the very next day I was carried away by a group of policemen to a cell where I was mercilessly kicked and beaten with sticks. I was admitted to a hospital with multiple fractures. The doctors had given up hope for my life. I spent six months in the hospital and finally recovered.

During all of this I do not recall a single moment when I was despondent. Gandhiji gave me his blessings. To me the whole of my suffering was the 'Agni Pariksha' out of which I had emerged pure and shining. My faith in nonviolence was only strengethened. Since this episode, everyone started to call me 'Gandhi' and to this day I am known As Ashgar Ali Gandhi.

The above accounts from the satyagrahis amply bring out the fact that some satyagrahis had almost a 'longing' for 'suffering'. It is also easy to see why some analysts claimed that noviolent action fostered masochism. We believe, however, that such a conclusion is based on a misunderstanding of the role of 'suffering' in the satyagraha context. Satyagrahis' desire to take self-suffering upon themselves has to be understood firstly in terms of religion and secondly in terms of its specific function during the satyagraha.

In Chapter I we elaborated the meaning Gandhi assigned to 'tapasya'—self-suffering—in the context of satyagraha system of action. Hindu religious practices emphasize the pursuit of 'Moksha' or salvation through prolonged meditation and specific austerities. Thus, ritual practices such as fasting and the concepts emphasizing the denial of sex, material goods and pursuits, etc., are all parts of the 'tapasya' which will finally lead the individual to Moksha. The word 'Daridranarayan' (God as manifested in the poor and the lowly) a common coin in India, is symbolic of the significance attached to the concept of tapasya. According to Iyer, tapasya gives the individual "a new power over his senses, the possibility of passing beyond their limits or suppressing them at will and thus he gains the self-knowledge and freedom of which moksha is the final form."[29] As we mentioned above, the emphasis on tapasya is reflected in various ritual religious practices in India. Once again regardless of the fact whether they understand the rationale of fasting, it is a common practice all over India, particularly among the twice-born castes, for men and women to observe fasts once a week on other religious days throughout the year. The fasts may range from missing a meal to going without eating or even drinking a drop of water throughout the whole day. So established and time-honored has been the practice of fasting in Indian homes that it is not unusual to find the children as well as the parents refusing to eat a meal as expression of anger, protest or frustration. Thus, any time an individual takes self-suffering upon himself through the established modes of behavior, he does it with a sense of inner satisfaction.

Gandhi with his interpretation of nonviolent action (as manifested through the satyagraha) as an excise in tapasya, the self-suffering and service needed for the realization of satya, brought it from the realm of the the individual and the family to the realm of politics and society. For him the human body was meant solely for service, never indulgence. "To achieve the highest ideal of suffering love, one must share the lot of the poorest and the lowliest. There is no limit whatsoever to the measure of sacrifice that one may make in order to realize the oneness with all life."[30]

Gandhi's insistence on suffering is somewhat reminiscent of the teaching of Christianity—which Gandhi was very fond of quoting—that "He that humbleth himself shall be exalted." It is also somewhat similar to Kierkegaard's emphasis on the concreteness of suffering men against the concept of man as animal rationale. According to Kierkegaard, as gold is purified by fire so is soul by suffering. Unlike passive and impotent suffering, anguish that is purposive and deliberate takes away the impure elements from human nature.[31]

In the light of the above analysis, it should not be difficult to understand the satyagrahis' willingness to invite suffering upon themsleves. Being socialized to considering purposive self-suffering as an intrinsic good it gave them a deep-seated sense of repose; and their capacity and willingness to refuse to hurt the opponent despite the wrongs perpetrated by the latter, gave the satyagrahis a sense of superiority vis a vis the opponent. Self-suffering and refusal to inflict suffering on the opponent enabled them to feel that they were better men, "better" in the spiritual and moral sense. When asked whether jail-going increased or decreased their involvement in the satyagrahas, over 70% of the satyagrahis who spent time in jail reported that it increased involvement; 30% reported no change in involvement. There was not even one satyagrahi who admitted that jail-going had any adverse effect on him. On the other hand, the courage and heroism involved in purposive suffering not only improved their self-image but provided opportunities to identify with their charismatic leaders and at the same time earn the gratitude of the whole community. It is in this sense that suffering was "positively desired." Far from being pathological, it was in the best traditions of courage, sacrifice and service to the people.[32] What Erikson wrote about Gandhi's fast during Ahmedabad Mill Workers' Strike is, in general, reflective of the role of suffering in the three satyagrahas under study:

> The acceptance of suffering and in fact death which is so basic to his 'truth force', constitute an active choice without submission to anyone: whatever masochism we may find in it, it is the highest affirmation of individualism in the service of humanity. It is at once a declaration of non-intent to do harm to others and an expression of a faith in the opponent's inability to persist in harming others beyond a certain point.[33]

We do not want to give an impression that there were absolutely no cases involving pathological masochism. In a movement where so many people are involved there are bound to be stray cases where satyagrahis take futile self-suffering upon themselves. On an individual level this may only represent a personality problem for the individual himself. On a social psychological level, as far as the total movement is concerned, it is likely—and this is just a tentative suggestion—that greater the social and psychological distance between the subordinate and the dominant group, the greater the possibility that in a non-violent action, the subordinate group would invite more suffering upon itself than when the distance was not great. Thus, in the context of our three satyagrahas, the social and psychological distance between the subordinate group and the dominant group in Pardi was much larger than for Rajkot and Bardoli. In spite of all the protestations of love, satyagraha is after all a veiled aggression against the dominant group. To the degree the subordinate group considered itself inferior to the dominant group, the former is likely to be cowed down by feelings of guilt caused by the expression of hostile and aggressive impulses in the satyagraha. These feelings of guilt might seek satisfaction in the need for punishment. Self-suffering would seem to satisfy that need. By this line of reasoning, one would assume that one would find greater heroics in suffering in Pardi satyagraha than in Rajkot or Bardoli. Does it explain Pardi satyagrahi's greater resilience in carrying on their satyagraha for almost ten years without blemish, in spite of their sufferings? Or does it explain the vigorous insistence by at least a few Pardi satyagrahis that they "did not want to see the landlords or their families hurt" or "could not bear the thought of inflicting injuries on the landlords" and "did not care that much what happened to me personally"? The confirmation of preceding inference should wait until more sophisticated tools for proper empirical analysis are available.

'SELF-SUFFERING' AS MASOCHISM

As far as the individual pathological masochism is concerned, it should be noted that the leaders of all the satyagrahas were aware and admitted that individual masochism was possible. They insisted, however, that a vigilant leadership could minimize or even completely eliminate it. Gandhi himself admitted the possibility that masochism and total unwillingness to embarrass the opponent might be exploited by the latter to the ruin of the nonviolent group. Therefore, "the satyagrahi must not exercise the virtue of self-restraint to the extent of self-extinction or suicidal self-suppression, for then the virtue becomes a vice."[34]

U.N. Dhebar, the important leader of Rajkot satyagraha, also said that,

There might be some masochism but it was not general. In a satyagraha, the leaders have a continuing responsibility that the self-suffering is meaningful and geared to the resolution of the problem for which the satyagraha was originally launched. During the Rajkot satyagraha I remember a couple of cases in which I personally discouraged or even disallowed volunteers from participation in a direct action project where I thought their exuberance might hurt them unnecessarily.

One of the remarkable features of all the three satyagrahas was that in our interviewing we did not come across a single satyagrahi who expressed dissatisfaction with satyagraha or who had any bitter memories to report. In spite of all the deprivations and suffering involved, the satyagrahis had only the positive aspects on their mind.[35] What is more, it was amazing that in spite of the fact that literally thousands of people were involved in these satyagrahas, there were few indications of serious individual or collective frustration.[36] The question to be posed at this stage, then, is what were the factors which led to the rivetting of the satyagrahis' involvement in the satyagrahas so completely.

The question has already been partly answered. The occasions for frustration were few not only because of their faith in the efficacy of nonviolence for the redress of their grievances but also because they found psychological satisfaction in the opportunity to identify with their charismatic leaders and serve their people.

SATYAGRAHA AND REFERENCE GROUPS

Another factor which must be considered significant was the extent of involvement of the relatives, friends and peer groups of the satyagrahis. One would expect that in any society where a protesting group had the total approval of the reference groups within the community, a significant contributing factor in guilt and frustration would be eliminated. By reference groups we mean here "those groups to which the individual relates himself as a member and aspires to relate himself psychologically."[37] The groups have special salience in the derivation and functioning of attitudes of the individual.

Perhaps, nowhere are reference groups more important than in the context of Indian culture. The Western culture with its accent on individualism makes it possible for an adult to deviate from his family's or peer group's norms at least to some degree, without causing too much guilt or anxiety. In India, however, an individual's attitude and goals are so firmly anchored within the family and peer groups that it would be impossible for him to shift his goals and attitudes without acquiring intense feelings of guilt and anxiety unless there was a corresponding shift in the attitudes of the reference units themselves. In his study of a Gujarat village, Steed, trying to delimit the sociological horizons of personality formation in which he might try to ascertain the widest range of circumference of an individual's experiences, found that "while individuals move through several realms of interpersonal associations, each individual's personal history remains moored firmly within Kasandra's (the name of the village) society of caste, kinship, and family."[38]

In our study of the three satyagrahas we found that besides the satyagrahis, many of the elderly and powerful persons, important reference individuals, were not only psychologically involved but were personally involved in the movements.

In our study of all the three satyagrahas, respondents reported active participation by parents, relatives, friends and teachers, the most important reference individuals, when asked if they participated in the movement.

As the following table indicates, there was active participation of the reference individuals in all the three satyagrahas. The percentages, however, for all the four categories of reference individuals is higher for the Pardi satyagrahis, showing a greater involvement than in case of the Gandhi satyagrahas. We find the same patterns of responses in regard to the parental approval of the satyagrahis' participation in the movement. When asked if their parents liked the satyagrahis' participation, a greater percentage in Pardi indicated that their parents liked it.

TABLE 19
PROJECTIVE RESPONSES ON THE QUESTION WHETHER THE FOLLOWING REFERENCE INDIVIDUALS PARTICIPATED IN THE SATYAGRAHAS

Response	Gandhi Satyagraha	Pardi Satyagraha
Parent Participation		
Yes	11(19.0)	33(30.3)
No	47(81.0)	77(70.0)
Total	58(100.0)	110(100.0)
Teacher Participation		
Yes	9(15.3)	3(2.7)
No	50(84.7)	107(97.3)
Total	59(100)	110(100)
Friends' Participation		
Yes	54(91.5)	106(96.4)
No	5(8.5)	4(3.6)
Total	59(100)	110(100)
Relatives Participation		
Yes	41(69.5)	100(90.9)
No	18(30.5)	10(9.1)
Total	59(100)	110(100)

TABLE 20
PROJECTIVE RESPONSES TO THE QUESTION IF FATHER LIKED SON'S PARTICIPATION IN THE SATYAGRAHA
(Percentages in parentheses)

Response	Gandhi Satyagraha	Pardi Satyagraha
Liked	18(30.5)	81(75.0)
Disliked	17(28.8)	
Indifferent	2(3.4)	
Don't know	15(25.4)	27(25.0)
Father deceased	7(11.9)	
Total	59(100)	108(100)

TABLE 21
PROJECTIVE RESPONSES TO THE QUESTION IF MOTHER LIKED SON'S PARTICIPATION IN THE SATYAGRAHA
(Percentages in parentheses)

Response	Gandhi Satyagraha	Pardi Satyagraha
Liked	18(30.5)	89)83.2)
Disliked	14(23.7)	
Indifferent	5(8.5)	
Don't know	17(28.8)	18(16.8)
Mother deceased	5(8.5)	
Total	51(100)	107(100)

The data indicates that 75% of the fathers and 83.2% of the mothers in case of the Pardi satyagrahis liked the participation of their sons in the satyagrahas. The percentage of the fathers and mothers liking the sons' participation is comparatively low in the Gandhi satyagrahas. Some reported that their parents came around to liking their participation after the movement had been in progress for some time. Some parents and other reference individuals, subsequently, came under the spell of the charismatic leaders, themselves. Some were influenced enough to actually join the movement.[39] The greatest change in the attitudes of the parents was, however, brought about as a result of the satyagrahis' jail-going. Most of the satyagrahis reported that their esteem went up in the eyes of their parents, friends, teachers and relatives. This was true even in the case of the Gandhi satyagrahis, where the overwhelming majority said that their stock went up tremendously in the eyes of their parents and others as a result of their jail-going.

One respondent from the Rajkot sample reported that his parents, particularly the father, bitterly opposed his participation in the satyagraha. He said,

> We had a roaring business. Most of my relatives where also in business. I was already so much impressed with Gandhiji's work that I was ready to join him as soon as the first opportunity arose. I had to wait, however, until the Rajkot

satyagraha. As my determination to join the movement became clear, my father tried to prevent me first by persuasion, then by threats. He told me, 'Satyagrahas are not for us. All our business and affluence are dependent upon the government's special favour. You will ruin everything.' I was not impressed. The first day I participated in a demonstration my father told me, 'If you go again the doors of this house will be closed for you forever.'
And that is the way it happened. Even some of my close relatives spurned me. Many of my friends and teachers gave me moral support. I made new friends due to the satyagraha and had the privilege of being associated with the great leaders of Gujerat and the whole country. I was, however, constantly ridden with guilt for having failed my family. Sometimes when I thought about my family, I was so depressed that I wanted to die. Whenever I read reports about the brutal beating of the satyagrahis by the police, I wished I was there to take their place. It still rankles like a thorn in my heart that my father never pardoned me until the end. However, I have remained convinced to this day that he was wrong.

SATYAGRAHA AND CONSTRUCTIVE ACTIVITY

The almost total involvement of the communities and the strict observance of the discipline of nonviolence must also be attributed to the role constructive activity played in the satyagraha. At the time of the Bardoli Satyagraha Gandhi declared,

> They (the satyagrahis) will not become a nonviolent organization unless they undergo a process of what may be called continuous corporate clearing. This they can only do by engaging in carrying out a well thought out constructive program promoting common good . . . in other words they must receive education in nonviolence.[40]

Actually, Gandhi ascribed the resounding success of the Bardoli satyagraha to the fact that a constructive economic or social program of reform had been going on for six or seven years prior to the actual launching of the satyagraha. During the Rajkot satyagraha also Gandhi strongly exhorted the volunteers to carry on constructive activity. "There should not be one house in Rajkot with which you have not established contact from the point of view of pure service."[41]

That the constructive activity did play an important part in the satyagrahas is indicated by the fact that almost 88% of the satyagrahis in the Gandhi sample and 83% in the Pardi sample were either aware of or participated in the constructive activity associated with the satyagraha. An important consequence of constructive activity, apart from the inculcation of the knowledge and discipline of nonviolence was that it fostered economic and psychological interdependence among the participants which, in turn, bound them together in interpersonal ties of love, respect and togetherness.[42] The following respondent from Bardoli emphasized the economic aspect of the constructive activity.

> There is a direct relationship between nonviolence and constructive activity. Gandhiji believed, and I agree, that during a satyagraha some means of subsistence have to be open for the satyagrahis. To the extent constructive activity does that it is part of satyagraha.

The following satyagrahis from Bardoli and Rajkot emphasized the economic aspect and the relationship of constructive activity to nonviolence:

> Gandhiji considered the charkha (the spinning wheel) to be a symbol of ahimsa. Through charkha we could wear our own 'swadeshi' (self-produced) cloth. The British had made this country totally dependent upon them. The idea of the constructive activity was to, once again, gain self-dependence through mutual love, cooperation and nonviolence through constructive activity.
> —A satyagrahi from Bardoli

> Nonviolence develops the power of self-dedication. Constructive activity needs the same self-dedication since the satyagrahis learn to subsist on self due to the constructive activity. Activities involved in the constructive activity,

e.g., adult education, eradication of untouchability, spinning, etc., all create a basic sense of love, cooperation and belief in the basic unity of all mankind.

—A satyagrahi from Rajkot

Still another factor which contributed to the rivetting of the satyagrahis' attention on the satyagraha, and reduction of tension and anxiety was the shouting of slogans and singing of songs. A prominent feature of all the three satyagrahas—and for that matter any satyagraha in India—has been the shouting of slogans. The most common slogan was 'Mahatma Gandhi Ki Jay'—Victory to Gandhi. The same slogan, then, would be raised in the name of Ishver Bhai for Pardi and Sardar Patel and U. N. Dhebar for Bardoli and Rajkot respectively. Through these slogans, the satyagrahis constantly reinforced their sense of identification with their charismatic leaders. Other slogans, such as 'Hamaari Mange Puri Karo'—fulfill our demands—etc., raised by all the satyagrahis in unison reinforced their determination to fight on and concentrate their energy and efforts on the declared goals.

Similarly, songs sung in unison by the satyagrahis during a direct action project and other occasions greatly helped the satyagrahis in developing a spirit of camaraderie and fearlessness. Songs also helped the satyagrahis relax in a meaningful way, namely, they were not only entertaining but constantly reminded them of their avowed goals and pledges to nonviolent behavior.[43]

Hakumat Bhai Desai, the Pardi leader recounting the role of songs and slogans in the Pardi satyagraha said:

The songs and slogans to be raised were chosen with great deal of care. Slogans helped to keep the satyagrahis to the highest pitch of excitement and interest particularly when a direct action project was in progress. Singing usually included 'Bhajans'—devotional songs or hymns—and songs emphasizing the Gandhian virtues of humility, love, service, courage and ahimsa. In tense situations, as for example, when police were arresting or beating the satyagrahis, slogans and songs also helped to relieve the tension and calm the satyagrahis.

From the above discussion it is clear that apart from the crucial factor of charisma which helped the satyagrahis imbibe the ideal of nonviolent behavior, the satyagrahas reinforced the ideal continually through the speeches of their leaders, through emphasis on constructive activity rather than destructive and through the singing of songs emphasizing the humane qualities. Is it any wonder then, that we do not find any serious evidence of individual or collective frustration? We believe that the impact of the charismatic leaders, coupled with the reinforcement of the ideal of nonviolent behavior through leaders' speeches, constructive activity, singing, etc., led to the internalization of the norms of nonviolent behavior to such an extent that the satyagrahis found the suffering engendered by the satyagrahas to be truely satisfying. Also, in singing, sloganeering and inviting self-suffering upon themselves they found a useful 'expressive outlet'[44] from any traces of frustration which might have been caused by conflict.

SATYAGRAHA AND FRUSTRATION

Finally, we would like to emphasize that while all the three satyagrahas were remarkably free of any evidence of frustration in general, there were individual cases of frustration. No satyagraha can be totally without blemish. In the more vigorous phases of the satyagraha, the repression let loose by the enemy may be so severe, the sacrifice demanded of the satyagrahis so great and the tension so unbearable that some satyagrahis may be compelled to seek release from tension by indulging in highly expressive acts which may include even violence[45] particularly, where the satyagrahis have not internalized the behavioral norms of nonviolence may feel frustrated and find it difficult to remain nonviolent. The necessity of 'expressive outlet' under such circumstances will be greater.[46] For the satyagrahis who have not sufficiently internalized the nonviolent norms but still feel obligated to nonviolent action as a matter of discipline, the attempt at self-suppression under conditions of frustration may result in a compromise response.

Thus, Uttam Bhai, the adivasi leader of Pardi proudly stated that his satyagrahis were nonviolent at all times. Even under extreme provocation from the police and landlords they were able to remain peaceful. During the phase of the satyagraha when we decided to refuse to cut the landlords' standing grass on the pastures, the latter decided to hire labor from outside Pardi. We surrounded one grassland and started shouting slogans when we learned that the landlord has hired some outside help. The policemen who were around tried to intimidate a few satyagrahis by pushing them away from the boundary of the grassland. One policeman used his stick to push a satyagrahi while the other pushed another satyagrahi so hard that he fell down on the ground injuring himself. This provoked the satyagrahis so much that about a dozen of them entered the grassland in anger and madly started trampling the grass under their feet. The situation was soon brought under control by me. This is the only kind of incident involving violence by the satyagrahis that I can remember.

Similarly, during the Rajkot satyagraha, following the arrests of leaders, when the mounted police came with loudspeakers to make announcements, the demonstrators would shout slogans so loudly that the announcements could not be heard.[47]

To summarize, the impact of the satyagrahas on the participants was far reaching and went much beyond the objectives for which the satyagrahas were originally launched. Before the three satyagrahas were launched all the would-be participants were weighed down by a deep sense of inferiority and powerlessness. In the case of the Rajkot and Bardoli satyagrahis, this was largely the result of the British people's stereotyping of them as weak and cowardly. The condition of the tribals in Pardi was worse. Being branded as low caste and miserably poor they were under the total subjection of the landlords.

Satyagraha with its emphasis on militant nonviolent action provided them with an opportunity to explode the stereotype about their being weak and cowardly. Also, linking of nonviolent action with their religious and traditional norms and roles gave them a sense of superiority vis a vis the opponent that they were morally and spiritually 'better' men. Other activities connected with the satyagrahas such as constructive activity bound the satyagrahis in close ties of interdependence, while other activities such as communal singing and slogan-raising fostered a new spirit of camaraderie and cooperation. All the satyagrahis displayed a new sense of courage and self-confidence which was born of the satyagraha discipline and united action.

NOTES and REFERENCES

[1] This section of the chapter draws considerably from the incisive analysis of this problem, by Lloyd I. Rudolph and Susanne Hoeber Rudolph in *The Modernity of Tradition: Political Development in India* (Chicago and London: University of Chicago Press, 1967).

[2] The twice-born castes, namely Brahmins, Kshatriyas, and Vaishyas, are distinguished from the non-twice-born namely, Shudras in their ability to command the services of Brahmin priests to perform Vedik rituals and wear sacred thread.

[3] John Strachy, *India, Its Administration and Progress* (London: 1888), pp. 411-12, cited from Rudolph, pp. 164-165. The Rudolphs also point out that Percival Spear's book, *The Nabobs* (London: 1932), lists twenty-six quotations, expressing European sentiment about Indians, which described Indians as "sober and effiminate people."

[4] See Hira Lal Seth, *The Iron Dictator* (Hero Publications, 1943), p. 84.

[5] Cited in *Collected Works of Mahatma Gandhi* (Delhi: 1958), I, p. 30.

[6] Lloyd I Rudolph, and Sussanne Hoeber Rudolph, *The Modernity of Tradition* (Chicago and London: The University of Chicago Press, 1967), p. 167.

[7] At least 50% of the satyagrahis in Bardoli said that they had participated in one or more Gandhian satyagrahas before they participated in Bardoli satyagraha.

[7a] *Harijan*, January 18, 1942.

[8] At least half a dozen appelations have been used to describe these people. Apart from the words 'tribes', 'tribal people', 'adivasis', the Government of India has officially used terms such as 'aborigines', 'backward classes', 'scheduled caste', 'scheduled tribes', 'depressed people', etc., in order to distinguish one tribe from another and from caste. For more light on this, see G.S. Ghurye, *The Aborigines—'so-called'—and Their Future*, Publication No. 2 (Poona: Gokhale Institute of Economics, 1943). Also "The Backward Classes," in *The Economic Weekly*, October 29, November 4 and 18, 1961, pp. 1665-8, 1695-1706, 1729-38.

Satyagraha and the Rank and File 159

[9] See G.S. Ghurye, *The Aborigines—'so-called'—and Their Future*, Chapter 1. Also F.G. Bailey, *Tribe, Caste and Nation* (Manchester: University Press, 1966), pp. 263-264.

[10] The term, first used by M.N. Srinivas, and now widely used to describe the emulation of high caste norms and practices by lower castes for purposes of social leveling and increased self-respect. *Religion and Society Among the Coorgs of South India* (London: 1952).

[11] An early case of sanskritization of a tribe to 'Kshatriya' caste is described by Martin Orans in which he talks about a Munda tribal who had established himself as a local 'Raja' (King) and attracted Brahmins to his court, who sanskritized his rituals and also manufactured a Rajput—an established Kshatriya caste—genealogy for him. For similar themes, see Surjit Sinha, "State Formation and Rajput Myth in Central India," *Man in India*, XLII (January-March, 1962).

[12] The term is taken from Erik Erikson. He uses it to describe self-images which are diametrically opposed to the dominant values of individuals upbringing, an identity which he can become only with a divided heart, but which he nevertheless finds himself compelled to become. See his *Young Man Luther* (New York: W.W. Norton, 1958), p. 102. For elaboration of the concept, see also his "Identity and the Life Cycle," Monograph 1, *Psychological Issues* (1959), pp. 1-171. Also "Psychoanalysis and Ongoing History: Problems of Identity Hatred and Nonviolence," *The American Journal of Psychiatry* (September 1965), p. 246.

[13] David G. Mandelbaum, *Society and Change in India: Change and Continuity* (Berkeley: University of California Press, 1970), pp. 618-619.

[14] L.M. Shrikant, in his study of the tribes of this region points out that it is still not known how they became slaves to absentee landlords in the districts of Surat and Bulsar. See his "Western Deccan Tribes" in Suresh K. Singh, *Tribal Situation in India* (Simla: Indian Institute of Advanced Study, 1972), p. 204. For a description of the tribes in the Southwest, see B.S. Guha, "Indian Aborigines and Who They Are", *The Adivasis* (Delhi: The Government of India, 1955).

[15] E.g., Jharkhand Party in Bihar. See in this connection, N.K. Bose, "Change in Tribal Cultures Before and After Independence" in *Man in India*, XLIV, No. 1 (1964).

[16] L.P. Vidyarthi, "The Historical March of the Jharkhand Party: A Study of Adivasi Leadership in Tribal Bihar," *Indian Sociological Bulletin*, 1, No. 2 (1964), p. 5. For the same conclusions see also Andre Beteille. "The Future of Backward Classes: The Competing Demands of Status and Power" in Philip Mason, *India and Ceylon: Unity and Diversity* (Bombay: Oxford Univerity Press, 1967).

[17] *Indian Village* (London: Routledge and Kegan Paul Ltd., 1955), p. 183.

[18] Susanne Rudolph, "A New Courage" in *World Politics*, 16 (1963). p. 113.

[19] H. Isaacs in his study of India's untouchables clearly brings out their plight. There is a continual implied comparison of the Harijans—

literally meaning God's people, the name given by Gandhi to the untouchables and low cast—with the Negroes in the United States. Harijan like Negro was part of society and yet outside it. He dared not enter the quarter where Brahmins lived and he must get out of the way when twice born approached and so on; he must use terms of respect when speaking to him and so on. Like the Southern Negro, outwardly, he was a conformist accepting his subordinate role. Like Uncle Tom trying to get respectability by accepting white values, the Harijans would sanskritize by accepting the values of the twice born, e.g., giving up meat eating, prohibition of widow marriages. All—like Negro—have some legal protection. See his *India's Exuntouchables* (New York: John Day, 1964).

It must be pointed out here that the adivasis were not 'untouchables' and hence not in as a bad condition. However, being low caste they certainly suffered many of the ignominies mentioned by Isaacs.

[20] Account of the tribals by several scholars corroborate the views expressed here. A. Aiyappan in his study of the tribesmen of the South states that the greatest danger that confronts them is a loss of self-confidence which had enabled them to live fearlessly in forests inhabited by wild beasts. The feelings of frustration and inadequacy "seem to make members of the small communities in the South suffer from a severe inferiority complex." This is a result of the attitude of the Hindu plainsman who uses any means to denigrate the tribes. See his "In the South in Tribal India," *Seminar 14* (Bombay: 1960). Cited in Christoph Von Fueres-Haimendorf, "The Position of Tribal Population in India" in Philip Mason, ed., *Unity and Diversity: India and Ceylon*, pp. 182-222.

[21] "The New Courage," *World Politics*, 16 (1963), 98-217.

[22] *Discovery of India* (New York: 1959), pp. 274-275.

[23] Vallabh Bhai Patel, the Bardoli leader, earned the title of 'Sardar'— meaning brave warrior—from Gandhi, for his role in the Bardoli satyagraha. He went on to become Deputy Prime Minister in independent India. U.N. Dhebar, the Rajkot leader, went on to become the Chief Minister of Saurashtra state and has, since, held numerous top posts in Congress Party and the Government of India. Jetha Lal Joshi, another Rajkot leader was, several times, elected to Indian Parliament. Similary, Uttam Bhai, the Pardi leader has since been regularly elected to the Gujerat State Assembly. The rank and file participants have also played prominent part in the life of their communities.

Actually, in some cases the impact was so far reaching that some satyagrahis in the process of shedding their inferiority complex developed a superiority complex causing resentment among the common people, by their arrogance, self-righteousness and insensitivity to the people's needs.

[24] Evidence from studies in the United States seems to support this finding. Thus, a report of a six-year follow up study of a group of black children who participated at the ages of five to fifteen in the first lunch counter sit-in in Oklahoma City stresses their persistent feeling of latent

power, based in part on a strong conscious sense of being able to control their own feelings in the service of ideals. See C.M. Pierce and L.J. West, "Six Years of Sit-in," *International Journal of Psychiatry*, 12 (1966), 29-34. In anoter report, extensive interviews with adolescents and young adults who participated in Freedom rides and sit-ins, revealed that by refusing to resort to violence the participants got a feeling of heightened manliness and a sense of moral superiority over their opponents. See Solomon and Fishman, "The Psychosocial Meaning of Nonviolence in Student Civil Rights Activities," *Psychiatry*, 27 (1964), 91-99.

[25] Article under Section 144 prohibits assembly of five or more persons at public places without government's permission.

[26] *Psychoanalysis of Gandhism. Problem of Freedom* (Calcutta: Renaissance Publishers, 1945), pp. 28-38.

[27] Leo Kuper, *Passive Resistance in South Africa* (New Haven: Yale University Press, 1957), pp. 78-94.

[28] Literally means 'fire test'. The term is derived from an episode in *The Ramayana*. Seeta, Lord Rama's wife was kidnapped by Ravana, the demon. Ravana was killed by Rama in the great battle that followed the incident; and Seeta was recovered. There was gossip among the local people that Seeta's modesty may have been outraged during her detention at Ravana's. To prove her purity, Seeta put her on a burning pyre and came out unscathed, thus proving her innocence. Hence, the term 'Agni Pariksha'.

[29] Raghavan Iyer, *"The Moral and Political Thought of Mahatma Gandhi* (New York: Oxford University Press, 1973), p. 236.

[30] The *Harijan*, December 26, 1936.

[31] Kierkegaard, *'Christian Discourses* (Oxford: 1961), p. 114. For a detailed elaboration and comparison of Gandhi's concept of suffering with Kierkegaard's see also Raghavan Iyer, pp. 224-250.

[32] In a study of eight children, ages 5 to 15, who participated in Oklahoma sit-in for integration of a luncheon counter at a drug store on August 19, 1958 and a follow up study of the same children after six years, Pierce and West report that the important motivation derived from participation in dangerous activities since "there are significant gratifications related to the channeling of hostile and aggressive impulses into an acceptable outlet" (p. 31). The authors further observed that the children "have been motivated by altruistic rather than masochistic strivings" (p. 31). Chester M. Pierce and Louis Jolyon West, "Six Years of Sit-ins: Psychodynamic Causes and Effects" in *International Journal of Social Psychiatry*, 12, No. 1 (1966) pp. 29-34.

[33] Erik Erikson, "Problem of Identity, Hatred and Non-Violence" in Paul Hare and Herbert Blumberg, *Nonviolent Direct Action* (Corpus Books, 1968), p. 509.

[34] Cited in Gopi Nath Dhawan, *The Political Philosophy of Mahatma Gandhi* (Ahmedabad: Navjeevan, 1957). p. 215.

[35] Pierce and West in the study cited earlier also report that in spite of the fact that the children were spat on, scolded, handled

roughly and insulted, they remembered after six years only the positive aspects of their nonviolent sit-in. The control of behavior, required by the discipline on nonviolent movement has also extended to the other aspects of their lives, namely, they are all motivated by altruistic strivings. In general their feelings "have generalized to the broader conviction that they will be able to do good." Op. cit., pp. 31-32.

[36] Johan Galtung (op. cit., pp. 69-72) has posed an interesting and fruitful question in this connection. First, he makes a distinction between instrumental and expressive behavior during a conflict situation. "An act may be said to be 'instrumental' to the extent that it has the function of contributing to conflict resolution and it may be said to be 'expressive' to the extent that it serves the function of tension release from the latent intensity." (p. 69).

A conflict is, by definition, frustrating because it means that there are social and personal impediments to the realization of a value. If frustration is a necessary and sufficient condition for 'aggression' where the aggression may be instrumental (as when directed against the enemy) and/or expressive (as when it is displaced and directed against third parties—scapegoats—one's own groups—self-hatred—or one's self-inner-directed), what kinds of outlet does a satyagraha provide for release from tension? (It should be clear that by 'aggression' we need not necessarily mean violent aggression; we have already characterized nonviolent action as 'passive aggression'.)

Usually both dimensions of behavior exist side by side. During conflict the same act may score high on 'instrumental' dimension but low on 'expressive' and vice versa (pp. 69-70). The question posed, simply, in regard to a satyagraha is this; while a satyagraha may be instrumental to conflict resolution, what means does it provide for expressive behavior, when expressive need is great? Any time expressive need is great, the gratification coming from an expressive act is immediate and certain.

Galtung partly answers his own question when he subsequently asks if it is possible that those who have internalized nonviolent ideology may find in nonviolent action conditions which satisfy both the instrumental and expressive needs. For example, the diplomatic expert who at the same time is deeply involved may obtain a great relief by watching the successful results of his diplomatic skills (p. 71).

Thus, in the three satyagrahas we studied, we believe that the satyagrahis had sufficiently internalized the norms of nonviolent behavior to get psychological satisfaction from their courage, sacrifice and service to the community.

[37] M.A. Williams, "Reference Groups: A Review and Commentary," *Sociological Quarterly*, 11 (1970), 552.

[38] Gitel P. Steed, "Notes on an Approach to a Study of Personality Formation in a Hindu Village in Gujerat" in McKim Marriott, ed., *Village India* (Chicago: The University of Chicago Press, 1955), p. 107.

[39] This is not at all unusual. Sociologists agree that "Families, an important reference group to most persons, may change in varying

degrees their attitudes, behaviors, standards or values in response to the influence of their children, as may secondary groups on the basis of what individuals bring with them to the group and the process that goes on between them. See M.A. Williams, "Reference groups: A Review and Commentary, "*Sociological Quarterly*, No. 11, (1970), p. 552.

[40]*The Young India*, August 16, 1928. Cited in M.K. Gandhi, *Politics and National Life and Affairs* (Ahmedabad; Navjeevan, 1968), III, pp. 121-122.

[41]M.K. Gandhi, *Nonviolent Resistance*, p. 101.

[42]According to Janis and Katz, constructive activity consists in "maintaining a consistent and persistent set of positive activities which are explicit (though partial) realizations of the group's objectives." See their "The Reduction of Conflict in Intergroup Hostility" in the *Journal of Conflict Resolution*, 3 (1959), 86.

[43]Dubois and Soong Li point out that songs help greatly in bringing the people together and having a meaningful time together in a social movement. "Today's songs popular with youth in the folk style of our time are often related to our social problems, not only to joy and longing, but also to hunger, struggle, pain and to our search for peace." Rachel Davis Dubois and Mew-Soong Li, *Reducing Social Tension and Conflict* (New York: Association Press, 1971), p. 54.

[44]For elaboration of the term 'expressive' see note 36.

[45]Even the satyagrahas led by Gandhi were periodically marred by scattered cases of violence by the satyagrahis. Thus during the nation-wide satyagraha against the Rowlatt Bills in 1919 nonviolence broke down as a result of violent repression by police. There were cases of stone-throwing in Delhi; elsewhere government buildings were set on fire, telegraph lines cut and both English and Indian officers injured. The violence was widespread enough for Gandhi to suspend the satyagraha. He also went on a three day 'penitential fast'.

For a brief description of the satyagraha against the Rowlatt Bills, See Joan Bondurant, op. cit., pp. 73-88.

[46]An interesting example of 'expressive behavior' is narrated by Dr. Rajendra Prasad. During the Salt Satyagraha of 1930-31, the satyagrahis of the little village of Bihrpur in Bhagalpur district of Bihar were picketing peacefully when they were pounced upon by a large number of policemen and beaten mercilessly with their lathis. Not an arm was raised against the policemen. As the police left, dozens of people were left injured and bleeding on the streets. The crowds were in a state of great excitement and anger. Dr. Rajendra Prasad, one of their leaders, tried to pacify them but one of the villagers said in an excited voice, "You have come here. We have lived to see you and other leaders beaten up in our very presence—Those few policemen would not have dared to raise their hands against any one let alone you. But what can we do? Gandhiji had tied down our hands;—If that were not so, we could have made short shrift of them regardless

of consequences." And they broke down then and began to cry like children. Dr. Rajendra Prasad, *At the Feet of Mahatma Gandhi* (Bombay: Hindi Kitabs Ltd., 1955), pp. 192-194.

[47]Such incidents have also been reported in American Civil Rights movement. Thus, Mabee reports an incident during efforts to desegregate a restaurant in Maryland "When a policeman asked a group of picketers to walk outside a certain line on the concrete sidewalk so as not to block a door, two of the picketers taunted the policeman by placing their feet as close to the line as possible watching their feet with exaggerated care and occasionally grinning at him." C. Mabee: "Will Commitment to Nonviolence Last," *Liberation* (April, 1963), 15.

9
Conclusion

Most of the writers on satyagraha have operated on two levels. They have either concerned themselves with a philosophical elaboration of the meaning of satyagraha or have sought to analyze it purely in terms of the role played by its chief architect, Mahatma Gandhi. One result of this has been the accentuation of the religico-ethical interpretation of satyagraha to the total neglect of its study as a system of action. Similarly the total preoccupation of the writers with the study of Gandhi failed to take into consideration the role played by millions of the rank and file satyagrahis. It may be argued that a Gandhi was only as much essential to the effectiveness of a satyagraha as the numerous satyagrahis and the subelites who helped translate the satyagraha into effective action.

This study has sought to explore the satyagraha from the point of view of these thousands of rank and file satyagrahis and subleaders. Although, nonviolent action comes through distinctly as a purely religico-ethical category through Gandhi's writings we have attempted to understand it as a sociological and social psychological category. In the satyagraha system of action nonviolence implies a system of values and meanings with a specific commitment to them as a way of life. Through a study of the attitudes of the rank and file and the subleaders, we have attempted to understand the perception and cognition of nonviolence and their commitment to it as a system of behavioral norms. We extended this study to three different satyagrahas, namely, Bardoli, Rajkot and Pardi which fitted Gandhi's model of an ideal satyagraha, in order to find a common denominator in the cognition and perception of nonviolence in all the three satyagrahas.

Cognitive level of understanding is important insofar as it is by far the most elemental and basic stage of its substantive existence in the consciousness of the people. The cognitive level of understanding of nonviolence may reveal not only the social-cultural processes in society in general, but also in the limited context of our three satyagrahas the functional viability of the norms of nonviolent behavior. The findings suggest that few among the rank and file satyagrahis had any religious or philosophical understanding of nonviolence, and fewer still of its eschatological underpinnings. This, however, was no bar to the internalization of nonviolence on the action level. They believed in nonviolence as a creed without necessarily understanding it. 'Creed' for all practical purposes, for a satyagrahi, simply meant that he was not to indulge in physical violence under any circumstances. Thus, the faith of the satyagrahis in nonviolence was more cathectic-emotive than rational or pragmatic. This cathectic-emotive response to nonviolent behavior, in turn, derived from their faith in the charismatic leaders of the three satyagrahas, Gandhi in the case of Rajkot and Bardoli and Ishver Bhai in the case of Pardi. As compared to the rank and file the approach of the subleaders to nonviolence was purely pragmatic. Many of the leaders had not internalized the norms of nonviolence. These leaders led and participated in nonviolent action in deference to the demands of the charismatic leaders, who alone commanded the respect of the masses, the real muscles of the movements. Thus, the subleaders were bound to the satyagrahas more by discipline than by their own faith in nonviolence.

Most of the writings on satyagraha suggest that an overwhelming number of people who participated in satyagrahas did not have faith in nonviolence. According to these writers the satyagrahas were held together only by a cadre of dedicated leaders who had strong faith in it. Our findings suggest the very opposite. The rank and file were deeply cathected on nonviolent behavior. On the other hand there were many leaders who did not have faith in nonviolence. Thus it was the people who helped preserve the nonviolent character of the satyagrahas rather than the leaders who were only doing a job out of a sense of discipline and responsibility.

As regards the social composition of the three satyagrahas, the participants were a 'vanguard' group. They were young, mostly in their twenty's, more active and elite in relation to the rest of the people. They were relatively more educated and showed a higher economic status. Our findings also suggest that the commitment to nonviolent movement can be sustained either on ideological goals or goals involving economic, personal or group gains of the participants.

Like the rank and file, the leadership was also dominated by people who were young, highly educated and had a greater degree of experience in satyagraha participation. The leadership in the Pardi satyagraha was dominated by Brahmins. This, coupled with the fact that the dominant group, the landlords in this case, mostly consisted of Brahmins also strongly suggests that the protests for an oppressed group are usually conducted or at least initiated by leaders who are equal or at least psychologically feel equal or even superior in status to the group being opposed. Sense of equality or superiority, however, is not something that ought to be necessarily a result of one's belonging to high caste. It could be besides, high caste, because of high education or high economic status or it may be because of the individual personality. We believe that in the social background of the leaders, the important factors lending homogeneity to the movements were the leaders' education and occupation, rather than their castes. Under the influence of Western liberal education they were more secular and egalitarian in their outlook toward the world. The leaders, in participating in the satyagrahas, had larger ideological goals in mind rather than the immediate issues. In their attitudes toward nonviolence the leaders reflected pragmatism and humanism and a total absence of religious orientation.

One of the most surprising findings from our point of view was the degree of influence that Gandhi exercised over the three satyagrahas and Ishver Bhai, over the Pardi satyagraha. It was expected that the influence of these two leaders would be widespread and strong. However, we also expected that the rank and file will bring to the movement a distinct socio-cultural personality of their own. The big surprise was the extent to which the impact of Gandhi was written all over the faces of the three satyagrahas. The inordinate impact of Gandhi's charisma on the satyagrahis incidentally also helped to explain another rather curious finding, namely, throughout our interviewing with the satyagrahis, references to religion or God were totally missing. This was curious because Gandhi presented and emphasized his program of nonviolent action purely in terms of religion.

In India, over the centuries, religion has been a way of life rather than a philosophy. In actual life, religion to an Indian means conforming to certain norms of behavior and prescribed ritual practices within the family, caste and clan. On the individual level it means the inculcation of certain virtues. If these virtues have proved difficult of adoption to most of the people, the individual who can realize these virtues becomes the center of worship and admiration from the people.

To most of the satyagrahis, Gandhi was a living example of purity, uprightness, continence, freedom from anger, compassion to all living beings, truth and nonviolence. He was the very incarnation of religious virtues which they aspired to realize but found themselves wanting. Therefore, the satyagrahis found relief from anxiety and tension caused by their failure by emotionally identifying with Gandhi. The satyagrahis sought this identification by adopting certain external symbols such as vegetarianism, nondrinking, austerity, and above all pledging unquestioning allegiance to nonviolent behavior under all circumstances. By this identification the satyagrahis not only vicariously experienced the power of the leader, but by adopting the nonviolent norms as established by the leader and interpreted in terms of their religion, they had the satisfaction of living the life of virtue that their religion prescribed. Thus, although we do not find any references to God and religion in the satyagrahis' perception of nonviolence, the fact is that religion was an integral part of their faith in nonviolent action.

Finally, the effects of satyagraha on the participants were far reaching. The findings from all the three satyagrahas indicate that where a people is weighed down by feelings of guilt and powerlessness, the ideal of heroic action and self-denial involved in the satyagraha have given rise to self confidence and a sense of power which were lacking before. Describing the impact of satyagraha, Nehru aptly wrote that Gandhi through his potent weapon of nonviolence "had instilled courage and manhood in (India's) people—courage is the one sure foundation of character, he had said; without courage there is no morality, no religion, no love."[1]

It is pertinent to observe at this point, that our emphasis in the above paragraphs on the roles of religion in the satyagrahis' perception of nonviolence does not warrant the conclusion, as has been done by most writers, that satyagraha was strongly culture bound and applicable only to India. The fact that Gandhi lived to see thousands of Hindus and Muslims butcher one another in cold blood following the partition of India, the fact that Gandhi himself met violent death at the hands of an assassin and the fact that India, today, is riven with conflict and violence on an unprecedented scale prove, if anything, that nonviolence is not necessarily typical to Indian culture. As far as Indian religions are concerned, they can be easily interpreted either to support violence or nonviolence. The fact that Gandhi successfully accentuated the nonviolent aspect of religion in presenting his 'satyagraha' before the Indian people, is as much attributable to historical circumstances as to the incredible genius of Gandhi himself. Bertrand Russel wrote about Gandhi, generations to come will scarcely believe that the little brown man ever walked this earth in reality. The disturbing implication of what we are saying here is that if Gandhi, because of his charisma was able to emphasize and establish the nonviolent aspects of Hinduism in support of his satyagraha, there is no reason to believe that some other charismatic leader would not be able to organize and conduct a violent movement by emphasizing the violent aspects of it. That the potential for violence is there is admitted by Gandhi himself. In his letter to C.F. Andrews from Nadiad, Gandhi denied that nonviolence had been given a very great importance in Hinduism. On the contrary, he said that he saw

> no sign of it (even) in the *Mahabharata* or the *Ramayana*— the incarnations are described as certainly blood thirsty, revengeful and merciless to the enemy. They have been credited with having resorted to tricks—for the sake of overcoming the enemy. The battles are described with no

less zest than now and the warriors are equipped with weapons of destruction such as could possibly be conceived by the human imagination. The finest hymn composed by Tulsidas in praise of Rama gives the first place to his ability to strike down the enemy—Shankaracharya did not hesitate to use unspeakable cruelty in banishing Budhism from India—and he succeeded.[2]

The successful use of nonviolent action in the United States by Martin Luther King, in the Civil Rights movement, only tends to confirm the observation made earlier. The fact that King was able to accentuate and impress the Christian aspect of his nonviolent action on his followers was as much the result of historical circumstance of the Negro as to his charismatic influence. Different symbols were used by the two leaders, but the underlying principle was the same. Thus, when Gandhi fasted he touched the hearts of millions of Indians; King had the same effect with his open prayers.

The important question to ask at this stage is, what are the prospects for satyagraha becoming the normal mode of social action in conflict situations? The answer to this question depends upon how far a society is capable of internalizing the norms of nonviolence. So far, most of the nonviolent movements, including the three studied here, have been sustained by a nonviolent ideology derived through religious beliefs and practices. The danger is that if the accent is on religion rather than nonviolence, the accent on nonviolence will change as the interpretation of religion changes. Thus, unless a secular nonviolent ideology becomes enshrined in the hearts and minds of men, the society will of necessity have to wait for the appearance of charismatic figures like Gandhi, Ishver Bhai or Martin Luther King. Until then effective satyagrahas will continue to be exceptions rather than the generally accepted modes of social action.

NOTES and REFERENCES

[1]Jawahar Lal Nehru, *Freedom From Fear: Reflections on Personality and Teachings of Gandhi* (Delhi: 1960), p. 12.
[2]*Collected Works of Mahatma Gandhi* (Delhi: 1958), XIV, p. 475.

A SELECT BIBLIOGRAPHY

Aiyappan, A. *Social Revolution in a Kerala Village : A Study in Cultural Change.* Bombay: Asia Publishing House. 1965.

Aiyer, S.P. *The Politics of Mass Violence in India.* Bombay: Manaktalas and Sons, Private Ltd., 1967.

Almond, Gabriel. *The Appeals of Communism.* Princeton, New Jersey: Princeton University Press, 1954.

Appadorai, A. "Gandhi's Contribution to Social Theory." In *Review of Politics,* 31, No. 3 (July, 1969) pp. 312-328.

Arendt, Hannah. *The Origins of Totalitarianism.* New York: Harcourt, Brace and Company. 1954.

──────. *The Origins of Totalitarianism.* Cleveland: World Publishing Company, 1958.

Argyris, Chris. *Personality and Organization: The Conflict Between System and the Individual.* New York: Harper, 1957.

Ashe, Geoffrey. *Gandhi.* New York: Stein and Day Publishers, 1968.

Axelford, Robert. "Conflict of Interest: An Axiomatic Approach." *Journal of Conflict Resolution.* Vol. II, No. 1 (1967), pp. 87-99.

Bailey, F.G. *Tribe, Caste and Nation.* London: Manchester University Press, 1966.

Barber, Bernard. "Acculturation and Messianic Movements." *American Sociological Review,* 6 (1941), 663-669.

Barry, Wm. Theodore. *Source of Indian Tradition.* New York: Columbia University Press, 1959.

Basham, A.L. *Studies in Indian History and Culture.* Calcutta: Sambodhi Publications, 1964.

──────. *Wonder That Was India : A Study of the History and Culture of the Indian Subcontinent.* New and revised edition. New York: Hawthorne, 1963.

Bass, Bernard M. *Leadership, Psychology and Organizational Behavior.* New York: Harper and Brothers, 1960.

Bay, Christian. *The Structure of Freedom.* New York: Atheneum, 1965.

Bayley, David H. "Public Protest and the Political Process in India." *Protest, Reform, and Revolt: A Reader in Social Movements.* Ed. Joseph R. Gusfield. New York: John Wiley and Sons, Inc., 1970.

Beals, Alan R. and Bernard J. Siegel. *Divisiveness of Social Conflict, an Anthropological Approach.* Stanford University Press, 1966.

Becker, Howard, *The Otherside : Perspectives on Deviance.* New York: Free Press, 1967.

—————. *Outsiders,* Glencoe, Illinois: Free Press, 1964.

—————. "Personal Change in Adult Life." *Sociometry.* Vol. 26, No. 1, 1964, pp. 40-53.

Belfrage, Sally. *Freedom Summer.* New York: Viking, 1965.

Bell, Daniel. "America as a Mass Society: A Critique," *The End of Ideology.* New York: Free Press, 1966.

—————. *The End of Ideology.* Revised edition. New York: Free Press, 1966.

Bell, David J. *Resistance and Revolution.* Boston: Houghton Mifflin Company, 1973.

Bell, Inge Powell. *Core and the Strategy of Nonviolence.* New York: Random House, 1968.

Bendix, R. "Reflections on Charismatic Leadership." *Asian Survey,* 7 (1967), 341-352.

Bernard, J. "Some Current Conceptualizations in the Field of Conflict." *American Journal of Sociology,* 70 (1965), 442-54.

Beteille, Andre. "Elites, Status Groups and Caste in Modern India." In Philip Mason: *India and Ceylon: Unity and Diversity.* Bombay: Oxford University Press, 1967.

—————. "The Future of the Backward Classes: The Competing Demands of Status and Power." *India and Ceylon: Unity and Diversity.* Philip Mason. Bombay: Oxford University Press, 1967.

Bhagavat Gita, The. Trans. Franklin Edgerton. Cambridge Mass.: Harvard University Press, 1952.

Blumer, Herbert. "Collective Behavior." *Principles of Sociology.* Ed. Alfred M. Lee. New York: Barnes and Noble, 1951.

Bibliography

Bondurant, Joan. *Conquest of Violence.* Revised edition. Berkeley: University of California, 1958.

————. *Conflict: Violence and Nonviolence.* New York: Atherton, 1971.

Bose, N.K. "Change in Tribal Cultures Before and After Independence." *Man in India.* XLIV, No. 1, 1964.

Bose, S.C. *The Indian Struggle 1920-34,* Calcutta: Thacker, Spink and Company, 1948.

Briggs, George Weston. *The Power of Nonviolence in India.* Madison, New Jersey, 1953.

Brim, Orville G. and Stanton Wheeler. *Socialization after Childhood: Two Essays.* New York: John Wiley and Sons, Inc., 1966.

Brissett, Dennis. "Collective Behavior: The Sense of a Rubric." *American Journal of Sociology,* 74 (July), 70-78.

Buhler, George. *The Laws of Manu.* Oxford: Clarendon Press, 1886.

Burkhart, James A. and Frank J. Kendrick. ed. *The New Politics: Mood or Movement.* New York: Prentice Hall, 1971.

Carpenter, William. "Reconstruction of Indian Polity: Defense of J.P." *Economic Weekly,* February 4, 1961.

Carstair, G. Morris. *The Twice Born: A Study of a Community of High Caste Hindus.* London: Hogarth Press, 1957.

Case, Clarence Marsh. *Nonviolent Coercion, A Study in Methods of Social Pressure.* New York and London: The Century Company, 1923.

Catlin, G. *Systematic Politics.* Toronto: University of Toronto Press. 1965.

Cenker, W. "Gandhi and Creative Conflict." *Thought,* 45 (1970), 421-432.

Choudhari, Nirad C. *The Autobiography of an Unknown Indian.* New York: The McMillan Company, 1951.

Coles, R. "Serpents and Doves: Nonviolent Youth in the South." *Youth: Change and Challenge.* Ed. E. Erikson. New York: Basic Books, 1963.

Coser, Lewis. *The Functions of Social Conflict.* Glencoe, Illinois: Free Press, 1964.

————. "Social Conflict and the Theory of Social Change." *British Journal of Sociology,* 8 (September, 1957), 197-220.

——————. "The Termination of Conflict." *Journal of Conflict Resolution.* (December, 1961).

Couch, Carl J. and John S. Murray. "Significant Others and Evaluation." *Sociometry,* 21, No. 4, p. 502-509.

Currie, Elliot and Jerome Skolnick. "A Critical Note of Conceptions of Collective Behavior." *Annals,* (September), 34-45.

Dahrendarf, Ralf. *Class and Class Conflict in Industrial Society.* Stanford: Stanford University Press, 1959.

——————. "Out of Utopia." *American Journal of Sociology,* 64 (1958), 115-127.

De Grazia, Sebastian. *The Political Community: A Study of Anomie.* Chicago: University of Chicago Press, 1948.

de Reuck, Anthony, Ed. *Conflict in Society.* Boston: Little Brown and Company, 1966.

Desai, A. R. *Social Background of the Indian Nationalism.* Bombay: Popular, 1959.

——————. *Social Background of the National Movement* Bombay: Popular, 1954.

Desai, Ishverlal. *Satyagraha, Democracy, and Gramdan.* Surat: V.M. Dalal, 1959.

Desai, Mahadev. *The Story of Bardoli,* Ahmedabad: Navajivan Press, 1957.

Dhawan, G.N. *The Political Philosophy of Mahatma Gandhi.* Ahmedabad: Navajivan, 1957.

Diwakar, R.R. *Satyagraha—Its Technique and Theory.* Bombay: Hind Kitabs, 1946.

Dollard, John. *Caste and Class in a Southern Town.* New York: Harper, 1949.

Dow, T.E. "Theory of Charisma." *Sociol. Qly,* 10 (1969), 306-318.

Driver, P.N. *Survey of Grasslands in Pardi Taluka.* Government of Bombay Agricultural Department, 1956.

Dube, S.C. *Indian Village.* London: Routledge, 1955.

Dubois, Rachel Davis and Mew-Soong Li. *Reducing Social Tension and Conflict.* New York: Association Press, 1971.

Durkheim, Emile. *The Elementary Forms of the Religious Life.* Glencoe, Illinois: Free Press, 1947.

Dyer, William G. *The Sensitive Manipulator.* Provo, Utah: Brigham Young University Press, 1972.

Ebert, Theodore. "Nonviolence: Doctrine or Technique." *Gandhi Marg*, II, No. 3, (July 1967), pp. 251-260.

Eckstein, Harry, ed. *Internal War*. New York: Free Press, 1964.

Erikson, Erik. *Gandhi's Truth*. New York: W.W. Norton and Company, Inc., 1969.

————. Identity and the Life Cycle. Monograph 1, *Psychological Issues*, 1 (1959), 1-171.

————. "On the Nature of Psycho-Historical Evidence in Search of Gandhi.". *Daedlus*, 97, No. 3, (Summer, 1968), pp. 695-730.

————. "Problem of Identity, Hatred and Nonviolence." In Paul Hare and Herbert Blumberg, *Nonviolent Direct Action*. Washington, D. C.: Corpus Books, 1968.

————. *Young Man Luther*. New York: Norton, 1958.

Etzioni, A. *A Comparative Analysis of Complex Organizations: On Power, Involvement and their Correlates*. New York: Free Press, 1961.

Fanon, Franz. *The Wretched of the Earth*. New York: Grove Press, 1968.

Feldman, Arnold S. "Violence and Volatility: the Likelihood of Revolution." *Internal War*. Ed. H. Eckstein. New York: Free Press, 1964.

Feures-Haimendorf, Christoph Von. "The Position of Tribal Population in India." *Unity and Diversity: India and Ceylon*. Ed. Philip Mason. Bombay: Oxford University Press, 1967, pp. 182-222.

Finn, James. *Protest: Pacifism and Politics: Some Passionate Views on War and Nonviolence*. New York: Random House, 1968.

Fischer, L. *The Life of Mahatma Gandhi*. New York: Harpers, 1950.

Foster, Arnold. "Violence on the Fanatical Left and Right." *Annals*, 364 (October 1966), 141-147.

Frank, Jerome D. and E.H. Nash. "Commitment to Peace Work I: A Preliminary Study of Determinants and Sustainers of Behavior Change." *American Journal of Orthopsychiatry*, 37 (1967), 112-119.

Frank, Jerome D. and Jacob Schoenfield. "Commitment to Peace Work II: A Closer Look at Determinants." *American*

Journal of Orthopsychiatry, 37, No. 1, (1967), pp. 112-119.

Frank, Jerome D. *Persuasion and Healing.* Baltimore: Johns Hopkins Press, 1961.

———. *Sanity and Survival, Psychological Aspects of War and Peace.* New York: Random House, 1967.

Friedrich, C.J. "Political Leadership and Charismatic Power." *Journal of Politics,* 23 (1961), 2-24.

Fromm, Erich. *Escape from Freedom.* New York: Holt Rinehart, and Winston, 1941.

———. *The Sane Society.* New York: Rinehart, 1955.

Galtung, Johan. "A Model for Studying Images of Participants in a Conflict, Southville." *Journal of Sociological Issues,* 15 (1959).

———. "Pacificism from a Sociological Point of View." *Journal of Conflict Resolution,* 3 (1959), 67-84.

Gameson, William. *Power and Discontent.* Homewood, Illinois: The Dorsey Press, 1968.

———. "Rancorous Conflict—Community Politics." *American Sociological Review,* 31 (February, 1966), 71-88.

Gandhi M.K. *The Collected Works of Mahatma Gandhi.* Ahmedabad: Ministry of Information and Broadcasting, Government of India, 1958.

———. *Constructive Programme.* Ahmedabad: Navajivan, 1941.

———. *Hindu Dharma.* Ahmedabad: Navajivan, 1958, p. 93.

———. *From Yerveda Mandir.* Trans. V.G. Desai. Ahmedabad: Navajivan, 1932.

———. *Nonviolence in Peace and War.* 2 vols. Ahmedabad: Navajivan, 1948 and 1949.

———. *Nonviolent Resistance.* New York: Schocken Books, 1968.

———. *Political and National Life and Affairs.* 2 vols. Ahmedabad: Navajivan, 1968.

———. *Satyagraha in South Africa.* Trans. from the Gujerati by Valji Govindvi Desai. Rev. 2nd ed. Ahmedabad: Navajivan, 1950.

———. *The Speeches and Writings of Mahatma Gandhi.* 4th ed. Madras: Natesan, 1934.

―――. *The Story of My Experiments with Truth.* Ahmedabad: Navajivan, 1956.

Gerth, H.H. and C. Wright Mills. *From Max Weber: Essays in Sociology.* New York: Oxford University Press, 1958.

Ghosh, Aurobindo. *The Doctrine of Passive Resistance.* Calcutta: Arya Publishing House, 1968.

Ghurye, G.S. *The Aborigines—'So-Called'—and Their Future.* Poona: Gokhale Institute of Politics and Economics. 2nd ed., 1943.

―――. "The Backward Classes." *The Economic Weekly,* October 29, November 4 and 18, 1961, 1665-8, 1695-1706, 1729-38.

―――. *The Scheduled Tribes.* Bombay: Popular Press, 1963.

Gittler, J.B. "Collective Behavior." *Review of Sociology: Analysis of a Decade.* New York: John Wiley and Sons, 1957.

Gordon, L.A. *Bengal's Gandhi: A Study in Modern Indian Regionalism, Politics and Thought in Bengal Regional Identity.* Ed. David Kopf. East Lansing, Michigan: Asian Studies Center, Michigan State University, January, 1969.

Gouldner, A.W. "Organization Analysis." *Sociology Today: Problems and Prospects.* Eds., R.K. Merton, L. Broom, and S. Cottrell. New York: Basic Books, 1959.

―――. *Patterns of Industrial Bureaucracy.* London: Routledge and Kegan Paul, 1955.

Gregg, Richard. *Power of Nonviolence.* New York: Schocken Books, 1966.

Guha, B.S. "Indian Aborigines and Who They Are." *The Adivasis.* Delhi: Government of India, 1955.

Gurr, Ted. *Why Men Rebel.* Princeton: Princeton University Press, 1970.

Gurr, Ted. "Psychological Factors in Civil Violence." *World Politics,* 20 (1967-1968), 245-278.

Gusfield, Joseph R. "Mass Society and Extreme Politics." *American Sociological Review,* 27 (1962), 19-30.

―――. *Protest, Reform and Revolt: A Reader in Social Movements.* New York: John Wiley and Sons, 1970.

Haimendorf, Christoph Von Fueres. "The Position of Tribal Population in India." *Unity and Diversity: India and Ceylon.* Ed. Philip Mason. Oxford University Press, 1967, pp. 182-222.

Hammond, K.R. "New Directions in Research on Conflict Resolution." *Journal of Social Issues,* 21 (1965), 44-66.

Hare, Paul and Herbert Blumberg. *Nonviolent Direct Action, American Cases: Social Psychological Analyses.* Washington, D.C. : Corpus Books, 1968.

Harijan. Ahmedabad, India, 1933-1948.

Heberle, Rudolf. *Social Movements: An Introduction to Political Sociology.* New York: Appleton-Century Crofts, 1951.

Hoedemaker, Edward. "Distrust and Aggression: an Interpersonal International Analogy." *Journal of Conflict Resolution,* 12 (1968), 69-81.

Hoffer, Eric. *Temper of Our Time.* New York: Harper and Row, 1967.

————. *True Believers.* New York: Harper and Brothers 1951.

Horsburgh, H.J.N. *Nonviolence and Aggression: A Study of Gandhi's Moral Equivalent of War.* London: Oxford University Press, 1968.

Husain, Abid. *The Way of Gandhi and Nehru.* London: Asia Publishing House, 1959.

Hyman, Herbert. "Reflections of Reference Groups." *Public Opinion Quarterly,* 24 (1960), 383-396.

Isaacs, H. *India's Exuntouchables.* New York: John Day, 1964.

Iyer, Raghavan. *The Moral and Political Thought of Mahatma Gandhi.* New York: Oxford University Press, 1973.

————. "On Gandhi." *Civil Disobedience.* H.A. Freeman, R. Rustin, R. Lichtman, et. al. New Youk: Fund for the Republic, 1966.

Jain, R.C. *The Great Revolution.* Sri Ganganagar: Institute of Bharatalogical Research, 1967.

Janis and Katz. "The Reduction of Conflict in Intergroup Hostility." *Journal of Conflict Resolution,* III, No. 1, 1959.

Kadt, Emanuel. "Conflict and Power in Society." *International Social Science Journal,* 17 (1965), 454-471.

Kahn, Richardsan Herman. *On Escalation: Metaphores and Scenarios.* New York: Praeger, 1965.

Kaplan, Norman. *Reference Groups Theory and Voting Behavior.* Ann Arbor: Microfilm, Ph. D. Thesis, Columbia.

Kelley, B.H. "Two Functions of Reference Groups." *Readings in Social Psychology*. By. G.E. Swanson and T.M. Newcomb and E.L. Hartley. New York: Holt, 1952.

Kemper, Theodore D. "Reference Groups, Socialization and Achievement." *American Sociological Review*, 33, No. 1, (1968).

Kerdiner, Abraham and Lionel Ovesey: *The Mark of Oppression: A Psycho Social Study of American Negro*. New York: Norton, 1951.

Kierkegaard, Sorel. *Christian Discourses*. London: Oxford University Press, 1961.

Killian, Lewis. "Leadership in the Segregation Crisis: An Institutional Analysis." *Intergroup Relations and Leadership*. Ed. Muzafer Sherif. New York, 1962.

Killian; L. and Charles Gregg. *Racial Crisis in America: Leadership in Conflict*. Engelwood, New Jersey, 1964.

King, Martin Luther. *Why We Can't Wait*. New York: Signet Books, 1964.

King, Martin Luther. *Stride Toward Freedom*. New York: Ballantine Books, 1958.

Kluckhohn, Clyde, et. al. "Values and Value-Orientations in the Theory of Action, as Exploration in Definition and Classification." In Talcott Parsons and Edward Shils, *Toward A General Theory of Action*. Cambridge, Mass.: Harvard University Press, 1951.

Kornhauser, William. *The Politics of Mass Society*. Glencoe; Illinois: The Free Press, 1961.

Kothari, Rajni, *Caste in Indian Politics*. New Delhi: Orient Longman's, 1970.

Krech, D. and Crutchfield. *Theory and Problems of Social Psychology*. New York: McGraw Hill, 1948.

Kuhn, Manford H. "The Reference Group Reconsidered." *Symbolic Interaction*. Eds. Jerome G. Manis and Bernard N. Meltezer. Boston: Allyn and Bacon, 1967, 171-184.

Kuper, Leo. *Passive Resistance in South Africa*. New Haven: Yale University Press, 1957.

————. *Race Relations*. Boston: Houghton Mifflin and Company, 1951.

Lakey, George. "The Sociological Mechanisms of Nonviolent Action." *Research Review*, 2, No. 6 (1968).

———. *Strategy for a Living Revolution.* San Francisco: W.H. Freeman, 1973.

Lane, James H. "The Movement: Negro Challenge to the Myth." *New South,* 18 (1963), 9-17.

Lasswell, H. "Conflict and Leadership: The Process of Decision and the Nature of Authority." *Conflict in Society.* Ed. Anthony de Reuck. Boston: Little Brown and Company, 1966.

Leadership and Groups in a South Indian Village. Government of India, 9th pub., June 1955.

Lenski, G. "Status Crystallization: A Nonvertical Dimension of Social Status." *American Sociological Review,* 19, August (1954), 405-413.

Levine, Robert. "Political Socialization and Cultural Change." *Old Societies and New State.* Glencoe, Illinois: Free Press, 1963.

Levy, Hyman, *The Universe of Science.* 2nd ed., rev. London: Watts and Company, 1967.

Lorenz, K. *On Aggression.* New York: Harcourt, Brace and World, 1966.

Mabee, C. "Will Commitment to Nonviolence Last?" *Liberation.* April 1963, p. 15.

Macaulay, T.B. "Warren Hastings." *Critical and Historical Essays.* Boston, 1900.

Mahabharata, The. Trans. M.N. Dutta. Calcutta: R.M. Sircar, 1902.

Mahadevan, T.K. "A Search for Meaning: an Indian Approach to the Negro Revolution." *Gandhi Marg,* 42 (1962), 128-132.

Maier, N.R. *Frustration, the Study of Behavior Without a Goal.* New York: McGraw-Hill, 1949.

Mandelbaum, David G. *Society in India: Change and Continuity.* Berkeley: University of California Press, 1970.

Mannheim, Karl. *Ideology and Utopia an Introduction to Sociology of Knowledge.* London: Routledge and Kegan Paul, 1952.

———. *Man and Society in an Age of Reconstruction; Studies in Modern Social Structure.* New York: Harcourt, Brace and Company, 1940.

Marriott, McKim. *Village India*. Chicago: University of Chicago Press, 1955.

Mashruwala, K.M. *Practical Nonviolence*. Ahmedabad: Navajivan Press, 1941.

McNeil, Elton B. "Violence and Human Development." *Annals*, 364 (October, 1966).

Mason, Philip. *India And Ceylon: Unity and Diversity*. Bombay: Oxford University Press, 1967.

Masotti, Lovis H. and Don R. Bowen, ed. *Riots and Rebellion*. Beverly Hills, California: Sage Publications, 1968.

Mead, Margaret. "Bio-Social Components of Political Processes." *Journal of International Affairs*, 24, No. 1 (1970), pp. 18-28.

―――――. *Collective Guilt*. International Conference On Medical Psychotherapy, August 1968.

Menon, V.P. *The Story of the Integration of Indian States*. New York: Arm Press, 1956.

Merton, Robert K., ed., *Contemporary Social Problems*. New York: Harcourt and World, 1966.

―――――. *Social Theory and Social Structure*. Glencoe, Illinois: Free Press, 1958.

Merton, R.K. and Alice Rossi, ed. "Contributions to the Theory of Reference Group Behavior" and "Continuities in the Theory of Reference Groups and Social Structure." *Social Theory and Social Structure*. Glencoe: Free Press, 1950, 40-105.

Merton, Robert, and Marjorie Fiske and Patricia Kendall. *The Focused Interview: A Manual of Problems and Procedures*. Glencoe, Illinois: Free Press, 1956.

Merton, Thomas. *Gandhi on Nonviolence*. New York: New Directions Paperback, 1965.

―――――. "The Meaning of Satyagraha." *Gandhi Marg*, V, 10 (1966), 108-116.

Meyer, P. "Aftermath of Martyrdom: Negro Militancy and Martin Luther King." *Public Opinion Quarterly*, 33 (1969), 160-173.

Miller, William. *Nonviolence: A Christian Interpretation*. New York: Association Press, 1964.

Mitscherlich, Alexander. *Society Without the Father*. New York: Harcourt, Brace and World, 1969.

Morris, Desmond. *Naked Ape.* New York: McGraw-Hill, 1968.

Morris-Jones, W.H. "India's Political Idioms," *Politics and Society in India.* Ed. C.H. Philips. London: Allen and Unwin, 1963.

——————. "The Unhappy Utopia, J.P. Wonderland." *Economic Weekly,* June 25, 1960.

Murphy, Gardner. *In the Minds of Men; the Study of Human Behavior and Social Tensions in India.* New York: Basic Books, 1953.

Murti, Satchidananda and A.C. Bouquet. *Studies in the Problems of Peace.* Bombay: Asia Publishing House, 1960.

Murti, V.V. Raman. "Gandhian Concepts of Social and Political Change." *Interdiscipline,* 7, No. 1 (1970), pp. 78-88.

Myrdal, Gunner. *An American Dilemma.* New York: Harper, 1944.

Naess, Arne. *Gandhi and Nuclear Age.* Engelwood, New Jersey, 1965.

——————. *Gandhi and Group Conflict.* Universitetsforlaget. 1974.

——————. "Systematization of Gandhian Ethics of Conflict Resolution." *Journal of Conflict Resolution,* 2 (1958)

Nakhre, Amrut W. "Religion and Charisma in Nonviolent Action." *Gandhi Marg.* Vol. 1. No. 9 (1979), pp. 559-574.

——————. "Meanings of Nonviolence, A Study of Satyagrahi Attitudes." *Journal of Peace Research.* 13, No. 3 (1976)

Nagpal, O.P. and Nakhre, Amrut W. *Selected Political Thinkers.* Allahabad: Kitab Mahal, 1972.

Nanda, B.R. *Mahatma Gandhi.* London: Allen and Unwin, 1958.

——————. *The Nehrus: Motilal and Jawaharlal.* New York: John Day Co., 1962.

Nandy, Ashish. "The Culture of Indian Polity." *The Journal of Asian Studies,* 30, No. 1 (November 1970), pp. 57-79.

Narayan, Jay Prakash. "Reconstruction of Indian Polity." Ed. Bimla Prasad. *Socialism, Sarvodaya, and Democracy.* London, 1964.

Nehru, Jawaharlal. *Discovery of India.* New York: John Day, 1956.

―――――. *Mahatma Gandhi.* New York: Asia Publishing House, 1966.
Newfield, Jack. "SOS: From Port Huron to La Chinoise." *Evergreen*, (1969), 59.
Niehburg, H.L. *Political Violence.* New York: St. Martin's Press, 1969.
Nisbet, Robert. *Quest for Community.* New York: Oxford University Press, 1953.
Oomen, T.K. "Charisma, Social Structure and Social Change." *Comp. Stud. Soc. and Hist.*, 10 (1967), 85-99.
―――――. "Political Leadership in India: Image and Reality." *Asian Survey*, 9 (1969), 515-521.
Oppenheimer, Martin and George Lakey. *A Manual for Direct Action.* Chicago: Quadrangle Paperbacks, 1965.
Ostergaard, G. and M. Currell. *The Gentle Anarchists.* London: Oxford University Press, 1971.
Page, Kirby. *Is Mahatma Gandhi the Greatest Man of the Age?* New York: Harcourt, Brace and Company, 1930.
Panikkar, K.M. *Indian States.* London: Oxford University Press, 1944.
Panter-Brick, Simone. *Gandhi Against Machiavellism; Nonviolence in Politics.* Bombay: Asia Publishing House, 1966.
Pardi Development Committee. Gujerat Bhoomidan Samiti, Vedchi, 1955.
Parel, Anthony. "Symbolism in Gandhian Politics." *Canadian Journal of Political Science*, 2, No. 4 (1969), pp. 513-517.
Parikh, N.D. *Sardar Vallabh Bhai Patel.* 2 vols. Ahmedabad: Navajivan, 1952.
Park, Richard and I. Tinker, Ed. *Seminar on Leadership and Political Institutions in India.* Princeton, New Jersey: Princeton University Press, 1959.
Parrinder, Geoffrey. *Upnishads, Gita and Bible.* New York: Harper Torch Books, 1972.
Parsons, Talcott. *Structure and Process in Modern Societies.* Glencoe, Illinois: Free Press, 1960.
―――――. *The Structure of Social Action.* Glencoe, Illinois: Free Press, 1968.
Parsons, T. and Robert F. Bales. *Family, Socialization and Interaction Process.* Glencoe, Illinois: Free Press, 1960.

Pear, Tom H. *The Moulding of Modern Man: A Psychologist's View of Information, Persuasion and Mental Coercion Today.* London: Allen and Unwin, 1961.

——————. *Psychological Factors of Peace and War.* London: Hutchinson, 1950.

Pelton, Leroy H. *The Psychology of Nonviolence.* Pergamon Press Inc. 1974.

Perloe Sidney; David Olton and David Yaffe. "Attitudes and Nonviolent Action." *Hare and Blumberg: Nonviolent Direct Action.* Corpus Books, 1968, pp. 407-447.

Pierce, Chester M. and Louis Jolyon West. "Six Years of Sit-ins: Psychodynamic Causes and Effects." *International Journal of Social Psychiatry,* 12, No. 1 (1966), 29-34.

Policy Statement Regarding Grasslands at Pardi. (In Gujerati), 1964.

Prabhu, R.K. and U.R. Rao. *The Mind of Mahatma Gandhi.* Ahmedabad: Navajivan, 1967.

Prasad, Rajendra. *At the Feet of Mahatma Gandhi.* Bombay: Hind Kitabs, Ltd., 1955.

——————. *Satyagraha in Champaran Mahatma*: Ahmedabad: Navajivan, 1949.

Proudfoot, Merrill. *Diary of a Sit-in.* Chapel Hill, North Carolina: University of North Carolina Press, 1962.

Pyarelal. *Gandhian Techniques in the Modern World.* Ahmedabad: Navajivan, 1953.

——————. *Mahatma Gandhi: The Early Phase.* Ahmedabad: Navajivan, 1965.

——————. *Mahatma Gandhi, the Last Phase.* 2 vols. Ahmedabad: Navajivan, 1958.

Radhakrishnan, S. *Religion and Society.* London: George Allen and Unwin, Ltd., 1947.

Rajgopalachari. *Hinduism, Doctrine and Way of Life.* Bombay: Bhartiya Vidya Bhavan, 1964.

Ramchandran, G. and T.K. Mahadevan, ed. *Nonviolence After Gandhi: A Study of King.* Delhi: Gandhi Peace Foundation, 1968.

Rastogi, G.D. *Psychological Approaches to Gandhi's Leadership.* Delhi: U.B.S. Publishers, 1969.

Ratnam, K.J. "Charisma and Political Leadership." *Political Studies,* 12 (1964), 341-345.

Ray, Sibnarayan, ed. *Gandhi and the World: An International Symposium*. Melbourne: Hawthorne Press, 1970.

Rajamey, Pie. "The Mystique of Nonviolent Action." *Thought*, 41, pp. 381-389.

Retzlaff, Ralph. *Village Government in India: A Case Study*. Bombay: Asia Publishing, 1962.

Rex, J. *Key Problems of Sociological Theory*. London: Routledge, 1961.

Robin, Jenkin. "Who Are These Marchers?" *Journal of Peace Research*, No. 1 (1967), pp. 46-60.

Roethlisberger, F.J. and W.L. Dickinson. *Management and the Worker*. Boston: Harvard University Press, 1939.

Rolland, Romain. *Mahatma Gandhi*. London: Allen and Unwin, 1924.

Rosen, B.C. "Conflicting Group Membership: A Study of Parent Peer Group Crosspressures." *American Sociological Review*, 20 (1955), 155-161.

Rothermund, Indira. *The Philosophy of Restraint*. Bombay: Popular Publishing House, 1963.

Roy, M.N. *Psychoanalysis of Gandhism: Problem of Freedom*. Calcutta:Renaissance Publishers, 1945.

Rudolph, Lloyd I. and Susanne Hoeber Rudolph. *The Modernity of Tradition, Political Development in India*. Chicago and London: The University of Chicago Press, 1967.

—————. "Political Role of India's Caste Associations." *Pacific Affairs* 33 (1960),1-22.

Rudolph, Susanne H. "The New Courage: An Essay on Gandhi's Psychology" *World Politics*, 16 No. 1 (October 1963), pp. 98-117.

Rustow, Dunkwart A. *Philosophers and Kings: Studies in Leadership*. New Yotk; George Braziller, 1970.

Samartha, S.J "Is Nonviolence Out of Date?" *Religion in Life*, 39 (1970), 393-395.

Santhanam, K. *Satyagraha and the State*. London: Asia Publishing House, 1961.

Scheter, Betty. *The Peaceable Revolution*. Boston: Houghton Mifflin Company, 1963.

Schelling, T.C. *The Strategy of Conflict*. New York: Oxford University Press, 1963.

Searing, D.D. "Models and Images of Man in Society in Leadership Theory." *Journal of Politics,* 31 (1969), 3-31.

Sellers, James E. "Love Justice, and Nonviolence." *Theol. Life* 18 (1962), 422-433.

Selznick, Philip. *The Organization Weapon.* New York, McGraw Hill, 1952.

Seshachari, C. *Gandhi and the American Scene,* Bombay: Nachiketa Publications, Ltd., 1969.

Seth, Hiral Lal. *The Iron Dictator.* New Delhi: Hero Publications, 1943.

Sharp, Gene. *Exploring Nonviolent Alternatives.* Boston: Porter Sargent Publication. 1970.

————. "Gandhi as a National Defense Strategist." *Gandhi Marg,* 14 No. 3 (1970), pp. 254-273.

————. *Gandhi as a Political Strategist, with Essays on Ethics and Politics.* Porter Sargent Publications Inc. 1979.

Sharp, Gene. "The Need of A Functional Substitute for War." *International Relations,* 3, No. 3 (1967). pp. 187-207.

————. *The Politics of Nonviolent Action.* Boston: Porter Sargent Publisher. 1973.

Shastri, Chandrashekhar, *Rashtra Nirmata Sardar Patel.* New Delhi: Society for Parliamentary Studies, 1963.

Shelitz, Claire, Maries Jahoda, Morton Deutsch and Stuart Cook. *Research Methods in Social Relations.* London: Methuen and Company, Ltd., 1962.

Sherif, M. "Conformity-deviations. Norms and Group Relation." *Conformity and Deviation.* Eds. G. Berg and B.M. Bass. New York: Harper, Row, 1961.

Sherif, M., and Carolyn Sherif. *An Outline of Social Psychology.* New York: Harper, 1956.

————. *Reference Groups: Exploration into Conformity and Deviation of Adolescents.* New York: Harper and Row, 1964.

————. *An Outline of Social Psychology.* New York: Harper and Row, 1969.

Shils, Edward. *The Intellectual Between Tradition and Modernity: The Indian Situation.* The Hague: Mouton, 1961.

————. "The Intellectuals and the Powers" *Comp. Stud. in Society and Hist.* 1958-59 pp.5-22

Shridharani, K. *War Without Violence.* New York: Harcourt, Brace and Company, 1939.

Shrikant, L.M. "Western and Eastern Deccan Tribes." *Tribal Situation in India.* Ed. Suresh K. Singh. Simla: Indian Institute of Advanced Study, 1972.

Sibley, Mulford, *The Quiet Battle.* Boston: Beacon Press, 1969.

Singh, Suresh K. ed. *Tribal Situation in India.* Simla: Indian Institute of Advanced Studies, 1972.

Sinha, Surjit. "State Formation and Rajput Myth in Central India." *Man in India.* XLII (January-March, 1962).

Sjoberg, Gideon. *The Preindustrial City: Past and Present.* New York: Free Press, 1960.

Smelser, Neil J. "Some Additional Thoughts on Collective Behavior." *Social Enquiry,* 42 (Spring), 97-103.

Smelser, Neil J. *Theory of Collective Behavior.* New York: Free Press. 1962.

Smelser, N.J. and James A. Davis. *Sociology, the Progress of a Decade: a Collection of Articles.* Engelwood Cliffs: Prentice-Hall, 1961.

Smith, Donald E. *India as a Secular State.* Princeton: Princeton University Press, 1963.

Solomon, Frederick and Jacob Fishman. "The Psycho-Social Meaning of Nonviolence in Student Civil Rights Activities." *Psychiatry,* 27, No. 2 (May, 1964), pp. 91-94.

Sorokin, P. *The Ways and Power of Love.* Boston: Beacon Press, 1954.

Spear, Percival. *The Nabobs, a Study of the English in 18th Century India.* London: Oxford University Press, 1932.

Spodek, Howard. "On the Origins of Gandhi's Political Methodology: The Heritage of Kathiawar and Gujerat." *Journal of Asian Studies,* 30, No. 2 (1971), pp. 361-372.

Srinivas, M.N. *Cast in Modern India and Other Essays.* Bombay: Asia Publishing House, 1962.

———. *Religion and Society Among the Coorgs of South India.* London: Oxford University Press, 1952.

Stagner, Ross and Hjalmar Rosen. *Psychology of Union-Management Relations.* Belmont, California: Wadsworth, 1965.

Steed, Gitel P. "Notes on an Approach to a Study of Personality Formation in a Hindu village in Gujerat." *Village India.*

Ed. McKim Marriott. Chicago: The University of Chicago Press, 1955.

Steihm, Judith. *Nonviolent Power.* London: D.C. Heath and Company, 1972.

―――. "Nonviolence is Two." *Nonviolent Direct Action American Cases: Social Psychological Analyses.* Eds. Paul Hare and Herbert Blumberg. Washington, D.C.: Corpus Books, 1968, pp. 447-459.

Strachy, John. *India, Its Administration and Progress.* London: Oxford University Press, 1888.

Swarup, S. "Ambivalence of Nonviolence." *Political Quarterly,* 41 (1970), 207-215.

Tagore, R. *Nationalism.* New York: McMillan Company, 1917.

Tagore, R. *Truth Called Them Differently: Tagore-Gandhi Controversy.* Ahmedabad: Navajivan, 1961.

Tandon, P.D. and R.E. Wolsley. *Gandhi, Warrior of Nonviolence.* New Delhi: National Book Trust, 1969.

Taylor, W.S. "Basic Personality in Orthodox Hindu Culture Pattern." *Journal of Abnormal and Social Psychology,* 43 (1948), 3-12.

Templin, Ralph Todd. *Democracy and Nonviolence: The Role of Individual in World Crisis.* Boston: Porter Sargent, 1965.

Tendulkar, D.G. *Mahatma: Life of Mohandas Karamchand Gandhi,* 8 vols. Bombay: V.K. Jhaveri and D.G. Tendulkar, 1951-54.

Tercheck, Ronald J. "Theory Application of Gandhian Tactics in Three Disparate Environments: India, the U.S. and Czechoslovakia." Paper presented at the American Political Science Association Meeting in New York City, 1969.

Thompson, G.D. "Organizational Management of Conflict." *Administration Science Quarterly,* 4 (1960), 389-409.

Tinker, Jerry. "The Political Power of Nonviolent Resistance: the Gandhian Technique." *West. Pol. Qly.,* 24 (1971), 775-788.

Toch, Hans. *The Social Psychology of Social Movements.* Indianapolis: Bobbs-Merrill Company, Inc., 1965.

Tucker, E.H. "Theory of Elites." *Daedlus,* 97 (1968), 695-730.

Unnithan, T.K. *Gandhi and Free India.* Groningen, Netherlands: T.B. Walters, 1956

Unnithan, T.K. and Yogendra Singh. *Sociology of Nonviolence and Peace: Some Behavioral and Attitudinal Dimensions.* New Delhi: Research Council for Cultural Studies, 1969.

Vander, Zanden James W. "The Nonviolent Resistance Movement Against Segregation." *American Journal of Sociology,* 68 (1973), 544-550.

Vekatrangaiya, M. *Gandhiji's Gospel of Satyagraha.* Bombay: Bhartiya Vidya Bhavan, 1966.

Vidyarthi, L.P. "The Historical March of the Jharkhand Party: A Study of Adivasi Leadership in Tribal Bihar." *Indian Sociological Bulletin,* 1, No. 2 (1964).

Vidyarthi, L.P., B.N. Sahay, and B.K. Shrivastava. *Gandhi and Social Sciences.* New Delhi: Bookhive Publishers and Book Sellers. 1972.

Von Eschen, Donald, Jerome Kirk and Pinard Maurice. "The Disintegration of the Negro Nonviolent Movement. *Journal of Peace Research,* No. 3 (1969), pp. 215-234.

Wadkow. Aurthur I, *From Race Riot to Sit-in 1919 and 1960's: A Study in the Connections Between Conflict and Violence.* New York: Doubleday, 1966.

Watson, Francis, and Maurice Brown, ed. *Talking of Gandhiji.* Calcutta: Orient Longmans, 1957.

Weber, Max. *On Charisma and Institution Building.* Chicago, University of Chicago Press, 1968, p. 285.

———. *The Sociology of Religion.* Boston: Beacon Press, 1964.

Weekly Janata, Ahmedabad, India, 1951-54.

Weller, J.M. and E.L. Juarantelli. "Neglected Characteristics of Collective Behavior." *American Journal of Sociology,* p. 682-5.

Weseley, William A. "Escalation of Violence Through Legitimation." *Annals,* 364 (October 1966), 120-126.

West, Morris L. "The Struggle for Identity." *Conflict Resolution and World Education.* Ed. Stuart Mudd. Bloomington: Indiana University Press, 1967.

Williams, Margaret Asterud. "Reference Groups: A Review and Commentary." *Sociol. Qly.,* No. 11 (1970), pp. 545-553.

Wynne-Edwards, V.C. *Animal Dispersion in Relation to Social Behavior*. Edinburgh: Oliver and Boyd. New York: Hafner 1962.

Yinger, Milton J. *Religion in the Struggle for Power: A Study of the Sociology of Religion*. New York: Russel and Company, 1961,

Young India. Ahmedabad. India, 1919-1932.

Young India Selection, 3 vols. Madras: Madras Publishing, 1927-29.

APPENDIX A

Interview Schedule
Rank & File

Respondent No.

1. In how many Satyagrahas have you participated?
2. How did you first become familiar with ahimsa? Check any two.

Through local leaders (name them)	i
Reading (give specific references)	ii
Gandhi's speeches	iii
Through participation in the constructive activities sponsored by the party. (name them)	iv
Any other	v

3A. Did you get any training in nonviolent direct action?

Yes	i
No	ii

3B. If yes to 3A describe how much, when and where you got the training.

4. During the movement, did you consider ahimsa to be (Please explain your reason for the response)

only a political tactic	i
a creed i.e. a way of life	ii
other (specify)	iii

4B. Do you still hold the same opinion (as in 4A)

Yes	i
No	ii
Other (specify)	iii

4C. If no to 4B why and what change.
5. In what ways do you think ahimsa is effective during conflict?

6. During the movement whom does it (i.e. ahimsa) affect most?

   Participants   i
   opponents   ii
   nonparticipants   iii
   other (specify)   iv
   DK   v

7A If a protracted nonviolent action over a particular period of time does not produce the desired result, do you think that the nonviolent participants are bound to turn violent?

   Yes   i
   No   ii

7B (If yes to 7A Explain the conditions for turning violent)
8A Did you, at any time, in connection with the movement use physical violence?

   Yes   i
   No   ii

8B If yes to 8A, describe in detail the incident and its effect on you.
9A Did you have any experiences during the movement where you were afraid that you might not remain nonviolent?

   Yes   i
   No   ii

9B If yes to 9A, describe the incident and say what prevented you from getting violent.
10. Which two of the following best describe your feelings regarding why you participated in this satyagraha?

    Faith in the efficacy of nonviolence   i
    Faith in local leadership (Name them)   ii
    Faith in your religious principles   iii
    Faith because of Gandhi's support and
    blessings   iv

11. What did you think about your local leaders, whether nonviolence for them was

    Only a tactic   i
    a creed   ii
    Other (specify)   iii
    DK   iv

Appendix

12. Knowing that your movement succeeded in its objective, did you think that the opponent was

Coerced i.e. forced into submission	i
Persuaded	ii
Converted	iii
Other (specify)	iv
DK	v

13. From your experience of participation which of the following do you think is more effective for nonviolent action?

Mass participation with a loose discipline	i
Small group with a tight discipline	ii
Both (Explain why)	iii
Other (specify)	iv
DK	v

PERSPECTIVES ABOUT GOALS

14A. When satyagraha started, did you think the nonviolent way was going to work?

Yes	i
No	ii
Other	iii
DK	iv

14B. How did you first become aware of the goals for which the movement was started?

Through leaders' speeches (Name them)	i
Personal contacts	ii
Reading	iii
Other (specify)	iv
DK	v

15. At what stage did you join the movement?

From the beginning (year)	i
Midway (year)	ii
Toward the end (year)	iii
DK	iv

16. When did you become acutely aware of the goals for which Satyagraha was being offered?

From the beginning	i
Midway	ii
Toward the end	iii
DK	iv

17. When you decided to join the movement, what benefits would, you thought, accrue if it succeeded? (Watch for ideological Vs. bread and butter orientation. Also other changes that might be brought about in terms of welfare, cultural standards, etc.)
18. How did your father react when you decided to join the movement?

    Liked   i
    Disliked   ii
    Indifferent iii
    DK   iv

19. How did your mother react when you decided to join the movement?

    Liked   i
    Disliked   ii
    Indifferent iii
    DK   iv

20. How many hours a week did you spend in the movement activities including meetings, action projects, etc.?
21. How does this compare with other organizations that you spent your time in?
22. How many times did you participate in demonstrations, picketing and other nonviolent projects during this movement?
23A Were you given any special assignments in connection with the movement such as recruiting volunteers, leading a particular group, etc.?

    Yes i
    No   ii

23B If yes to 23A specify. Also describe whatever significant problems you had in your assignment and how you tackled them.
24A (Preface the question with the comment that although communalism and casteism, not in accordance with the principles of Satyagraha, some Satyagrahis have complained about them).
    Did you notice any casteism, communalism among the participants in any form?

	casteism	communalism
Yes	i	i
No	ii	ii

24B If yes to 24A specify

CONSTRUCTIVE ACTIVITIES

25. Could you please tell me which political party led this movement?

    Congress   i
    P S P   ii
    P M   iii
    Other   iv
    DK   v

26. Apart from sponsoring the Satyagraha what other contributions readily come to your mind that the party made to your community?   (Record all)
27A Are you aware if there were any constructive activities carried on by the party before or during the movement?

    Yes   i
    No   ii

27B If yes to 27A specify what activities.
27C If yes to 27A also say whether those activities influenced you to join the Satyagraha?

    Yes   i
    No   ii

28A Did you or your family personally benefit from the constructive activities of the party?

    Yes   i
    No   ii

28B If yes to 28A describe in what way.
28C What do you think is the relationship between nonviolence and constructive activity?

IMPORTANT EXPERIENCES

29A Were you offered any monetary gratification in return for participation in this movement?

    Yes   i
    No   ii

29B If yes to 29A describe what kind, when, how, etc.
30. In retrospect, as you think of the satyagraha which incident or incidents come to your mind most? (Give a brief description of the event)

31. Did the following participate in the movement?

	Yes	No
Your parents	i	ii
Other relatives	i	ii
Your teachers	i	ii
Your friends	i	ii

32A Did you sustain any economic loss as a result of participation in the movement?

Yes i
No ii

32B If yes to 32A specify what kind of loss.
32C If yes to 32A did you regain what you lost after the conclusion of the movement?

Yes i
No ii

33. How many times in all have you been to jail in connection with Satyagraha movements?
34A Have you been to jail in connection with this movement?
34B If yes to 34A how many times?
34C If yes to 34A how much time did you spend in jail?
34D If yes to 34A how did it affect your involvement in the movement?

Deepened your involvement i
Reduced your involvement ii
No change in the involvement iii
Other iv
DK v

35. How did the following react to your going to jail?

	Esteem went up	Went down	Indifferent	DK
Parents	i	ii	iii	iv
Relatives	i	ii	iii	iv
Teachers	i	ii	iii	iv
Friends	i	ii	iii	iv

36A In connection with the movement did you have any experiences with insults or physical violence?

Yes i
No ii

Appendix

36B If yes to 36A did it

    deepen your involvement in the movement   i
    Reduce "   " " "   ii
    No Change   iii
    DK   iv

ACTIVE PARTICIPATION IN PARTY ACTIVITIES

37. Formal Membership of Organizations: name them

Before you joined the movement	During the movement	Present Membership

(List all organizations political; religious; professional; caste, etc.) (Ask the reasons for all switch overs from one political party to another, if any)
If not a member of the party, skip to 41A

38A Did you hold any offices in your party during the movement?

    Yes   i
    No   ii

38B If yes to 38A give details of offices held and the kind of work that you had to do, etc.
39. How often did you interact with the members of party outside of formal party activity?

    Very often   i
    Often   ii
    Not too often   iii
    Not at all   iv
    DK   v

40. How much did you think party was important to you as compared to other organizations?

    Very important   i
    Important   ii
    Not so important   iii
    Not important   iv
    DK   v

PERSONAL DATA

(We are almost at the end of our interview. Before we close I would like to get some personal data about you. It will take only a few minutes)

41A May I ask how old were you at the time of participation in the movement and your present age?

Age at the time of participation   years

41B Present Age   years
42. Religion:

Hindu	i
Sikh	ii
Muslim	iii
Christian	iv
Parsi	v
Jain	vi
Other (specify)	vii

43. Your Caste Status

| High | i |
| Low | ii |

44. Caste

Brahmin	i
Kshatriya	ii
Vaishya	iii
Shudra	iv

45. Marital Status at the time of participation.

Single	i
Married	ii
Widowed	iii
Divorced or separated	iv

46A Education level at the time of participation.

| Literate | i |
| Illiterate | ii |

46B If literate ask level of education.
(continued)

Appendix

	During participation	Now
Literate but no formal education	i	i
Primary	ii	ii
Middle	iii	iii
Matric	iv	iv
Above matric	v	v

47. Are you

    Vegetarian   i
    Non Vegetarian   ii

48. Do you drink wine or liquor:

    Yes   i
    No   ii

49. Your Occupation

	At the time of participation	Now
Main		
Subsidiary		

50. Your annual Income

Annual income	at the time of partipation	Now
From main occupation		
From subsidiary occupation		

51. Your Father's Occupation

Occupation	At participation time	Now
Main		
Subsidiary		

52. Father's Annual Income

Annual income	At participation time	Now
From main occupation		
From subsidiary occupation		

53. Now before we close, would you like to say anything else which you consider important with regard to your participation, that I might have left out? (Note down in detail)

(Well, I am very grateful to you for having given so much of your time. It was a very fruitful interview. You have given a wealth of information which will be of immense use for this research.)
(Beyond this point fill in yourself)

54. Sex:
    Male   i
    Female   ii

55. Was the respondent wearing Khadi?

    Yes   i
    No   ii

56. When interviewed?

    Morning   i
    Afternon   ii
    Evening   iii

57. Where interviewed?

    Home   i
    Street   ii
    Office/Work   iii
    Other   iv

58. Except the personal data part would you like the rest of the interview also to be confidential?

    Yes   i
    No   ii

59. Remarks by the interviewers
    I here by attest that this is an interview strictly in accordance with your directions.

                    Signed_____
                    Date_____

APPENDIX B

Leader Interview

No.
1. Sex?
2. Age?
3. Education?
4. Religion?
5. Caste Status?
6. Marital Status at the time of the satyagraha?
7. Occupation at the time of the satyagraha?
8. Present occupation?
9. Annual income at the time of the satyagraha?
10. Father's occupation during satyagraha?
11. Father's annual income at the time of the satyagraha?

COGNITION AND PERCEPTION OF NONVIOLENCE

12. In how many satyagrahas have you participated?
13. How did you first become familiar with nonviolence?
14. Did you get any training in nonviolent direct action?
15. During the movement, did you consider ahimsa to be a tactic or a creed? Please explain.
16. In what ways do you think ahimsa is effective during conflict?
17. During the movement whom does it (i.e., ahimsa) affect the most, participant, opponents, nonparticipants or others? Please explain.
18. If a protracted nonviolent action over a particular period of time does not produce the desired result, do you think that the nonviolent participants are bound to turn violent? Please explain the conditions for turning violent.
19. Did you, at any time, in connection with the movement use physical violence? Please describe.
20. Did you have any experiences during the movement where you were afraid that you might not remain nonviolent?
21. Please explain the circumstances and what you did.

22. What did you think about the other leaders, whether nonviolence for them was a creed or a tactic?
23. What did you think of the effect of satyagraha on the opponent? Did you think the opponent was coerced, persuaded or converted?
24. When this movement started, were you optimistic that it was going to succeed?
25. At what stage did you join the movement?
26. When you decided to join the movement, did you have ideological goals or did you have only the immediate issues in mind?

SATYAGRAHA ACTIVITIES

27. How many hours a week did you spend in the movement activities including meetings, action projects, etc.?
28. How does this compare with other organizations that you spent your time in?
29. How many times did you participate in demonstrations, picketing and other nonviolent projects in the movement?
30. What special assignments did you have in connection with the movement?

CONSTRUCTIVE ACTIVITY

31. What kinds of constructive activities went on during the satyagraha?
32. What do you think is the relationship between nonviolence and constructive activity?

EXPERIENCES DURING SATYAGRAHA

33. In retrospect, as you think of the satyagraha which incident or incidents come to your mind most?
34. How did your father react when you decided to join the satyagraha?
35. How did your mother react when you decided to join the satyagraha?
36. Did you sustain any economic loss as a result of participation in the movement?
37. Did you regain what you lost after the conclusion of the movement?
38. How many times did you go to jail in connection with the satyagraha movements?
39. Have you been to jail in connection with this movement? How many times? How much time did you spend in jail each time?

Appendix

40. How did jail-going affect your commitment to the movement?
41. Did your parents, relatives, teachers and friends participate in the movement?
42. How did they react to your jail-going?
43. Did you have any experiences with insults or physical violence in connection with the movement?
44. How did it affect your commitment to the satyagraha?

ORGANIZING THE MOVEMENT

45. Through what kinds of activities did you recruit new members? Was it an organized activity? Specify.
46. What kinds of people did you lose and why?
47. Was there any procedure by which an active member was distinguished from an ordinary member?

MAJOR DIRECT ACTION PROJECTS

48. Did you have any disciplinary problems in the direct action projects?
49. How were the direct action projects promoted? What kinds of advertising, community and group contacts did you use?
50. From what segments of the community did you draw most support?

MASS PARTICIPATION ACTIVITIES

51. Was there a downgrading of group morale when mass support ebbed away? How was this handled?
52. What kinds of activities do you think are best for volunteers' morale?
53. For which kinds of activities did you have most trouble in getting the services of the qualified members. Routine things, e.g., secretarial, preparing mailing lists, etc.? or facing arrest or violence? things requiring education; negotiating, writing, speaking? or assuming leadership or responsibility?
54. Were there any people who called for more radical measures than the others? Were there any systematic splits with particular kinds of people being on a particular side?

PARTY ACTIVITIES

55. Please name the past and present organizations (political, religious, professional, caste, etc.) of which you held formal membership?
56. How did your political party get involved in the satyagragha?
57. Did you hold any offices in your party during the movement? Please explain the kind of work that you did, etc.
58. How much did you think the party was important for the satyagraha?

FOUNDING OF LOCAL BRANCH

59. When was the local branch of the party founded?
60. Who took part in founding it? Were there national leaders to help in founding?
61. Was it founded in response to a particular situation? Specify.
62. Did members of the party maintain a distinction from the other activists who joined a movement temporarily? and How?
63. Did you have and encourage any outsiders (to the region) to participate in direct action projects in your region?
64. How were the finances of local party managed? Did you put money into the party without expecting it back? Where did the bulk of money for the local branch come from?
65. From your experience what would you think are the most important qualities a person needs to lead a nonviolent direct movement?
66. How far do you think that the local groups were mobilized and activated for participation in a nonviolent direct action project under your influence or under the influence of Gandhiji or some other national leaders? (Name them)

CONTACTS WITH NATIONAL ORGANIZATIONS

67. Did you have frequent contacts with national office? (How?)
68. Did you have to stop a local activity because of the attitude of national office?
69. Did you ever feel dissatisfied with the policies and projects of national office?
70. Did you ever defy the directives of the national office?
71. Remarks by the leader.
72. Day and date of interview.
73. Time of interview.
74. Place of interview.
75. Remarks by the interviewer.

Index

Act of 1858 42
Agricultural wages 52
'Ahimsa' 15, 78, 80, 95, 98-100, 120 138
Ahmedabad Mill Workers Strike 147
Almond, Gabriel 110
American Civil Rights Movements 164, 170
American Constitution 125
Anderson 37
Andrews, C.F. 169

Babu Bhai, Professor 31
Bardoli Satyagraha 9, 28-32, 37, 38, 64, 65-68, 74, 76, 80, 87, 88, 112, 113, 131, 133, 142, 148, 153-157, 166
Bass, Bernard 123
Bell, Daniel 7, 8, 105
Bhatt, Braham Kumar 99, 105, 106
Bhave, Vinoba 116, 117
Bhoodan 49, 51, 52, 56, 140
Blumer, Herbert 8
Bombay Government 52
Bombay Tenancy and Agricultural Lands Act 56
Bondurant, Joan 15, 103
British cloth industry 25

Canning, Lord 42
Chandrashekhar, Acharya 62
'Charismatic leadership' 94, 95, 103, 104, 108, 113, 114, 117-121, 123, 127, 147, 152, 155, 166
Christianity 146

Civil disobedience 20, 21, 23, 25, 26
Communist Party 110
Congress Party Organisation 38, 47, 48, 51, 93, 136
Constitution of India 47, 93
Constructive activities 21, 22, 38, 54, 76, 153, 154, 156
Coser, Lewis 2, 6, 7

Dahrendorf, Ralf 2
Dantwala, Prof. 51
'Daridranarayan' 145
Desai, Dr. Amul 130
Desai, Hakumat Bhai 66, 101, 155
Desai, Mahadev 40
Desai, Morarji 50
Dharamshastras 124
Dhawan, G.N. 22
Dhebar, U.N. 34, 35, 46, 74, 90, 97, 99, 100, 148, 155, 160
'Dhurna' 25
'Dnyan' 117
Dolci, Danielo 21
Driver Commission 51
Dube, S.C. 137

East India Company 42
Economic boycotts 20, 25
Einstadt 117
Erikson, Erik 7, 147
'Ethical prophet' 113
'Exemplary prophet' 112

Fasting 24, 25

Galtung, Johan 1
Gandhi 4, 5, 13, 19, 21, 24, 32, 40, 44, 59, 61, 65, 74-80, 84, 88, 90, 94, 95, 97, 99, 101, 104, 105, 113, 116, 121-123, 126, 127, 133, 139, 143, 144, 146, 148, 153, 165, 167-169; as charismatic leader 114, 115; fast unto death 46; on ahimsa 80, 98; on khadi 119; on non-violence 16; on religion 111, 112; on self-suffering 17, on tapasya 16; on truth 14, 15
Gandhian Satyagraha 1, 8, 15, 17, 18, 21, 22, 26, 93, 96, 106, 108, 115, 118, 138, 140
Gandhi, Ashgar Ali 144, 145
Gandhi Ashramas 75, 76
Gandhi, Karam Chand 43
Gandhi Library 29
Gandhi, Mrs. Indira 53
'Gandhi Sample' 34, 35, 54, 58-61, 64, 65, 67, 69, 73, 74, 78, 80, 81, 85, 86, 142, 152, 154
General Elections of 1952 48
Gibson, R.C. 45, 46
Gita, the 125, 127
Godavari 110
Gujerat Vidyapith Library 29
'Gurumantra' 111
Gwyer, Sir Mourice 46

Harijan 119
'Hartal' 24
Hinduism 61, 62, 119, 123, 124, 169
'Hizrat' 25
'Hunger Strikes' 24

Indian Culture 150
Ishver Bhai 48-51, 74, 77-79 84, 88, 90, 97, 102-106, 111-117, 120-123, 141, 155, 167
Italy 21

Jail-going 152
Jainism 61, 76
Jasper, Carl 100
Jayaprakash Narain 49, 117

Jethwa, Prof. P.S. 31
Joshi, Jetha Lal 34, 45, 46, 90, 97, 98, 102, 160

Kaira District Satyagraha 38
Kali, Goddess 142, 143
Kasturba (Gandhi) 36
Khadi 61, 91, 118-120, 127
Khadi and Village Industrial Commission 99
Kierkegaard 146
K.P. Commerce College 31
Kripalani, Acharya 51
Kumudben, Mrs. 102, 137
Kuper, Leo. 143

Land Ceiling Act 52
Land Tenancy Act of 1956 52
Lathi charges 45
Laws of Manu 124, 125
Levy, Hymen 37

Macaulay, Lord 131
Mandelbaum, David G. 135
Mahabharata 88, 124, 169
Marquess of Linlithgo 46
Martin Luther King 170
Marx, Karl 2
Mehta, Asoka 49-52
'Moksha' 145
Munshi, K.M. 39

Naess, Arne 4
Nanda, B.R. 114
Negro movement 93
Nehru, Jawaharlal 139, 169
Noncooperation 20, 25, 50
Nondrinking 127, 168
Non-violence as 'creed' 72, 73, 76, 78-80, 82, 86-88, 91, 96, 99-101, 103, 107, 108, 119, 166; as 'faith' 78, 79, 88; as 'tactic' 72, 73, 76, 82, 84, 86, 87, 91, 98, 99, 102, 103, 107
Non-violence of the strong' 71
'Non-violence of the weak' 71

Paraja Mandal Party 45

Index

Praja Socialist Party 29, 33, 48, 50, 122, 136
Pardi Samle 34-36, 54, 58, 61, 64, 69, 73, 74, 78-80, 85, 86, 96
Pardi Satyagraha 9, 28-36, 47-52, 59, 63-67, 69, 73, 74, 77, 78, 81, 82, 84, 90, 91, 93, 95, 102, 103, 105, 106, 108-113, 118, 122, 130, 131, 134-140, 142, 148, 150, 152, 154, 156, 157, 166, 167
Parikh, Utsav 53
Parsons 115
Passive aggression 140
Patel, Ramabhai Devabhai 103
Patel, Sardar Vallabh Bhai, 38-40, 45, 46, 65, 74, 75, 77, 133, 143, 145, 160
Proclamation of Queen Victoria 42
'Prohibition' 119

Radhakrishnan, Dr. S. 123
Rajadharma 124-126
Rajendra Prasad, Dr. 163
Rajkot floods 36
Rajkot Satyagraha 9, 28-34, 42-46, 64, 68, 74, 77, 82, 88, 90, 91, 97-103, 112, 113, 131, 133, 134, 142, 144, 148, 149, 154, 155, 157, 166
Raj, Lakhaji 44
Ramayana 169
Rashtriya Shala Library 29, 45
Ravishankar Maharaj 51
'Reactive measurement' 36
Representative Government 44, 46, 67
Rowlatt Bills 59, 163
Roy, M.N. 143
Rudolfs, L.I. and S.H. 87

Salt Satyagraha 163
Sanskritization 135, 136

Satyagraha 5, 9, 17, 19-21; defined 13, 16, 18; stages of 22, 23; as a means of conflict resolution 1, 2, 4, 13, 14, 18-20, 24, 72, 85, 87, 162
Satyagraha of 1930-31 22
Saurashtra University 31
Self-suffering 17, 21, 54, 143-149, 156
Shah, Vaju Bhai 101
Shridharani, K.S. 28
Smelser, Neil J. 8
Socialism 93, 94
South Africa 38
Steim, Judith 18
'Swadeshi' 154
'Swaraj' 65, 67
Swaraj Ashram 29, 38

'Tapasya' 16, 145, 146
Tapti-Valley Railway 37
Tennyson 61
Thakore, Dharmendra Singh 44-46, 134
Theory of Mass Society 8
Toch, Hans 65
Twice-born castes 131, 132, 146, 158

Untouchability 119, 125
Upanishads 124
U.S.A. 21
Uttam Bhai 33, 69, 74, 77, 90, 97, 103, 110, 113, 121, 135, 141, 156

Vakil, Govindji 100
Vegetarianism 61, 118, 119, 127, 168
Vidyarthi, L.P. 136

Weber, Max 112-115

Young India 22, 39, 74